ESSAYS ON SOCIALIST HUMANISM

Essays on Socialist Humanism

in honour of the Centenary of Bertrand Russell 1872-1970

Edited by Ken Coates
With Contributions from:
Gunther Anders
Charles Atkinson
Lelio Basso
Stephen Bodington
Michael Barratt Brown
Keith Buchanan
Noam Chomsky
Vladimir Dedijer
John Hughes
V. G. Kiernan
A. J. Liehm
Mihailo Marković
Lucio Lombardo Radice
Jean-Paul Sartre

SPOKESMAN BOOKS
1972

U.S. DISTRIBUTOR
DUFOUR EDITIONS
CHESTER SPRINGS,
PA 19425-0449
(215) 458-5005

Printed by The Russell Press Limited
Set in 10pt. Press Roman

Published by The Bertrand Russell Peace Foundation Limited,
Bertrand Russell House, 45 Gamble Street, Forest Road West,
Nottingham NG7 4ET for *The Spokesman.*

Acknowledgments

This book would never have been produced in time, had it not been for the continuous help of Christopher Farley, who struggled with the proofs at a moment of intense activity when he had many other calls upon his time, and of Ken Fleet, Mike Cushman, John Daniels, and all the staff of the Russell Press.

Stephen Bodington and Marion Sling produced clear translations of complex texts in a miraculously short time.

Two of the papers included here were also submitted to the Russell Memorial Seminar on Spheres of Influence in the Age of Imperialism, which was conducted under the presidency of Vladimir Dedijer and the generous auspices of the Vienna Institute for Development. A full account of the proceedings of this seminar is being prepared for the press by Professor Dedijer.

Contents

Introduction

This book is published during the centenary year of Bertrand Russell. Since Russell died only two years earlier than this event, and since he remained energetically committed to a whole complex of humanist and socialist causes until the very moment of his death, it is quite difficult for our generation to appreciate that he would have been a hundred years old in 1972. Although he was too old for military service during World War I, he is today remembered for his quite remarkable services to the movement of opposition to World War III, and seems in consequence to be a strikingly contemporary figure. Yet it remains true that his birth was the subject of concerned enquiry by Queen Victoria, that his first book was published after intensive enquiries in the Germany of Bebel and the elder Liebknecht, that Beatrice Webb had welcomed him as a bright young member of the Fabian set, and that he was run over by Bernard Shaw, on a bicycle, long before that sage's greatest plays had ever been conceived.

This astonishing life-span of Russell's, all spent in intensive activity, provides a remarkable link between the radical movements of our own day and the pioneering efforts of the founding fathers of modern socialism. In writing about Vietnam, Russell naturally cast his thoughts back to his advocacy on behalf of the victims of imperial oppression in the Belgian Congo, in the days of Nevinson and Casement. When he enthusiastically greeted the formation of the Institute for Workers' Control in England, in 1968, he wrote as a survivor of the original movement for Guild Socialism, and as the author of the best-selling accounts of socialist and syndicalist ideas, which had first been published fifty years before. When he corresponded with Krushchev, he carried with him the memory of his previous encounters with Lenin and Trotsky, in the very earliest days of the Russian Revolution.

During all this time Russell frequently had occasion to modify his views, and was never afraid to confess that he had changed his mind. This fact led shallow men to accuse him of inconsistency, even capriciousness. But it is clear that in certain crucial respects there is a very real continuity between the basic ideas of the Russell who campaigned for women's suffrage in 1907, and the Russell who denounced the apostasies of the Wilson Labour administration during 1964 to 1970. There are those people, perhaps all too many of them, who claim to see an inconsistency between the activities of Russell the propagandist for Vietnam, and Russell the defender of the Prague Spring in Czechoslovakia, or who find "illogical" the simultaneous support for victims of anti-semitic persecution in Eastern Europe and for Arab refugees in Palestine. Such persons will not like the essays in this book, which have all been prepared by men who supported Russell in one or other of his various crusades, and which are all conceived in a spirit of concern to develop, advance and realise the main aspirations which he made his own.

The authors of these papers do not write in a spirit of piety and they would not, in general, lay claim to an agreement with every one of Russell's political and social prescriptions. One certain thing can be said of him, and it is that he would have found any such volume as would result from such deference to be distasteful in the extreme. Often he whimsically claimed to like flattery, but in fact there was never a man who had less taste for sycophancy. These essays are full of the disagreements and variations of opinion which might be felt to be natural in any living movement for social change. They are seen as modest attempts to carry on the fundamental struggle in which Russell was totally engaged, which was a struggle for human liberation in the fullest sense of that word. Perhaps there can be no higher hope than that they may help also, at the same time, to defend that uncompromising tolerance and open-mindedness of which he was so conspicuous an example, and which is to crucially necessary to any socialist movement which hopes to resist the baneful onset of dogma, leading, as this does, inevitably to atrophy and irrelevance.

Some of the contributors to this volume have set out to discuss Russell's own ideas, and to argue their relevance in the modern context. Others have preferred to wrestle directly with some of the major problems with which he was involved. But all have written in the intention that these arguments will provoke others to join the discussion, and so help to assure the practical continuity of the movements which gained so much from Russell's selfless dedication. That is the only tribute he would have wished, and it is the best we could hope to offer him.

CHAPTER I

Russell's Critique of Socialist Theory and Practice

Charles Atkinson and John Hughes

The motive in exploring systematically Russell's views on socialism is to emphasise the continuing relevance of his views. Russell's writings on the subject — stretching over more than half a century — succeed in identifying the most critical problems both of theory and practice that beset socialist and labour movements. Moreover, there is a consistency and continuity of approach on his part that offers the material for a comprehensive view of what socialist objectives and labour movement practice should consist in.

Indeed, Russell emerged as a major force in the critical analysis of socialist theory and practice with his very first book on "German Social Democracy" (published in 1896). Deeply influenced by Hegelian philosophy, he set out to examine the theory and practice of Marxism by a critical study of Marxist philosophy, not least the economics, and of the nature and operational practice of social democracy in Germany (as the labour movement most directly and openly influenced by Marxist ideas). Thus from early years, Russell was systematically studying — and also sharply criticising — the most powerful of all socialist theories. We revert to the detailed significance of his views on German social democracy subsequently.

Russell, who perceived what one might call the Englishness of much of Marx's analysis of capitalist economic relationships, was himself very concerned with events and movements of thought in Britain. He was, alas, sufficiently influenced by Sidney Webb to become for a brief time "an imperialist, and even supported the Boer war."[1] But his acquaintance with the theorists and practitioners of state socialism in Britain does not seem to have modified his earlier critical reaction to the same phenomenon in Marxist philosophical clothing. It is clear from his writings that the emergence of syndicalist, and in Britain "guild" socialist, ideas of socialism and of the strategy required to reach a socialist society greatly extended his critical response to the growing debate on socialism. He joined the Labour Party in 1914, but by then his positive views on socialism and

13

"social reconstruction" already form a systematic whole whose reach far distanced orthodox British socialism. In 1915 he was writing lectures that provided the gist of his analysis (subsequently published as "Principles of Social Reconstruction"); the same analysis recurs – but with much more detailed reference across to Marxist, anarchist, syndicalist and guild socialist schools of thought – in "Roads to Freedom" which was written later on in the course of the first world war and completed just before the unfreedom of a period of imprisonment.

Subsequent studies, not least "The Practice and Theory of Bolshevism" and "The Prospects of Industrial Civilisation" fill out Russell's mature view of society and of the special problems of socialism in "undeveloped" countries. In view of the elements both of continuity and repetition in all these writings, and in subsequent ones, we have attempted to distil from them in brief form the main arguments that Russell was accepting from socialist thought and practice, and the main critical and positive contribution he was himself making.

Russell's acceptance of the socialist critique of capitalism.

It is clear how completely Russell accepted the main critical arguments that socialist thought directed against capitalism as a social and economic system. He also added additional elements of his own. He took over from "The Communist Manifesto" ("this magnificent work" he called it in his first book, even while he was sharply challenging many aspects of Marxist orthodoxy) the recognition of the destructive and dynamic drive of industrial capitalism; he took over from Marxism also the notion of the permanent importance and irreversible nature of the internal drive of capitalist enterprise to concentration of large-scale production and an ever extending integration of production processes. If anything he extended traditional socialism's view of the alienating, de-humanising, and destructive nature of capitalism. In its shortest expression Russell puts his view of capitalism:

"Except slavery, the present industrial system is the most destructive of life that has ever existed. Machinery and large-scale production are ineradicable, and must survive in any better system."[2]

It is particularly important for an understanding of his positive views on socialism to notice the emphasis Russell placed on the denial of *initiative* under capitalism to most people. In this he echoes Marx's point in the "Manifesto" that capitalism has expropriated most people's *property*[3] but extends the point to emphasise the denial of a creative role in society:

"The chief defect of the present capitalistic system is that work done for wages very seldom affords any outlet for the creative impulse. The man who works for wages has no choice as to what he shall make; the whole creativeness of the process is concentrated in the employer who

14

orders the work to be done . . . the work becomes a merely external means to a certain result, the earning of wages . . . And so the process of production, which should form one instinctive cycle, becomes divided into separate purposes, which can no longer provide any satisfaction of instinct for those who do the work."[4]

Beyond this, of course, Russell accepted the socialist argument that capitalism as a system of distribution denied any opportunity for justice and was "indefensible from every point of view." As he put it in a satirical passage:

"We may distinguish four chief sources of recognised legal rights to private property (1) a man's right to what he has made himself; (2) the right to interest on capital which has been lent; (3) the ownership of land; (4) inheritance. These form a crescendo of respectability: capital is more respectable than labour, land is more respectable than capital, and any form of wealth is more respectable when it is inherited than when it has been acquired by our own exertions."[5]

It reads as a very English comment directed at the aristocratic society from which Russell had disengaged himself. But his further criticism of the nature and direction of capitalism has a more universal significance, and raised sixty years ago the issue that modern critics of capitalism are increasingly emphasising.

As Russell put it, one of the least questioned assumptions of capitalism was that production ought to be increased by every possible means; this belief in the importance of production had "a fanatical irrationality and ruthlessness":

"The purpose of maximising production will not be achieved in the long run if our present industrial system continues. Our present system is wasteful of human material . . . The same is true of material resources; the minerals, the virgin forests, and the newly developed wheatfields of the world are being exhausted with a reckless prodigality which entails almost a certainty of hardship for future generations."[6]

So, the final contradiction in capitalism is that in the name of "growth" it strips and robs the human and material resources of the planet; the technical progress which is claimed as the contribution of capitalism operates within a destructive, robber, economy which is bringing closer the prospect of decay and diminishing returns.[7]

The "philosophy of life" which accompanies this worship of production is that what "matters most to a man's happiness is his income," a philosophy says Russell that is harmful because

"it leads men to aim at a result rather than an activity, an enjoyment of material goods in which men are not differentiated, rather than a creative impulse which embodies each man's individuality."[8]

15

We do not think that later socialist writings on the distorting and manipulating effects of capitalist organised consumption have improved on that sentence of Russell which embodies both his criticism of capitalism and his social goal.

Russell's Critique of Socialism

Russell did not move from acceptance of socialist criticism of capitalism (and his own further extension of that critique) to an acceptance of the social goals posed by the state socialists of his time. This arose partly from his sense of the *inadequacy* of socialist views of the principles and nature of a socialist society,[9] partly it arose from a much more specific concern as to the implications of the extended role of the state that orthodox socialism appeared to be stressing. This critique of state socialism is particularly important in understanding Russell's views on the political and economic development of the labour movement. For, as we shall see subsequently, the discussion of the *transition* to socialism posed for him not only the question of whether the agencies of social action and change could reach as far as the overcoming of capitalism, *but also* whether they offered a road to an adequate social system, to a socialism that would not contain its own seeds of degeneration and denial of human creativity.

In various ways Russell sought to emphasise the achievement of human creativity as a necessary ingredient for post-capitalist society: "to promote all that is creative, and so to diminish the impulses and desires that centre round possession."[10] His concern about the role of the state was linked to his identification of the state so far as the embodiment of possessive forces, both internally and externally, and to the coercive role of the state ("the repository of collective force"). Moreover he saw that a transfer of the property claims from the individual capitalist to the state could produce a perpetuation of the wages system, a kind of bureaucratised state capitalism. After the criticism of the wage-earner/employer relationship that was quoted earlier, he went on to say:

> "This result is due to our industrial system, but it would not be avoided by state socialism. In a socialist community, the state would be the employer, and the individual workman would have almost as little control over his work as he has at present. Such control as he could exercise would be indirect, through political channels, and would be too slight and roundabout to afford any appreciable satisfaction. It is to be feared that instead of an increase of self-direction, there would only be an increase of mutual interference."[11]

That sounds all too accurately like an appraisal of British nationalised industries. His initial pessimistic view of the denial of creativity if state socialism produced an enforced discipline reads all too obviously like a

16

prescient view of the Soviet Union, or Czechoslovakia, seventy-five years later:

> "State socialism means an increase of the powers of absolutism and police rule, and ... acquiescence in such a state, whatever bribes it may offer to labour, is acquiescence in the suppression of all free speech and all free thought, is acquiescence in intellectual stagnation and moral servility."[12]

Russell's underlying argument is that there are four requirements for a humanly adequate industrial system, four tests which can be applied to actual or proposed systems. They are (i) the maximising of production, (ii) justice in distribution, (iii) a tolerable existence for producers, and (iv) "the greatest possible freedom and stimulus to vitality and progress." As we have seen, capitalism could only lay claim to an interest in the first of these goals, and in Russell's view would by its nature fail to achieve it and instead bequeath a robbed and stripped planet to future generations. State socialism aimed primarily at the second and third objective; that is, it concentrates on justice, on the removal of inequality. But, says Russell, while justice may be a necessary principle it is not a *sufficient* one on which to base a social reconstruction. In its assertion of justice "the labour movement is morally irresistible ... all living thought is on its side." But, justice "by itself, when once realised, contains no source of new life."[13]

Russell's concern is twofold. Partly, that there are tendencies in the evolution of the labour movement (and in the resistance it has to overcome to achieve its objectives) that might make it repressive and hostile to "the life of the mind."[14] (Interestingly, he is concerned that labour discipline and the requirement that all should contribute to society should not be pushed so far as to produce intolerance to those who might want to drop out, to make only a minimum contribution, in the pursuit of individual creativity). He is also concerned at the danger of conservatism in methods of production, since technical progress may involve permanent loss to wage-earners. But the way to overcome this, he argued, was to give to labour "the direct interest in economical processes" which otherwise belongs to the employer, whether capitalist or state. The capitalist system has robbed most men of initiative; the danger of state socialism is that it might perpetuate this by taking over into the hands of a state bureaucracy the initiative, the power, and the autocracy that are the hallmarks of the industrial capitalist.

Russell does not seek to reduce the severity of the problem posed by the kind of retreat from large-scale industry that at least one school of British socialists had envisaged. We have seen that he postulates continued concentration of production into technically progressive large-scale industry. Instead he argues for the democratisation of the industrial process:

"Economic organisations, in the pursuit of efficiency, grow larger and larger, and there is no possibility of reversing this process. The causes of their growth are technical, and large organisations must be accepted as an essential part of civilised society. But there is no reason why their government should be centralised and monarchical. The present economic system by robbing most men of initiative, is one of the causes of the universal weariness which devitalises urban and industrial populations . . . If we are to retain any capacity for new ideas . . . the monarchical organisation of industry must be swept away. All large businesses must become democratic and federal in their government. The whole wage-earning system is an abomination, not only because of the social injustice which it causes and perpetuates, but also because it separates the man who does the work from the purpose for which the work is done."[15]

So, "industrial federal democracy" is the direction that has to be taken to reconstruct the industrial system. Industrial capitalism has separated the several interests of consumer, producer, capitalist, and the community. Co-operative systems offer some link between consumer and capitalist; syndicalism offers a link between producer and capital. No form of organisation links all these interests and makes them quite identical with the community's interest. Russell, in other words, envisages a pluralist society of participating democracies, although recognising that this still leaves the need to harmonise these differing organisations with their separate initiatives. The state appears, in this approach, as arbitrator and co-ordinator.

One advantage of this perspective is, as Russell puts it, that "it is not a static or final system: it is hardly more than a framework for energy and initiative." It offers the greater flexibility of combining geographical units of government with industrial democracies whose constituencies are trades and industries. Such an approach clearly begins to raise in a relevant way a socialist view of the future of what are already multi-national enterprises, and the need for an international as well as national framework for socialist societies. The sources of creative initiative are multiplied in such a federal and democratic framework; the opportunities for voluntary membership of industrial organisation, instead of legal or economic compulsion,[16] are enhanced.

It becomes obvious at this point that Russell is not only depicting the dynamic framework required for a creative form of socialism. He is also arguing for the development of this organisational base, particularly the development of the federal democracy of trade unions with an increased emphasis on encroaching control, as the way to strengthen the democratic and labour movement under capitalism. He is writing both about a socialism that does not rest on the worship of state power, and about the "roads to freedom," about the transition to socialism. He is writing about a creative and dynamic form of socialism but also about the way to create a dynamic for change within capitalism. We need, therefore, to look more systematically at Russell's critical appraisal of the operational experience of labour movements, and at his views of the organisational and policy requirements that these movements expressed.

Russell's Views on the Transition to Socialism

The conventional argument within the labour movement over several generations has been between reformist and revolutionary modes of progression. The concealed assumption, which Russell was critical of from the beginning, was the emphasis on political party organisation and activity and the devaluing of the role of trade union and industrial action. Russell's analysis – both of German social democracy in its early days and of Lenin's views – makes it clear that instead of Communist Party organisation in the advanced countries developing as the revolutionary polar opposite of earlier reformism, it tended to reproduce the oscillation between ostensible revolutionary ideology and practical ineffectiveness and political accommodation that he found in Germany in the 1890s. In our view, Russell offers the clues for a major re-consideration of the development of labour and socialist movements; the flaw in the pattern of socialist response Russell traced back to Marx himself. The outturn, as it appears to us, is either political compromise within advanced capitalist systems increasingly having recourse to a state apparatus with what one might call Bismarckian tendencies, or political revolution in less developed countries in periods of social breakdown with the likely outturn of a repressive state "socialism."

Russell saw the transition to socialism as a compelling problem because it was not *simply* a matter of superseding capitalism; it was not true that we could rely on "living happily ever after" by whatever road we came. There was also involved the wider struggle between the creative needs of humanity and the complex and potentially coercive nature of modern large-scale production (which, remember, Russell saw as common both to advanced capitalism and to post-capitalist society.) The double requirement to ask of socialist movements, therefore, was that they should be capable of transforming society instead of getting trapped in some accommodation within capitalism, and that they should at least begin to reflect the organisation and attitudes needed to humanise the industrial society of the future.

It was therefore of the utmost importance for Russell that socialists followed a course that led to the actual liberation of man, not "proletarian revenge":

"While I am as convinced a socialist as the most ardent Marxian, I do not regard socialism as a gospel of proletarian revenge, nor even *primarily* as a means of securing economic justice. I regard it primarily as an adjustment to machine production demanded by considerations of common sense, and calculated to increase the happiness not only of proletarians, but of all except a tiny minority of the human race."[17]

Nor should the labour movement follow a course that produced a type of economic justice superimposed on the fabric of an authoritarian state.[18] Russell's first study of social democracy in Germany is relevant because for the first time he begins to express the nature of his concern about the transition as well as making a penetrating criticism of the philosophy and tactics of the most powerful political labour movement at that time (the 1890s).[19] The Social Democrats were directly dependent on Marx's analysis and ideology and were agitating for socialism in an industrially advanced (at least, rapidly advancing) country. Russell criticised the Social Democrats for dogmatically adhering to tenets of Marx some of which he thought held little validity for Germany at the time. More particularly he felt that they had uncritically accepted and then made more rigid Marx's views on wages. Lassalle indeed injected into German Social Democracy his so-called "Iron Law" of wages – what one might call an ultra-pessimistic view of the scope for trade union economic pressure. Russell unfortunately sometimes seems to transfer this rigid notion from Lassalle to Marx.

"The Iron Law has for the moment a certain amount of validity. Marx's doctrines have therefore a sufficient kernel of truth to make them seem self-evident to German workmen. It is unfortunate, however, that their apparent necessity, under a capitalistic regime, should make German labourers very lukewarm as to trade union and all non-political means of improving their condition. The exclusively political character of Social Democracy, which is mainly due to Marx, is thus of very doubtful validity."[20]

As early as 1896, then, Russell foresaw a distinctive role for trade unions in the development of a viable transition to socialism, and later he was to fault Lenin for his inability to comprehend the potential power of trade unions. Russell's point is *both* that there may be distinct gains in terms of real wages and conditions to be secured from strong trade unions, *and* that the organisational experience (as he would have later put it, of "federal democracy") and ability to advance the frontier of unionised control were additional gains of lasting significance.[21] If, Russell felt, the trade unions were under-valued as a force for change then the ability of the predominantly political-party organisation to break through beyond capitalism was reduced, and there might be little hope for the extended role of trade unions as an independent source of social initiative after any successful revolution, because the orthodox Marxist approach would invite greatly increased state power, would emerge as state socialism.

The view implicit in this, and advanced by Russell with more confidence once syndicalist and guild socialist ideas became influential, is that a programme for the transition to socialism had to overcome the limitations of state socialism not least by acknowledging an extended role for trade unions.

Meanwhile, the Social Democrats, in Russell's view, were in difficulties in developing a coherent policy that attracted a mass base. On the one hand recognition of gradations in class structure and the political attitudes of different social groups[22] were causing the German Social Democrats to "revise their beliefs and to adopt an evolutionary rather than revolutionary attitude . . . Such doctrines diminish revolutionary ardour and tend to transform socialists into a left wing of the Liberal Party."[23] On the other hand, the ruling class were able to separate them from the general public, mobilising "popular enmity" against them by a distorted projection of their revolutionary philosophy and aspirations:

> "When a party proclaims class-warfare as its fundamental principle, it must expect the principle to be taken up by the classes against which its war is directed. But the popular enmity which was necessary to the passing of the Law,[24] though in large measure due to misrepresentation of bourgeois press and bourgeois politicians, was also, and principally, a religious antagonism to the new philosophy of life which Marxianism had introduced."[25]

In fact, this combination of practical ineffectiveness and accommodation within the system together with an ostensible revolutionary philosophy and purpose seems to have dogged both social democratic and communist parties within advanced capitalist countries. In diluted form what was true of German social democracy in the 1890s appears relevant to the successive political failures of the British Labour Party, or is exemplified too in the French Communist party.

Russell saw the need to remove the "popular enmity" that reaction could mobilise against the socialist and labour movement, and to secure instead a mass base of popular support as the guarantee for a successful revolution. He was deeply conscious of the risks involved in an all out revolutionary confrontation in advanced countries:

> "What was true of the late war" (i.e. 1914-18) "would be true in a far higher degree of a universal class war, because it would be longer, more desperate, and of greater extent. It may be taken as nearly certain that such a war would not end in the establishment of either capitalism or socialism, since both are forms of industrialism and both depend upon the existence of a more or less civilised community."[26]

Hence his emphasis on the need for popular support for a transition to socialism, and his recoil from revolutionary adventurism. His view was that political revolution was in fact less likely in the advanced countries and the opportunities ·greater in less developed ones, but this again led to further problems of the post-revolutionary transition.

In the specific case of Russia, Russell was conscious of the inadequacies of the Bolshevik programme. The continuous civil war and near world war after the revolution brought about extreme poverty and the inability to inculcate Communist ideals, and the seriousness of this situation led to the establishment of a despotic bureaucracy that could only be removed by a new revolution. The seizure of power by a few guaranteed the separation of these men from the genuine proletarian, and hence was the origin of a new ruling class. Russell did not believe that the Bolshevik model would produce the socialism that the Bolsheviks earlier aspired to.

The shock of this recognition was so great that Russell comments:

> "My first impulse was to abandon political thinking as a bad job, and to conclude that the strong and reckless must always exploit the weaker and kindlier sections of the population."[27]

Fortunately, hope and intellectual resilience being stronger Russell continued to try to analyse the faults in the Bolshevik model.[28] He decided that the concentration on economic inequality, while accurate, avoided a problem of equal magnitude – the inequality of power. (As we have seen, in his writing during the first world war, Russell had seen this as a critical weakness in state socialism; thus he was not unprepared intellectually for this outcome).

Perhaps, Russell reasoned in "The Prospects of Industrial Civilisation", the failure of the Bolsheviks was also connected with their attempt "to establish communism in a country almost untouched by capitalist industrialism" thus raising the question of whether capitalism is a necessary stage on the road to socialism or whether industry can be developed "socialistically from the outset in a hitherto undeveloped country." Significantly, he added that this was a question of vital importance "for the future of Russia and Asia."[29]

The undeveloped countries, in Russell's view, have one major advantage in any attempted transition, favourable political conditions – they do not have a ruling elite of powerful capitalists, and their wage earners are not so bemused as the workers in advanced countries who "continue to elect as their chosen representatives men whose delight it is to oppress, starve and imprison all who advocate the interests of the wage-earners."[30] But technical and economic conditions are a distinct disadvantage. The needed accumulation of capital seems to require that industrialism must be autocratically governed, and provide bare subsistence wages. Foreign capital and technology may also be important for an undeveloped country, and this interference by foreign capitalists leads to "loopholes for corruption." Moreover, even if revolutionary ardour suffices during the first militant phase of the transition, the second "constructive" phase is very long and the revolutionary zeal will diminish. Pessimistically, Russell concludes:

"there is, it would seem, only one force which could keep communism up to the necessary pitch of enthusiasm, and that is nationalism developing into imperialism as foreign aggressions are defeated."[31]

Nevertheless, Russell conceded the possibility that the Bolsheviks might succeed, and "if they do, they may quite possibly become a model for China and India." Another possibility was that of the Russian state replacing the foreign capitalist as the exploiter; what Russell here envisages is Russia playing the role of provider of capital, goods, and technology, to these countries in a state capitalist form, and help these countries to "escape . . . private capitalism."[32]

Thus the cumulative problems of a political revolution as a major element in the transition to socialism were seen by Russell as the risk of material devastation, the special and protracted problems of an economic transition for undeveloped countries which offered the best hope of political transition, and the likelihood that these conditions would result in the wielding of power through a state bureaucracy with a resulting repression of human creativity.

Russell's main hope of a transition to socialism therefore remained based on the possibilities within advanced countries, where the technical and economic conditions were most favourable, and combined with a wage-earning class not only educated and accustomed to industrial processes but also capable of more developed trade union organisation. But this is to come back to the question of how to break out beyond the confined achievement of traditional political social democracy (and the latter-day repetition of the same process through traditional communist party activity).

Russell's central idea is the importance to be attached to a persistent extension of the scope and direction of trade union organisation and power. The under-valuing of trade union organisation was one of the main criticisms he directed at the German Social Democrats. It was the injection of this idea of the potential sweep of trade unionism in transforming industrial society — rather than the practicality of particular methods proposed — that he held to be the permanent achievement of syndicalism:

"There is no doubt that the ideas which it" (i.e. syndicalism) "has put into the world have done a great deal to revive the Labour Movement and to recall it to certain things of fundamental importance which it had been in danger of forgetting. Syndicalists consider man as producer rather than consumer. They are more concerned to procure freedom in work than to increase material well-being. They have revived the quest for liberty, which was growing somewhat dimmed under the regime of parliamentary socialism, and they have reminded men that what our modern society needs is not a little tinkering here and there, nor the kind of minor readjustments to which the existing holders of power may readily consent, but a fundamental reconstruction, a sweeping away of all the sources of oppression, a liberation of men's constructive energies, and a wholly new way of conceiving and regulating production and economic relations. This merit is so great that, in view of it, all minor defects become insignificant, and this merit syndicalism will continue to possess even if, as a definite movement, it should be found to have passed away with the war."[33]

The sympathy that breathes through this passage is evident, and indeed the change of tone in the discussion of socialism as between the writing of "German Social Democracy" and the books he was writing from 1915 onwards seems to owe much to the increased confidence that a more realistic "road to freedom" was being depicted, one that would be capable of leading to a humanised industrial society.

Thus, on one side, Russell defended syndicalism against the criticisms of would-be revolutionary anarchism with its emphasis on the need for "armed insurrection and violent appropriation":

"Syndicalists might retort that when the movement is strong enough to win by armed insurrection it will be abundantly strong enough to win by the General Strike. In Labour movements generally, success through violence can hardly be expected except in circumstances where success without violence is attainable."[34]

Russell's view is that better trade union organisation can establish the power base needed to ensure that the rights of labour are respected and to extend labour's economic control.[35] Trade unionism and the accompanying reasoned propaganda of socialist opinion must not only win over "the less well-paid industrial workers." In addition:

"It is necessary to win over the technical staff . . . It is necessary to win over a considerable proportion of the professional classes and of the intellectuals."[36]

Socialists, he says, have been "too impatient" and this has inspired their emphasis on force instead of reason, and on "the dictatorship of the communist party." But if "all who will really profit by socialism have become persuaded of the fact" the force needed to take the capital from the capitalists "will be only a very little force."

Moreover, trade unionism has been moving in the right direction in establishing increased control over work processes in ways which directly challenge the repressive production-worshipping values of capitalism:

"The first steps towards a cure for these evils are being taken by the trade unions, in those parts of their policy which are most criticised, such as restriction of output, refusal to believe that the only necessity is more production, shortening of hours . . . It is only by these methods that industrialism can be humanised . . . It could be used to lighten physical labour, and to set men free for more agreeable activities . . . The trade unions have clearly perceived this, and have persisted in spite of lectures from every kind of middle and upper-class pundit. This is one reason why there is more hope from self-government in industry than from State Socialism."[37]

Nor was Russell to be turned aside from this belief by the repudiation of self-government in industry by the Bolsheviks; they were opposing self-government in industry everywhere because it had failed in Russia and their self-esteem prevented them admitting that this was due to backwardness:

"I would go so far as to say that the winning of self-government in such industries as railways and mining is an essential preliminary to complete Communism. In England, especially, this is the case. Trade unions can command whatever technical skill they may require; they are politically powerful; the demand for self-government is one for which there is widespread sympathy . . . moreover (what is important with the British temperament) self-government can be brought about gradually by stages in each trade, and by extension from one trade to another."[38]

This broad sympathy of Russell for the advocates of self-government in industry shows through in his extensive discussion of Guild Socialist ideas (particularly in "Roads to Freedom"). However, he did not believe that the Guild Socialists had in any way solved the problem of the institutional form that decision making, and the relations between "self-governing" industries and the state would take.[39] He thought also that they misrepresented in suggesting that the state would be the repository of consumer interests as against the producer interests centred in the guilds. "Neither the interests of the producer, nor those of the consumer, can be adequately represented except by ad hoc organisations . . . If capitalism were eliminated, the political strength of production as against consumption might be greatly increased. If so, the need of organising consumers to protect their own interest would become greater."[40]

The warning seems justified, though the ever-more evident social costs attaching to capitalist production, the rapid emergence of major problems of ecology and pollution, may well be providing the stimulus that will accelerate the development of consumer interests and the greater recognition of these by local and national (and international?) government.

Russell clearly sees the extension of trade union organisation and power, its developing interest in control, its assertion of a human scale of values, as critically important for the transition to socialism in mature countries. We should remember, though, that this is to him part of a more general advocacy of a pluralism of voluntary and autonomous organisations, acting as centres of creative initiative; that is, federal and democratic trade unionism is part of his general view of the structure of a democratic society:

> "It is not only geographical units, such as nations, that have a right, according to the true theory of democracy, to autonomy for certain purposes. Just the same principle applies to any group which has important internal concerns that affect the members of the group enormously more than they affect outsiders... The theory of democracy... demands (1) division of the community into more or less autonomous groups; (2) delimitation of the powers of the autonomous groups by determining which of their concerns are so much more important to themselves than to others that others had better have no say in them... In an ideal democracy, industries... would be self-governing as regards almost everything except the price and quantity of their product... Measures which they would then be able to adopt autonomously they are now justified in extorting from the Government by direct action."[41]

In a way, Russell's long-term belief in the reasonableness of his view of the progress of industrial society to communism, is derived — as was Marx's — from a sense of the incompatability between private property claims (with a legal form relevant to a predominantly agrarian and handicraft economy) and the more and more extensive co-operation of productive forces required by modern industrial society.[42] Looked at in that way, it is the capitalist form of industrial society that is temporary:

> "Capitalism is essentially transitional, the survival of private property in the means of production into the industrial era, which has no place for it owing to the fact that production has become co-operative. Capitalism, by being ill adapted to industrialism, rouses an opposition which must in the end destroy it. The only question is whether labour will be strong enough to establish socialism upon the ruins of capitalism, or whether capitalism will be able to destroy our whole industrial civilisation in the course of the struggle..."[43]

Reading Russell one is struck, time and again, with his remarkable predictive abilities, his power of constructing an analysis of social and economic processes that describe with great accuracy the movement of history after he has written. That he bears comparison with Marx in this respect is no mere accident.

Russell was able to use his critical understanding of Marx to penetrate and comprehend the complex class and power relationships created by the development of capitalism; this understanding extended to the processes as they would affect undeveloped countries as well as the advanced industrial countries.

His analysis served a twofold purpose; first to inject the dialectic of social process with a new life, and give it more humanised form. Secondly, to give a direction to those processes that might break through the capitalist integument of industrial society — its values as well as its property relationships. Echoing Marx's "Economic and Philosophic Manuscripts of 1844,"[44] but in a far less abstract manner, Russell attempted to analyse the positive effects of industrialism. If wage-earners (and by extension, technical and professional workers) could gain control of the productive apparatus, then they could use the efficiency of the process for the development of human creativity. Through group autonomy and collective control the de-humanising aspects of the process could be overcome — partially even within capitalism, and completely after its demise (to which this control contributes).

Russell once commented that Marx was "the last of the great system builders," but it is Russell's analysis of the whole process involved in the evolution of industrial society, not simply the economic process, that enabled him to be so prescient. Like Marx, there is tremendous consistency in the structure of his ideas, but like Marx we have to cull these from the writings of a lifetime. Like Marx, Russell's concern is with "real men" in their real social and material relationships, and it was this concern that led him to regard authoritarian power structures as anathema to the development of the creative powers of man.

Hence his persistent criticisms of state socialism as the social goal, and his critical attack on representative formal political democracy as an inadequate defence against autocracy and the centralisation of power. Participatory democracy, based particularly on trade unions and other functional organisations is, in Russell's view, the way to release men's energy and creativity, the road to the harmonisation of the industrial system and its requirements with human needs, the "road to freedom."

FOOTNOTES

1 B. Russell, "My Mental Development," from "The Philosophy of Bertrand Russell," sel. by P.A. Schilpp, 1951, reprinted in "The Basic Writings of Bertrand Russell," ed. by R.E. Egner & L.E. Denonn, 1961.
2 "Principles of Social Reconstruction," p.244.
3 "The Communist Manifesto:" "You are horrified at our intending to do away with private property. But in your existing society, private property is already done away with for nine-tenths of the population; its existence for the few is solely due to its non-existence in the hands of those nine-tenths."
4 "Principles of Social Reconstruction" p.136.
5 *Op. cit.* p.123.
6 *Op. cit.* p.123.
7 Besides, says Russell, the greater productivity arising from industrialism has "enabled us to devote more labour and capital to armies and navies for the protection of our wealth from envious neighbours, and for the exploitation of inferior races, which are ruthlessly wasted by the capitalist regime," *Op. cit.* p.119

8 *Op. cit.* p.244.
9 Russell is scathing about "the old type of Marxian revolutionary socialist" who never dwelt on the life of communities after the "millenium:" "He imagined that, like the prince and princess in a fairy story, they would live happily ever after."
10 *Op. cit.* p.236.
11 *Op. cit.* p.137.
12 "German Social Democracy", pp.113-114. See also, "Roads to Freedom" (1966 edn.) p.91-92: "State socialists argue as if there would be no danger to liberty in a State not based on capitalism. This seems to me an entire delusion." Russell's argument rests in part on what he sees as inherent defects in the working of *representative* (as against more participatory) democratic institutions; cf. "Roads to Freedom", p.93.
13 "Principles of Social Reconstruction," pp.123-131.
14 This is expressed also in "Roads to Freedom", where on pages 79 and 80 he expresses his fears of orthodox socialism, and in Ch.VIII ("Science and Art under Socialism") argues for tolerance for creative activity.
15 *Op. cit.* p.138.
16 *Op. cit.* p.139-142. "If organisation is not to crush individuality, membership of an organisation ought to be voluntary, not compulsory, and ought always to carry with it a voice in the management."
17 Essay on "The Case for Socialism," in "In Praise of Idleness' (first publ. 1935), 1970 edn. p.76.
18 Russell did not assume that the Russian revolution must of necessity lead to that. On his early hopes see "The Prospects of Industrial Civilisation," 1923, p.8.
19 Subsequently, of course, Michels quarried in the same place. Although Russell grasped the oligarchical degeneration of representative political organisation and processes that Michels emphasised, Michels never appears to have seen the even more vital points that Russell goes on to make. Astonishingly, Michels in "Political Parties" shows no sign of knowing — he certainly does not refer to — Russell's work.
20 "German Social Democracy", 1896, pp.27-28.
21 In 1923 he wrote: "The iron law of wages, invented by orthodox economists to discourage trade unions, and accepted by Marx to encourage revolution, was an economic fallacy." ("Prospects of Industrial Civilisation", pp.105-106) This aphorism of Russell's distorts Marx's views, although it is quite accurate when applied to most of the German "marxists" at the time in question. Marx in fact combined pessimism about the possible economic achievements of trade unionism with understanding of the wider importance of their persistent organisation: "Now and then the workers are victorious, but only for a time. The real fruit of their battle lies not in the immediate result but in the ever expanding union of the workers," but then by a curious elision goes on: "This organisation of the proletarians into a class, and consequently into a political party ...." ("The Communist Manifesto").

CHARLES ATKINSON AND JOHN HUGHES

22 "Roads to Freedom", pp.34-35.
23 *Op. cit.* p.35
24 The "Exceptional Law" which had deprived socialists of many of their rights.
25 "German Social Democracy," pp.92-93.
26 "The Prospects of Industrial Civilisation," p.128. See also "The Communist Manifesto", "The history of all hitherto existing society is the history of class struggles . . . . a fight that each time ended either in a revolutionary reconstruction of society at large, or in the common ruin of the contending classes."
27 "Practice and Theory of Bolshevism", 1920, p.157.
28 Russell saw this evaluation as imperative because: "The civilised world seems almost certain, sooner or later, to follow the example of Russia in attempting a communist organisation of society. I believe that the attempt is essential to the happiness of mankind during the next few centuries, but I believe also that the transition has appalling dangers . . . in the interests of communism, no less than in the interests of civilisation, I think it imperative that the Russian failure should be admitted and analysed." "Practice and Theory of Bolshevism", 1920, p.135.
29 "Prospects of Industrial Civilisation", pp.106-107.
30 *Ibid.*, p.119.
31 "The Prospects of Industrial Civilisation", p.117.
32 *Ibid.*, p.113.
33 "Roads to Freedom", pp.66-67
34 *Op. cit.* p.60
35 "Prospects of Industrial Civilisation", pp.240-241.
36 *Ibid.*, pp.138-139.
37 "Prospects of Industrial Civilisation", p.175.
38 "Practice and Theory of Bolshevism", pp.182-183.
39 "Roads to Freedom", pp.94-95.
40 "Prospects of Industrial Civilisation", p.238.
41 "Democracy and Direct Action", 1919, reprinted in "The Spokesman," No.22, April 1972.
42 This emphasis on the total productive process as the co-operative production of wealth seems to be the main force behind Russell's criticism of Marx's labour theory of value, or of the equivalent emphasis of pre-Marxist socialists on "a man's right to the produce of his own labour." This could not be used as "the basis of a just system of distribution" says Russell for "in the complication of modern industrial processes it is impossible to say what a man has produced." ("Principles of Social Reconstruction," p.124, and "German Social Democracy", p.17).
43 "The Prospects of Industrial Civilisation", pp. 62-63.
44 We are not implying that Russell used the "Manuscripts;" we have found no evidence that he used them (they were not published until 1932).

29

CHAPTER II

Anarchism

Noam Chomsky

A French writer, sympathetic to anarchism, wrote in the 1890s that "anarchism has a broad back, like paper it endures anything" – including, he noted, those whose acts are such that "a mortal enemy of anarchism could not have done better."[1] There have been many styles of thought and action that have been referred to as "anarchist." It would be hopeless to try to encompass all of these conflicting tendencies in some general theory or ideology. Even if we proceed to extract from the history of libertarian thought a living, evolving tradition, as the French writer Daniel Guerin does in his book *Anarchism,*[2] it remains difficult to formulate its doctrines as a specific and determinate theory of society and social change.

In his work *Anarchosyndicalism,* the German anarchist historian Rudolf Rocker[3] presented a systematic conception of the development of anarchist thought toward anarchosyndicalism along lines that bear comparison to Guerin's work. He wrote that anarchism is not

... a fixed, self-enclosed system, but rather a definite trend in the historical development of mankind, which, in contrast with the intellectual guardianship of all clerical and governmental institutions, strives for the free unhindered unfolding of all the individual and social forces in life. Even freedom is only a relative, not an absolute concept, since it tends constantly to become broader and to affect wider circles in more manifold ways. For the anarchist, freedom is not an abstract philosophical concept, but the vital concrete possibility for every human being to bring to full development all the powers, capacities, and talents with which nature has endowed him, and turn them to social account. The less this natural development of man is influenced by ecclesiastical or political guardianship, the more efficient and harmonious will human personality become, the more will it become the measure of the intellectual culture of the society in which it has grown.

One might ask what value there is in studying a "definite trend in the historic development of mankind" that does not articulate a specific and detailed social theory. Indeed, many commentators dismiss anarchism as

31

utopian, formless, primitive, or otherwise incompatible with the realities of a complex society. One might, however, argue differently: that at every stage of history our concern must be to dismantle those forms of authority and oppression that survive from an era when they might have been justified by the need for security or survival or economic development, but that now contribute to – rather than alleviate – material and cultural deficit.

If so, there will be no doctrine of social change fixed for the present and future, nor even, necessarily, a specific and unchanging concept of the goals of social change. Surely our understanding of the nature of man or of the range of workable social forms is so rudimentary that any far-reaching doctrine must be treated with great scepticism, just as scepticism is in order when we hear that "human nature" or "the demands of efficiency" or "the complexity of modern life" requires this or that form of oppression and autocratic rule.

Nevertheless, at a particular time there is every reason to develop, in so far as our understanding permits, a specific realisation of this "definite trend in the historic development of mankind," appropriate to the tasks of the moment. For Rocker, "the problem that is set for our time is that of freeing man from the curse of economic exploitation and political and social enslavement;" and the method is not the conquest and exercise of state power, not stultifying parliamentarianism, but rather "to reconstruct the economic life of the peoples from the ground up and build it up in the spirit of Socialism:"

> But only the producers themselves are fitted for this task, since they are the only value-creating element in society out of which a new future can arise. Theirs must be the task of freeing labour from all the fetters which economic exploitation has fastened on it, of freeing society from all the institutions and procedures of political power, and of opening the way to an alliance of free groups of men and women based on co-operative labour and a planned administration of things in the interest of the community. To prepare the toiling masses in city and country for this great goal and to bind them together as a militant force is an objective of modern Anarchosyndicalism, and in this its whole purpose is exhausted."

As a socialist, Rocker would take for granted "that the serious, final, complete liberation of the workers is only possible on one condition: the appropriation of capital, that is, raw materials and all the tools of labour, including land, by the whole body of workers" (Bakunin). As an anarchosyndicalist, he insists, further, that the workers' organisations create "not only the ideas but also the facts of the future itself" (Bakunin) in the pre-revolutionary period, that they embody in themselves the structure of the future society – and he looks forward to a social revolution that will dismantle the state apparatus as well as expropriate the expropriators. "What we put in place of the government is industrial organisation:"

> "Anarcho-syndicalists are convinced that a Socialist economic order cannot be created by the decrees and status of a government, but only by the solidaric collaboration of the worker with hand and brain in each special branch of production; that is, through the taking over of the management of all plants by the producers themselves under such form that the separate groups, plants, and branches of industry are independent members of the general economic organism and systematically carry on production and the distribution of the products in the interest of the community on the basis of free mutual agreements."

Rocker was writing during the Spanish Revolution, when such ideas had been put into practice in a dramatic way. Just prior to the outbreak of the revolution, the anarchosyndicalist economist Diego Abad de Santillan had written:

> " . . . in facing the problem of social transformation, the Revolution cannot consider the state as a medium, but must depend on the organisation of producers.
>
> We have followed this norm and we find no need for the hypothesis of a superior power to organised labour, in order to establish a new order of things. We would thank anyone to point out to us what function, if any, the state can have in an economic organisation, where private property has been abolished and in which parasitism and special privilege have no place. The suppression of the State cannot be a languid affair; it must be the task of the Revolution to finish with the State. Either the Revolution gives social wealth to the producers, in which case the producers organise themselves for due collective distribution and the State has nothing to do; or the Revolution does not give social wealth to the producers, in which case the Revolution has been a lie and the State would continue.
>
> Our federal council of economy is not a political power but an economic and administrative regulating power. It receives its orientation from below and operates in accordance with the resolutions of the regional and national assemblies. It is a liaison corps and nothing else."

Engels in a letter of 1883, expressed his disagreement with this conception:

> "The anarchists put the thing up-side down. They declare that the proletarian revolution must *begin* by doing away with the political organisation of the state . . . But to destroy it at such a moment would be to destroy the only organism by means of which the victorious proletariat can assert its newly conquered power, hold down its capitalist adversaries, and carry out that economic revolution of society

without which the whole victory must end in a new defeat and in mass slaughter of the workers similar to those after the Paris commune."[5]

In contrast, the anarchists — most eloquently Bakunin — warned of the dangers of the "red bureaucracy" that would prove to be "the most vile and terrible lie that our century has created." The anarchosyndicalist Fernand Pelloutier asked: "Must even the transitory state to which we have to submit necessarily and fatally be the collectivist jail? Can't it consist in a free organisation limited exclusively by the needs of production and consumption, all political institutions having disappeared?"[6]

I do not pretend to know the answer to this question. But it seems clear that unless there is, in some form, a positive answer, the chances for a truly democratic revolution that will achieve the humanistic ideals of the left are not great. Martin Buber put the problem succinctly when he wrote: "One cannot in the nature of things expect a little tree that has been turned into a club to put forth leaves." The question of conquest or destruction of state power is what Bakunin regarded as the primary issue dividing him from Marx. In one form or another, the problem has arisen repeatedly in the century since dividing "libertarian" from "authoritarian" socialists.

Despite Bakunin's warnings about the red bureaucracy and their fulfillment under Stalin's dictatorship, it would obviously be a gross error in interpreting the debates of a century ago to rely on the claims of contemporary social movements concerning their historical origins. In particular, it is perverse to regard Bolshevism as "Marxism in practice." Rather, the left-wing critique of Bolshevism, taking account of the historical circumstances of the Russian Revolution, is far more to the point:[8]

"The anti-Bolshevik, left-wing labour movement opposed the Leninists because they did not go far enough in exploiting the Russian upheavals for strictly proletarian ends. They became prisoners of their environment and used the international radical movement to satisfy specifically Russian needs, which soon became synonymous with the needs of the Bolshevik Party-State. The "bourgeois" aspects of the Russian Revolution were now discovered in Bolshevism itself: Leninism was adjudged a part of international social-democracy, different from the latter only on tactical issues."[9]

If one were to seek a single leading idea within the anarchist tradition, it should, I believe, be that expressed by Bakunin when, writing on the Paris Commune, he identified himself as follows:

"I am a fanatic lover of liberty, considering it as the unique condition under which intelligence, dignity and human happiness can develop and grow; not the purely formal liberty conceded, measured out and

34

regulated by the State, an eternal lie which in reality represents nothing more than the privilege of some founded on the slavery of the rest; not the individualistic, egoistic, shabby, and fictitious liberty extolled by the School of J.J. Rousseau and the other schools of bourgeois liberalism, which considers the would-be rights of all men, represented by the State which limits the rights of each — an idea that leads inevitably to the reduction of the rights of each to zero. No, I mean the only kind of liberty that is worthy of the name, liberty that consists in the full development of all the material, intellectual and moral powers that are latent in each person; liberty that recognizes no restrictions other than those determined by the laws of our own individual nature, which cannot properly be regarded as restrictions since these laws are not imposed by any outside legislator beside or above us, but are immanent and inherent, forming the very basis of our material, intellectual and moral being — they do not limit us but are the real and immediate conditions of our freedom."[10]

These ideas grow out of the Enlightenment; their roots are in Rousseau's *Discourse on Inequality,* Humboldt's *Limits of State Action,* Kant's insistence, in his defence of the French Revolution, that freedom is the precondition of acquiring the maturity for freedom, not a gift to be granted when such maturity is achieved.[11] With the development of industrial capitalism a new and un-anticipated system of injustice, it is libertarian socialism that has preserved and extended the radical humanist message of the Enlightenment and the classical liberal ideals that were perverted into an ideology to sustain the emerging social order.

In fact, on the very same assumptions that led classical liberalism to oppose the intervention of the state in social life, capitalist social relations are also intolerable. Humboldt, for example, in work which anticipated and perhaps inspired Mill, objects to state action because the state tends to "make man an instrument to serve its arbitrary ends, overlooking his individual purposes." He insists that "whatever does not spring from a man's free choice ... does not enter into his very being, but remains alien to his true nature; he does not perform it with truly human energies, but merely with mechanical exactness." Under the conditions of freedom, "all peasants and craftsmen might be elevated into artists; that is, men who love their own labour for its own sake, improve it by their own plastic genius and inventive skill, and thereby cultivate their intellect, ennoble their character, and exalt and refine their pleasures." When a man merely reacts to external demands and authority, "we may admire what he does, but we despise what he is." Humboldt is, furthermore, no primitive individualist. He summarises his leading ideas as follows:

" ... while they would break all fetters in human society, they would attempt to find as many new social bonds as possible. The isolated man is no more able to develop than the one who is fettered."

This classic of liberal thought, completed in 1792,[12] is in its essence profoundly, though prematurely, anti-capitalist. Its ideas must be attenuated beyond recognition to be transmuted into an ideology of industrial capitalism. The vision of a society in which social fetters are replaced by social bonds, and labour is freely undertaken, suggests the early Marx,[13] with his discussion of the "alienation of labour when work is external to the worker . . . not part of his nature . . . (so that) he does not fulfill himself in his work but denies himself . . . (and is) physically exhausted and mentally debased" — that alienated labour which "casts some of the workers back into a barbarous kind of work and turns others into machines," thus depriving man of his "species character" of "free conscious activity" and "productive life."

Similarly, Marx conceives of "a new type of human being who *needs* his fellow-men . . . (The workers' association becomes) the real constructive effort to creat a social texture of future human relations."[14]

It is true that classical libertarian thought is opposed to state intervention in social life, as a consequence of deeper assumptions about the human need for liberty, diversity, and free association. On the same assumption, capitalist relations of production, wage-labour, competitiveness, the ideology of "possessive individualism" — all must be regarded as fundamentally antihuman. Libertarian socialism is properly to be regarded as the inheritor of the liberal ideals of the Enlightenment.

Rudolf Rocker described modern anarchism as "the confluence of the two great currents which during and since the French Revolution have found such characteristic expression in the intellectual life of Europe: Socialism and Liberalism." The classical liberal ideals, he argued, were wrecked on the realities of capitalist economic forms, Anarchism is necessarily anticapitalist in that it "opposes the exploitation of man by man." But anarchism also opposes "the dominion of man over man." It insists that *"socialism will be free or it will not be at all.* In its recognition of this lies the genuine and profound justification for the existence of anarchism."

From this point of view, anarchism may be regarded as the libertarian wing of socialism. It is in this spirit that Daniel Guerin has approached the study of anarchism in the recently translated book *Anarchism* and in other works.[15] He quotes Adolph Fischer, who said that "every anarchist is a socialist but not every socialist is necessarily an anarchist." Similarly Bakunin, in his "anarchist manifesto" of 1865, the programme of his projected international revolutionary fraternity, laid down the principle that each member must be, to begin with, a socialist.

A consistent anarchist must oppose private ownership of the means of production and the wage-slavery which is a component of this system as incompatible with the principle that labour must be freely undertaken and under the control of the producer. As Marx put it, socialists look forward to a society in which labour will "become not only a means of life, but also the highest want in life,"[16] an impossibility when the worker is driven by external authority or need rather than inner impulse: "No form of wage-labour, even though one may be less obnoxious than another, can do away with the misery of wage-labour itself."[17] A consistent anarchist must oppose not only alienated labour but also the stupefying specialisation of labour that takes place when the means of developing production.

" . . . mutilate the worker into a fragment of a human being, degrade him to become a mere appurtenance of the machine, make his work such a torment that its essential meaning is destroyed; estrange from him the intellectual potentialities of the labour process in very proportion to the extent to which science is incorporated into it as an independent power . . ."[18]

Marx saw this not as an inevitable concomitant of industrialisation, but rather as a feature of capitalist relations of production. The society of the future must be concerned to "replace the detail-worker of today . . . reduced to a mere fragment of a man, by the fully developed individual, fit for a variety of labours . . . to whom the different social functions . . . are but so many modes of giving free scope to his own natural powers."[19]

The prerequisite is the abolition of capital and wage-labour as social categories (not to speak of the industrial armies of the "labour state" or the various modern forms of totalitarianism or state capitalism). The reduction of man to an appurtenance of the machine, a specialised tool of production, might in principle be overcome, rather than enhanced, with the proper development and use of technology, but not under the conditions of autocratic control of production by those who make man an instrument to serve their ends, overlooking his individual purposes.

Anarchosyndicalists sought, even under capitalism, to create "free associations of free producers" that would engage in militant struggle and prepare to take over the organisation of production on a democratic basis. These associations would serve as "a practical school of anarchism."[20] If private ownership of the means of production is, in Proudhon's often quoted phrase, merely a form of "theft" — "the exploitation of the weak by the strong"[21] — control of production by a state bureaucracy, no matter how benevolent its intentions, also does not create the conditions under which labour, manual and intellectual, can become the highest in life. Both, then, must be overcome.

In his attack on the right of private or bureaucratic control over the means of production, the anarchist takes his stand with those who struggle to bring about "the third and last emancipatory phase of history," the first having made serfs out of slaves, the second having made wage earners out of serfs, and the third which abolishes the proletariat in a final act of liberation that places control over the economy in the hands of free and voluntary associations of producers (Fourier, 1848).[22] The imminent danger to "civilisation" was noted by that perceptive observer, Tocqueville, also in 1848:

"As long as the right of property was the origin and groundwork of many other rights, it was easily defended — or rather it was not attacked; it was then the citadel of society while all the other rights were its outworks; it did not bear the brunt of attack and, indeed, there was no serious attempt to assail it. But today, when the right of property is regarded as the last undestroyed remnant of the aristocratic world, when it alone is left standing, the sole privilege in an equalised society, it is a different matter. Consider what is happening in the hearts of the working-classes, although I admit they are quiet as yet. It is true that they are less inflamed than formerly by political passions properly speaking; but do you not see that their passions, far from being political, have become social? Do you not see that, little by little, ideas and opinions are spreading amongst them which aim not merely at removing such and such laws, such a ministry or such a government, but at breaking up the very foundations of society itself?"[23]

The workers if Paris, in 1871, broke the silence and proceeded

". . . to abolish property, the basis of all civilisation! Yes, gentlemen, the Commune intended to abolish that class property which makes the labour of the many the wealth of the few. It aimed at the expropriation of the expropriators. It wanted to make individual property a truth by transforming the means of production, land and capital, now chiefly the means of enslaving and exploiting labour, into mere instruments of free and associated labour."[24]

The Commune, of course, was drowned in blood. The nature of the "civilisation" that the workers of Paris sought to overcome in their attack on "the very foundations of society itself" was revealed, once again, when the troops of the Versailles government reconquered Paris from its population. As Marx wrote, bitterly but accurately:

"The civilisation and justice of bourgeois order comes out in its lurid light whenever the slaves and drudges of that order rise against their masters. Then this civilisation and justice stand forth as undisguised savagery and lawless revenge . . . the infernal deeds of the soldiery reflect the innate spirit of that civilization of which they are the mercenary vindicators . . . The bourgeoisie of the whole world, which looks complacently upon the wholesale massacre after the battle, is convulsed by horror at the desecration of brick and mortar."

Despite the violent destruction of the Commune, Bakunin wrote that Paris opens a new era, "that of the definitive and complete emancipation of the popular masses and their future solidarity, across and despite state boundaries . . . the next revolution of man, international and in solidarity, will be the resurrection of Paris" – a revolution that the world still awaits. The consistent anarchist, then, should be a socialist of a particular sort. He will not only oppose alienated and specialised labour and look forward to the appropriation of capital by the whole body of workers, but he will also insist that this appropriation be direct, not exercised by some elite force acting in the name of the proletariat. He will, in short, oppose

" . . . the organisation of production by the Government. It means State-socialism, the command of the State officials over production and the command of managers, scientists, shop-officials in the shop . . The goal of the working class is liberation from exploitation. This goal is not reached and cannot be reached by a new directing and governing class substituting itself for the bourgeoisie. It is only realised by the workers. themselves being master over production."

These remarks are taken from "Five Theses on the Class Struggle" by the left-wing Dutch Marxist, Anton Pannekoek, one of the outstanding theorists of the Council Communist movement. And in fact, radical Marxism merges with anarchist currents.

As a further illustration, consider the following characterisation of "revolutionary Socialism:"

"The revolutionary Socialist denies that State ownership can end in anything other than a bureaucratic depotism. We have seen why the State cannot democratically control industry. Industry can only be democratically owned and controlled by the workers electing directly from their own ranks industrial administrative committees. Socialism will be fundamentally an industrial system; its constituencies will be of an industrial character. Thus those carrying on the social activities and industries of society will be directly represented in the local and central councils of social administration. In this way the powers of such delegates will flow upwards from those carrying on the work and conversant with the needs of the community. When the central administrative industrial committee meets it will represent every phase of social activity."

Hence the capitalist political or geographical state will be replaced by the industrial administrative committee of Socialism. The transition from the one social system to the other will be the *social revolution*. The political State throughout history has meant the government *of men* by ruling classes; the Republic of Socialism will be the government of *industry* administered on behalf of the whole community. The former meant the economic and political subjection of the many; the latter will mean the economic freedom of all – it will be, therefore, a true democracy.

These remarks are taken from William Paul's *The State, Its Origins and Function*, written in early 1917[25] – shortly before Lenin's *State and*

Revolution, perhaps his most libertarian work (see note 8). Paul was a member of the Marxist-De Leonist Socialist Labour Party and later one of the founders of the British Communist Party.[26] His critique of state socialism resembles the libertarian doctrine of the anarchists in its principle that since State ownership and management will lead to bureaucratic despotism, the social revolution must replace it by the industrial organisation of society with direct workers' control. Many similar statements can be cited.

What is far more important is that these ideas have been realised in spontaneous revolutionary action, for example in Germany and Italy after World War 1 and in Spain (specifically, industrial Barcelona) in 1936. One might argue that some form of council communism is the natural form of revolutionary socialism in an industrial society. It reflects the intuitive understanding that democracy is largely a sham when the industrial system is controlled by any form of autocratic elite, whether of owners, managers, and technocrats, a "vanguard" party, or a State bureaucracy. Under these conditions of authoritarian domination the classical libertarian ideals developed further by Marx and Bakunin and all other true revolutionaries cannot be realised; man will not be free to develop his own potentialities to their fullest, and the producer will remain "a fragment of a human being," degraded, a tool in the productive process directed from above.

The phrase "spontaneous revolutionary action" can be misleading, especially at a time when there is much loose talk of both "spontaneity" and "revolution." The anarchosyndicalists, at least, took very seriously Bakunin's remark that the workers' organisations must create "not only the ideas but also the facts of the future itself" in the prerevolutionary period. The accomplishments of the popular revolution in Spain, in particular, were based on the patient work of many years of organisation and education, one component of a long tradition of commitment and militancy. The resolutions of the Madrid Congress of June, 1931, and the Saragossa Congress in May, 1936, fore-shadowed in many ways the acts of the revolution, as did the somewhat different ideas sketched by Santillan (see note 4) in his fairly specific account of the social and economic organisation to be instituted by the revolution.

Guerin writes: "The Spanish revolution was relatively mature in the minds of the libertarian thinkers, as in the popular consciousness." And workers' organisations existed with the structure, the experience, and the understanding to undertake the task of social reconstruction when, with the Franco coup, the turmoil of early 1936 exploded into social revolution. In his Introduction to a collection of documents on collectivisation in Spain, the anarchist Augustin Souchy writes:

"For many years, the anarchists and syndicalists of Spain considered their supreme task to be the social transformation of the society. In their assemblies of Syndicates and groups, in their journals, their brochures and books, the problem of the social revolution was discussed incessantly and in a systematic fashion."[27]

All of this lies behind the spontaneous achievements, the constructive work of the Spanish Revolution.

The ideas of libertarian socialism, in the sense described, have been submerged in the industrial societies of the past half-century. The dominant ideologies have been those of state socialism or state capitalism (in the United States, of an increasingly militarised character, for reasons that are not obscure[28]). But there has been a rekindling of interest in the past few years. Theses I quoted by Anton Pannekoek were taken from a recent pamphlet of a radical French workers' group *(Informations Correspondance Ouvriere).* The quotation from William Paul on revolutionary socialism appears in a paper by Walter Kendall given at the National Conference on Workers' Control in Sheffield, England, in March, 1969.

The workers' control movement has become a significant force in England in the past few years. It has organised several conferences and has produced a substantial pamphlet literature, and counts among its active adherents representatives of some of the most important trade unions. The Amalgamated Engineering and Foundry-workers' Union, for example, has adopted, as official policy, the programme of nationalisation of basic industries under "workers' control at all levels."[29] On the continent, there are similar developments. May, 1968, of course accelerated the growing interest in council communism and related ideas in France and Germany, as it did in England.

Given the general conservative cast of our highly ideological society, it is not too surprising that the United States has been relatively untouched by these developments. But that too may change. The erosion of the cold war mythology at least makes it possible to raise these questions in fairly broad circles. If the present wave of repression can be beaten back, if the left can overcome its more suicidal tendencies and build upon what has been accomplished in the past decade, then the problem of how to organise industrial society on truly democratic lines, with democratic control in the work place and in the community, should become a dominant intellectual issue for those who are alive to the problems of contemporary society, and, if a mass movement for libertarian socialism develops, speculation should proceed to action.

In his manifesto of 1865, Bakunin predicted that one element in the social revolution will be "that intelligent and truly noble part of the youth which, though belonging by birth to the privileged classes, in its generous conviction and ardent aspirations, adopts the cause of the people." Perhaps in the rise of the student movement of the 1960s one sees the beginnings of a fulfillment of this prophecy.

In *Anarchism,* Daniel Guerin has undertaken what he describes elsewhere as a "process of Rehabilitation." He argues, convincingly I believe, that "the constructive ideas of anarchism retain their vitality, that they may, when re-examined and sifted, assist contemporary socialist thought to undertake a new departure ... (and) contribute to enriching Marxism."[30] From the "broad back" of anarchism he has selected for more intensive scrutiny those ideas and actions that can be described as libertarian socialist. This is natural and proper. This framework accommodates the major anarchist spokesmen as well as the mass actions that have been animated by anarchist sentiments and ideals. Guerin is concerned not only with anarchist thought but also with the spontaneous actions of popular forces that actually create new social forms in the course of revolutionary struggle. He is concerned with social as well as intellectual creativity. Moreover, he attempts to draw from the constructive achievements of the past lessons that will enrich the theory of social liberation. For those who wish not only to understand the world, but also to change it, this is the proper way to study the history of anarchism.

Guerin describes the anarchism of the nineteenth century as essentially doctrinal, while the twentieth century, for the anarchists, has been a time of "revolutionary practice."[31] ... (which is) the preliminary condition for Socialism inasmuch as Socialism can only be realised in a world enjoying the highest possible measure of individual freedom." This ideal, he notes, was common to Marx and the anarchists.[32] This natural struggle for liberation runs counter to the prevailing tendency toward centralisation in economic and political life.

A century ago Marx wrote that the workers of Paris "felt there was but one alternative — the Commune, or the empire — under whatever name it might reappear."

"The empire had ruined them economically by the havoc it made of public wealth, by the wholesale financial swindling it fostered, by the props it lent to the artificially accelerated centralisation of capital, and the concomitant expropriation of their own ranks. It had suppressed them politically, it had shocked them morally by its orgies, it had insulted their Voltairianism by handing over the education of their children to the *freres Ignorantins,* it had revolted their national feeling as Frenchmen by precipitating them headlong into a war which left only one equivalent for the ruins it made — the disappearance of the empire."[33]

The miserable Second Empire "was the only form of government possible at a time when the bourgeoisie had already lost, and the working class had not yet acquired, the faculty of ruling the nation."

NOAM CHOMSKY

It is not very difficult to rephrase these remarks so that they become appropriate to the imperial systems of the nineteen-seventies. The problem of "freeing man from the curse of economic exploitation and political and social enslavement" remains the problem of our time. So long as this is so, the doctrines and the revolutionary practice of libertarian socialism will serve as an inspiration and a guide.

FOOTNOTES

1 Octave Mirbeau, quoted in James Joll, *The Anarchists*, Little, Brown, 1964.
2 An English translation published by Monthly Review Press. Parts of the present essay appear as the Introduction.
3 Secker and Warburg, 1938.
4 *After the Revolution*, New York, Greenberg, 1937. In the last chapter, written several months after the revolution had begun, he expresses his dissatisfaction with what had so far been achieved along these lines. Though the matter still awaits a careful study, it seems to me that the results were impressive.
5 Cited by Robert Tucker, *The Marxian Revolutionary Idea*, Norton, 1969, in his discussion of Marxism and anarchism.
6 Cited by Joll. The source is *"L'Anarchisme et les syndicats ouvrières,"* Les Temps nouveaux, 1895. The full text appears in D. Guerin, ed., *Ni Dieu, ni Maître*, Lausanne, Le Cite Editeur, undated, an excellent historical anthology of anarchism.
7 Marx, of course, saw the matter entirely differently. For discussion of the impact of the Paris Commune on this dispute see Daniel Guerin's comments in *Ni Dieu, ni Maître;* these also appear, slightly extended, in his *Pour un Marxism libertaire*, Robert Laffont, Paris, 1969. See also note 24.
8 On Lenin's "intellectual deviation" to the left during 1917, see Robert Daniels, "The State and the Revolution: a Case Study in the Genesis and Transformation of Communist Ideology," *American Slavic and East European Review*, Feb. 1953.
9 Paul Mattick, *Marx and Keynes*, Porter-Sargent, 1969.
10 *"La Commune de Paris et la notion de l'Etat"* reprinted in *Ni Dieu, ni Maître.*
11 Bakunin's final remark on the laws of individual nature as the condition of freedom can be compared with the approach to creative thought developed in the rationalist and romantic traditions. See my *Cartesian Linguistics*, Harper & Row, 1966 and *Language and Mind*, Harcourt, Brace, 1968.
12 Reprinted in English translation by Cambridge University Press, 1969, edited and with an Introduction by J.W. Burrow.
13 The similarity is noted by Burrow. See also *Cartesian Linguistics*, particularly note 51.
14 Shlomo Avineri, *The Social and Political Thought of Karl Marx*, Cambridge, 1968, referring to comments in *The Holy Family*, 1845. Avineri

states that within the socialist movement only the Israeli Kibbutzim "have perceived that the modes and forms of present social organisation will determine the structure of future society." This, however, was a characteristic position of anarchosyndicalism, as noted earlier.

15 In addition to those already cited., see his *Jeunesse du socialisme libertaire*, Paris, Librairie Marcel Rivière, 1959.
16 *Critique of the Gotha Programme.*
17 *Grundrisse der Kritik der Politischen Ökonomie*, cited by Mattick, *op. cit.* In this connection see also Mattick's recent essay, "Workers' Control," in P. Long (ed.) *The New Left*, Porter-Sargent, 1969, and Avineri, *op. cit.*
18 Marx, *capital*. Quoted by Robert Tucker, who rightly emphasises that Marx sees the revolutionary more as a "frustrated producer" than a "dissatisfied consumer" *(The Marxian Revolutionary Idea)*. This more radical critique of capitalist relations of production is a direct outgrowth of the libertarian thought of the Enlightenment.
19 *Capital.* Cited by Avineri.
20 Pelloutier, *op. cit.*
21 *"Qu'est-ce que la propriété?"* The phrase "property is theft" displeased Marx, who saw in its use a logical problem, theft presupposing the legitimate existence of property. See Avineri, *op. cit.*
22 Cited in Buber's *Paths in Utopia.* 1945, Beacon, 1958.
23 Cited in J. Hampden Jackson, *Marx, Proudhon and European Socialism*, Collier, 1962.
24 Marx, *The Civil War in France*, 1871; International Publishers, 1941, Avineri observes that this and other comments of Marx about the Commune refer pointedly to intentions and plans. As Marx made plain elsewhere, his considered assessment was more critical than in this address.
25 Glasgow, Socialist Labour Press, undated.
26 For some background, see Walter Kendall, *The Revolutionary Movement in Britain*, Weidenfeld and Nicholson, 1969.
27 *Collectivisations, L'Oeuvre constructive de la Révolution Espagnole*, Editions, C.N.T., Toulouse, 1965. First edition, Barcelona, 1937.
28 For a good discussion, see Michael Kidron, *Western Capitalism Since the War*, Weidenfeld and Nicholson, 1968.
29 See Hugh Scanlon, "The way forward for Workers' Control," Institute for Workers' Control, 45 Gamble Street, Nottingham, Pamphlet Series No.1 1968. Scanlon is the President of the AEF. The Institute was established as a result of the sixth Conference on Workers' Control, March, 1968, and serves as a centre for disseminating information and encouraging research.
30 Introduction to *Ni Dieu, ni Maître.*
31 *Ibid.*
32 *A History of Bolshevism*, 1932, English translation, Russell & Russell, 1965.
33 *The Civil War in France.*

CHAPTER III

Shaking the Foundations

Lucio Lombardo Radice

Bertrand Russell made his first attack on conformism, tradition and the tyranny of common sense on the terrain of mathematical logic and the foundations of mathematics.

The question was: "for any given property P," does there exist "the set of precisely those objects (and no others) which satisfy the condition P?"[1] "It seems intuitively natural that every property should determine a set in the indicated manner. For example, the property 'to be red' or 'x is red' determines the set of all red things. The thesis that every property or condition does determine a set is known as the *principle of abstraction* (the set is 'abstracted' from the property)."

Such a principle is constantly used in everyday practice; it appears as 'undoubtedly' true to the common sense of the common man even today, seventy years after Russell's criticism. However, today the 'common sense' of every student of mathematics and/or philosophy (not to speak of the scholars of logic and the foundations of mathematics) has completely assimilated Russell's criticism of the principle of abstraction. Therefore, we must make an effort to put the clock back seventy years to the time, when the unrestricted validity of the principle of abstraction was taken for granted even by the most advanced logicians and mathematicians. "To Frege (and others of his time) the intuitive plausibility of the principal was fairly great, and Frege made it an axiom of his system . . ." This axiom asserts that "there is a y such that for all x, x is in y if and only if x satisfies the condition A(x)." Such an axiom was fundamental for the new *logical* foundation of mathematics, the goal to which the German scholar Gottlob Frege (1848-1925) dedicated more than twenty years of his activity, from 1879 to 1902.

Twenty-three years after his book on "ideography" *Begriffsschrift*, 1879), ten years after the publication of the first volume of his great work *Grundgesetze der Arithmetik* (1893)[2], Gottlob Frege believed he had attained his goal, of constructing mathematics on a foundation of pure logic.

45

But on the 16th of June, 1902, just as the second and conclusive volume of the *Grundgesetze der Arithmetik* was going to print, the young Russell[3], then thirty years old, wrote a famous letter to Frege, "shaking the foundations" of his edifice. Russell proved, in his letter, that the principle of abstraction in the unrestricted and "absolute" form accepted by Frege, led to contradictions. Let us summarise, in the words of W. S. Hatcher, the "paradox of Russell." "If every condition determines a set, then consider the set y determined by the conditions x ∉ x. That is, y is the set of all sets that are not elements of themselves. Presumably y is a large set, since most sets do not contain themselves as elements (the set of cats is not a cat, the set of real numbers is not a real number, and so on). Now, does y have itself as an element? By the rules of sentential logic, either it does or it does not. If it does, then y∈(x/x∉x) and so y must satisfy the defining condition of the set y; i.e. it must not belong to itself. On the other hand, if y does not belong to itself, then y satisfies the defining condition of y and is thus an element of itself."
itself."

Frege appended an acknowledgement of the contradiction to his work which reads in part:

"Hardly anything more unwelcome can befall a scientific writer than that one of the foundations of his edifice be shaken after the work is finished. I have been placed in this position by a letter of Mr. Bertrand Russell just as the printing of this (second) volume was nearing completion.

Frege saw very clearly that the criticism of Russell shook not only his own foundation of mathematics. "Everyone who in his proofs has employed abstractions, classes, sets, is in the same condition as I am myself. What is put in doubt here, is not just my method of foundations in particular, but the very possibility of a logical foundation in arithmetic."[4]

In order to avoid this paradox (and others similar to it) Russell evolved his famous theory of types: a discussion of which, however, would go beyond the purpose of this article.

Let us stop for a moment to consider the reader's opinion about the facts we have examined so far. I imagine there may be two completely different sorts of reactions. The mathematician might say: "I have no interest in reading it; it concerns things which are too well known." The answer of the scholar who has received a purely 'humanistic' education, and the answer of the purely politically engaged man, might be: "It is beyond my capacities and/or my will to make the effort to understand such subtle problems of mathematics and logic."

The two opposite answers have a common root: the belief in the existence of *two* Bertrand Russells. There is, we are told, Bertrand Russell number one, the mathematician and logician; and Bertrand Russell number two, the humanist engaged in so many political and idealistic struggles of his time. Yes, of course, it will be admitted there was a physical co-incidence between the two Russells: two souls, two minds in the same body. But, what is the difference between *two men*, and *one man* divided into two personalities? For the "average" conservative, Bertrand Russell is the good Doctor Jekyll of science and the bad Mister Hyde of politics; but we have to recognise that the "average" revolutionary has a not dissimilar reaction; with this difference, however: for him the "dark side" of Bertrand Russell the rebel is Russell the scientist — something *added*, something *foreign*. I do not deny that there can exist, indeed, very often there does exist, a gap *in the same man* between scientist and citizen, between the political and the scientific way of thinking. Now, such a phenomenon can be explained in two opposite ways. First scientific investigation and the "humanities" are separated areas of the human mind and of human praxis: they are two ways of thinking, "two cultures." Alternatively, there is the second view: that the contradiction lies in the individual man, as a member of a conflict-ridden, divided society, of a society that separates scientific criticism from social rebellion.

I believe that *culture is one*, that criticism searching for truth is the common character of all kinds of investigation, from pure mathematics to the study of mankind. Scientific revolutions are "isomorphic" to social revolutions, both having the same formal structure. Revolution, in science and/or history, begins by "putting in question" the traditionally accepted foundation: the absolute truth of the dynastic principle, or of the existence of a unique parallel line to a line on a plane through a point. All revolutions start with an act of "mental courage:" whether this confronts the heliocentric hypothesis or the hypothesis of a "social contract:" in other words, all revolutions begin with a counter-hypothesis, an antithesis to the "established" principles. Each revolution always opens with a "why not?"; this requires, in every field, the courage of testing very seriously the possibility that the "non-senses" of the established logic might become the foundations of a new and better logic. Thus we have benefited from the courage of those who have testified to the possibility that measurements of lengths and of time have no absolute character, accepting all the "non-sensical" consequences of such a new relativity principle; or from those who found the courage to put in question the priciple of private property as the necessary foundation of economic production and progress.

In capitalistic society, everything is contradictory; science also is full of contradictions. The law of profit requires an intensive development of production; such a development needs the free progress of science, or, in other words, unrestricted criticism: but, in contradiction, it also needs a lack of criticism as the basis for the social hierarchy of exploitation and privilege.

Clearly, the separation between social and scientific criticism is one way out of this contradiction which the bourgeoisie has discovered; but equally clearly, this convenient separation does not represent an intrinsic difference between scientific and humanistic research.

It is such a well-built separation that produces the *monstrum*: the scientist, who, while capable of shaking the foundations of his own discipline as a scientist, remains at the same time capable of accepting that the nonsensical establishment of imperialism, colonialism, and capitalism shall govern him as a citizen and as a man.

However, the contradiction explodes, even in everyday "average" scientific education; and the unity of scientific and social criticism becomes evident in all the great revolutionaries of science. It becomes clear in the marvellous, tragic youth of Evariste Galois, struggling against privilege in science and in society and the "kingdoms" in social and scientific organisation. It becomes clear and clearer in the long lives of Albert Einstein and of Bertrand Russell.

There is *one* Russell, therefore; no separation between the scientist and the social reformer, between the mathematician and the politician. The same man, the same attitude: shaking the foundations, testing "nonsensical" hypotheses.

FOOTNOTES

1. Here, and later, quotations are taken from the book of W.S. Hatcher, *Foundations of Mathematics*, W.B. Saunders Company, Philadelphia-London-Toronto, 1968, p. 87-110

2. M.Furth has published, in English translation, selected parts of Frege's major work (both the first and the second volumes), under the title: *The Basic Laws of Arithmetic.* (University of California, 1964).

3. It is well known that the first important published work of Russell was *A Critical Exposition of the Philosophy of Liebniz* (1900). (recently translated into Italian by Roberto Cordeschi, *La filosofia di Leibnez*, Newton Company Italiana, 1972). In my opinion there is some connection between this philosophical work and the criticism of Frege's logical foundation of mathematics two years later.

4. This quotation is taken from the fifth volume of the monumental work of Ledovico Geymonat and his school, *Storia del pensiero filosofico e scientifico*, Garzanti 1971; see Ch. 22 IV, "La sistemazione della logica moderna e la logicizzazione della matematica: Gottlob Frege".

CHAPTER IV

What Kind of Individuality?

Lelio Basso

One may say that the theme of humanism recurs from time to time in socialist literature. In recent times, there was a first wave after the publication of the writings of the young Marx in the thirties, which continued immediately after the war, when these writings began to circulate in the West. A second wave originated as a reaction to the revelations of the 20th Congress of the Soviet Communist Party on Stalinism, in 1956; and finally a third wave developed around the theme of 'socialism with a human face' developed by Dubcek. Today there exists a huge literature on this question and it is almost impossible to say in a few pages anything that is really new. Accordingly I shall limit myself to dealing with a particular facet of the problem, a facet that is, it seems to me, rather neglected by the authors who have tested this theme. I refer to the relationship between the individual and the social aspect of man's personality, in bourgeois society and in socialist society.

To understand this problem it is necessary to take it as a premise that there does not exist any immutable human nature, not even on the biological plane, still less on the historical and social plane. Mankind is a product of history, that is of Man himself, of his work: he is, at every moment, the product of a process of self-creation which is pursued indefinitely. Thus the 'nature' of man and, even more, the idea that man has of himself, varies continuously, in the course of the centuries, to the extent that praxis progressively transforms the environment (and hence the relationship between man and nature), and society (and hence the social relations between men themselves, the relations between subject and subject). In parallel, the men whose successive generations come into the light of day, each of which enters into a world which is no longer that of the preceding generation, take over from this world ideas, representations, conceptions, modes of existence, mentality, culture, and so on.

In this process of endless transformation there are nonetheless some fixed points of reference, which, though they are not immutable in the manner in which they show themselves, being subject to a continuous evolution, are nonetheless inseparable from the notion of man. The co-existence in the same person of an individual aspect and of a social aspect constitutes precisely one of these permanent characteristics, and the various postures that they take, the different relationship, the changing equilibrium between them, is a crucial indication of the changes that come about in society, a sign of such importance that it can contribute towards the characterisation of different historical epochs.

Few words are needed to explain what we mean by 'the individual aspect' and 'the social aspect' of a human personality. That every human being constitutes an individuality appears evident from the physical and biological appearances. But there is no doubt that the man of today has also a consciousness of this individual nature of his personality, so that he recognises himself before all else as an individual being. And yet Marx has rightly insisted on man's social character, on the fact that he is the ensemble of his social relations. The isolated individual has never existed: only in the modern epoch, only with the coming of capitalism, has it been possible to imagine 'Robinsonades'. Language itself, which is an essential characteristic of man, is an expression of the need to communicate, and therefore of social life. The individual aspect and the social aspect, clearly, co-exist in man.

But, as we have said, the relationship between these two aspects changes with the changing of social conditions. To the Western man of today the individual aspect appears as an immediate given fact, natural and evident, so much so that society comes often to be conceived as the simple sum of a mass of individuals, and therefore as something extrinsic to the individual himself, as an element added on, which could not exist if the individual decided otherwise. The idea of the 'social contract' expresses precisely the priority of the individual element, so that only at a certain point a person sacrifices a part of himself to put himself into society with others. If these assumptions are widespread, nonetheless in reality the social aspect is the prior aspect. Anthropogenesis, the birth of man, is a collective fact, not an individual fact: and primitive man, if indeed he had any sense of his own physical individuality, at the level of consciousness felt himself to be essentially a member of a group and could not conceive of his own existence outside of such a group.

Evidently we cannot here trace either the history of man or the history of the images that man has had of himself. We may assume that at the beginning man not only lacked consciousness of his own individuality as distinct from the group, but was not even aware of his own subjectivity with regard to nature. On the contrary, he felt himself to be merged with the world that surrounded him, part of this world, in which the boundaries between the material and the spiritual remained as indistinct as those between dream and reality. It is only in the course of a long, dramatic experience, whose traces remain still alive in the vast world of the unconscious, that man has acquired consciousness of his separateness from nature and of his power over nature, and has posited himself as subject, as 'I', interiorising, as attributes of the 'I', powers and faculties that hitherto were thought of as external 'forces', which did not belong to the quality of his being as man, and which might therefore flee away from him: escaping to be sure, from the actual orifices of his body, yet nonetheless not forming part of him in a bodily sense. As this process developed, those greater powers and those greater virtues that humanity did not yet know how to find in itself continued to be exteriorised, but these were no longer dispersed in nature, although they were transferred to a higher subjectivity, divinity. This process of distinction between man and nature, between subject and object, constitutes an important chapter in the history of the human spirit.

But then some further thousands of years were needed for the consciousness of individuality to be added to the consciousness of subjectivity. Though distinguished from his natural environment, man continued to make no distinction, except in a very obscure way, between himself and his social environment, between himself and his tribe, and his village, and his community. In this phase man felt the communal aspect of his being to be more authentic and actual than the individual aspect. Coming out of the group, going into isolation, if ever it had to happen, was a traumatic event which might well prove fatal. In this phase the group was the true historical subject and the collectivity was solidly responsible for the deeds and the sins of each of its members, just as sons were responsible for the sins of their fathers. What one had was not individual responsibility but collective responsibility, which always goes beyond the confines of the individual person, to embrace the whole collective subject, whether this was defined in space (tribe, village, etc.), or in time (successive generations). The curses such as we find in the bible and other ancient texts, which strike future generations and make the descendants bear the sins of their fathers, or the common lot that binds together all the members of a group, cause individual characteristics to be merged into the collective consciousness.

Many historical documents which have been preserved show us how, through thousands of years, humanity has proceeded towards a progressive discovery of individual consciousness and individual responsibility, emerging from the cloudy waters of collective responsibility. We find traces of this progressive discovery in the history of Egypt, where, through profound social, political and religious upheavals, ordinary people won recognition of their individual survival beyond the tomb, which had formerly been reserved only for the Pharaoh, acting as the symbol of the people as a whole, and then, at the very most, for important people, holding high office in the state, who possessed an individuality. We find traces of it in Babylonian history, for example in the codex of

Hammurabi, in which there is to be found the individualistic spirit of the ancient nomads of the desert, a population not tied to a group settlement, who from the very territorial mobility of their existence, were stimulated to enjoy a greater flexibility also in their inter-personal relations; and we find traces in the penitential psalms which sing of the drama of the just man in suffering, the drama of personal responsibility. We find also a very important trace in Hittite history, in the passionate prayer of the King Mursilis, who, stricken for long years by a plague that was destroying his people, and warned by the oracles that the plague was punishing the sins of his father (who had violated the peace with the Pharaoh of Egypt, after swearing an oath before the Gods), appealed to these very same Gods, maintaining, in a polemic that has the flavour of a break with tradition, that he ought not to be held responsible for the sins of his father, that man ought to be called upon to answer individually for his own acts.

So begins that process of distinction between the individual and the collectivity which was destined to triumph in the Western World, a process that asserts itself in a decisive way in Greek civilisation, is universalised in the Christian civilisation, and is the foundation of our present bourgeois civilisation. It would be a mistake, however, to believe that one is dealing with a unilinear and continuous process. On the contrary, we can state, if only in a general way, that as often as an agricultural civilisation triumphs in the course of history, that is to say, a civilisation which ties man to the earth and to the group that collectively cultivates this earth, man tends temporarily to lose his individual characteristics and to be reabsorbed into a collective consciousness: whilst every affirmation of a civilisation based on personal property, on money, on exchange, on trade, on transportation, as in the Greek civilisation or in the medieval communes, in the maritime republics or, finally, at the beginning of the modern age; causes a re-emergence of the individual's will to break with the bonds of tradition, to reaffirm his own individual being in distinction from that of the community.

This process of distinction between the individual and the collectivity tends to present itself to man's consciousness as a process of separation, which is thus immediately one of opposition. If, on the one hand, it represents a step forward in respect of the old confused consciousness, if it represents an advance in respect of the development of human capacities and the full unfettering of personality, it nonetheless enmeshes itself in new contradictions. As fast as the individual aspect gets the upper hand, as capitalism develops into the most extreme forms of egoism (one thinks of the formula 'each for himself and God for all', or 'homo homini lupus est' − man is a wolf to man − or 'bellum omnium contra omnes' − war of all against all, − and similar maxims), the social aspect, which remains an essential part of personality, comes to be exteriorised. This creates a false opposition between man and the collectivity in which he is implanted. In place of the old divinity there enters surreptitiously the state, as a mythical expression of a collective subjectivity, which is no longer the synthesis of the participatory aspects of each man, but an abstract entity, endowed with 'sovereignty,' superimposed on the individual men and opposed to them. By contrast with the ancient Pharaoh, who was the incarnation of his whole people, and who dominated over subjects who felt in much greater degree their quality as members of that collectivity than their quality as individual subjects: and by contrast with sovereignty in those doctrines of contract which were conceived as a self-imposed limitation upon the freedom of individuals, who thus acceded from the individual aspect to that of the collective, the sovereignty of the state in the nineteenth century reassumes and embodies the social and collective aspect of citizens who are strongly endowed with consciousness of their individuality, and feel state power as oppression: whilst the state itself conceives the liberty of the citizen as a self-imposed limitation of its own sovereignty.

This conception of liberty, as the right of the individual to be guaranteed a sphere of activity which cannot be violated by the state, today still common in the West, is nonetheless itself also the fruit of a long historical evolution. As, in the course of social transformations, the vision that man has had of himself has come to be modified in a continuous dialectic between social and individual aspects which exist in reality within his own person, and whose synthesis alone constitutes his personality; so the conception of the relations between the state and the citizen, between the public sphere and the private sphere, has, in a parallel way, come to be modified in the course of centuries. In this manner the notion of the liberty of the citizen has passed over from a communal participatory vision, which did not recognise any contrast between citizens and organised collectivity (the City State, or *Polis)* to an individualistic, typically bourgeois vision, which conceives of liberty not as a mode of participation in the collective life, but as the protection of a sphere of private autonomy reserved for the individual and forbidden to the collectivity.

Benjamin Constant, in his classical essay *De La Liberté des Anciens Comparée à Celle des Modernes* (A Comparison of the liberty of the Ancients with that of the Moderns) has put in relief the profound difference in the conception of human relations which underlies each of the two concepts of liberty. "Liberty, for the ancients," he writes, "means participation in the power of the state; liberty for the moderns is liberty before the state." Croiset has expressed an analogous notion. "Liberty, not only for the Athenians, but also for all the Greeks in general, was a privilege, the privilege enjoyed by the citizen. It consisted essentially in participation in government and in equality before the laws. It did not imply any necessary limitation on the rights of the state." And Jaeger: "In no other time was the state so fully identified with the dignity and worth of man. Aristotle defines man as a political being, and so distinguishes him from the animal by his characteristic of citizenship. This identification of *humanitas,* of the being of man, with the state, is only comprehensible if it is viewed in that vital structure of ancient civilisation, consisting of the Greek *polis* in which social existence is the norm of the most lofty existence, even to the point of acquiring a divine character." In other words, in the ancient civilisation there was no contradiction between individuals and collectivity: on the contrary, the distinctive characteristic of man is precisely his sociality, his belonging to the polis.

By contrast the individual shut up within himself, the private individual, as we are used to thinking of him today, may be said not to have existed. Kahler writes: "Until the end of the Roman Empire there existed no form of life of the kind that we today consider as 'private life.' In the polis a private life, as is indicated by the clearly negative meaning of the latin *privatus,* is a 'deprived' existence, robbed of all the rights and privileges of the community. The Greek word corresponding to 'privatus' has a negative character which is even more pronounced: *idiotes,* which signifies a man who is only interested in his own self, consequently a common man, without talent or education, a complete ignoramus." In no other time can the development of the personality be said to have touched such lofty peaks as in the Athens of the fifth and fourth century B.C., in which the citizen, though having consciousness of his own individuality, did not enclose himself within himself, or consider himself in contradiction to the *polis,* seen as something foreign to himself, but on the contrary, felt his own individual affirmation and his own participation in communal life to be inseparable, and thus attained a high degree of harmony between the individuals and the participatory aspects of his personality, each of which was seen as equally essential. So individualism was not always, as is today asserted, the foundation of human liberty and human dignity.

It may seem that we are now a long distant from our subject of socialist humanism. In reality we have simply wished to demonstrate that the consciousness that man has had of himself has changed in the course of the centuries, as social conditions have changed: and that this consciousness has passed from an exclusively group conception to an individualistic conception such as prevails today, linked as this is with the diffusion of the money civilisation. But we have seen that, in reality, man is the indivisible synthesis of a social aspect and an individual aspect. Both of these are interior to his being: it is not true that society is merely a sum of individuals, a thing superimposed upon and adjoined to their individual natures. And if it is true that the absence of the individual aspect can cause a herd mentality to endure, it is nonetheless true that the crushing of the social aspect impoverishes man and makes his life barren.

Capitalist society is par excellence the money society and at the same time the society of individualism, which tends, daily more and more, to deprive man of his participatory aspect, to render him continually more of an anonymous being, closed, privatised and thus 'deprived' in the ancient sense, that is to say, cut away from the life of other men and of the collectivity. It is significant that in his classical analysis of *The Condition of the Working Class in England.* in the chapter dedicated to the big cities, Frederick Engels dates from 1844, that is, from the beginning of capitalism, this aspect of dehumanisation which is occasioned by the loss of the participatory capacity, by the dominance of anonymity, by the isolation which is experienced even in the midst of the crowd, which is precisely characterised by the big city: an analysis that has often since been repeated by the present day sociologists of the 'Lonely Crowd.'

"After roaming the streets of the capital a day or two," writes Engels, "making headway with difficulty through the human turmoil and the endless lines of vehicles, after visiting the slum of the metropolis, one realises for the first time that these Londoners have been forced to sacrifice the best qualities of their human nature, to bring to pass all the marvels of civilisations which crowd their city, that a hundred powers which slumbered within them have remained inactive, have been suppressed in order that a few might be developed more fully and multiply through union with those of others. The very turmoil of the streets has something repulsive, something against which human nature rebels. The hundreds of thousands of all classes and ranks crowding past each other, are they not all human beings with the same qualities and powers, and with the same interest in being happy? And have they not, in the end, to seek happiness in the same way, but the same means? And still they crowd by one another as though they had nothing in common, nothing to do with one another, and their only agreement is the tacit one, that each keep to his own side of the pavement, so as not to delay the opposing streams of the crowd, while it occurs to no man to honour another with so much as a glance. The brutal indifference, the unfeeling isolation of each in his private interest becomes the more repellent and offensive, the more these individuals are crowded together, within a limited space. And, however much one may be aware that this isolation of the individual, this narrow self-seeking is the fundamental principle of our society everywhere, it is nowhere so shamelessly barefaced, so selfconscious as just here in the crowding of the great city. The dissolution of mankind into monads of which each one has a separate principle, the world of atoms, is here carried out to its utmost extreme."

Thirtyfive years after this description of London by Engels, a French socialist, Jean Jaurès, arrived in Paris and thus records his impressions in a book which appeared in 1910:

"I remember that on arriving in Paris 30 years ago, as a very young man, one winter's evening in the vast city, I found myself seized with a sort of social terror. It seemed to me that the thousands upon thousands of men who passed by without knowing one another, an innumerable crowd of solitary phantoms, had become separated from every attachment. And I was asking myself with a sort of impersonal terror how all these beings could accept the unequal distribution of goods and evils, how it was that the enormous social structure could avoid falling into dissolution. I did not see chains on their hands and feet, and I said to myself: by what miracle are these thousands of suffering and deprived individuals submitting to all that they submit to? I was not seeing the scene properly: the chain was on the heart, but it was a chain of which the heart itself did not feel the burden; thought carried bonds, but they were bonds of which thought itself did not know."

These reflections on the solitude of man in the midst of the mass with which he lives elbow to elbow every day in the great city have today become mere commonplace. But it is significant that it was socialists who were amongst the first to note this absurdity of capitalist society, which has developed forces of production to the highest possible degree of socialisation, which has created the greatest human conglomerations in history, but which at the same time has progressively killed in man his social capacity, all that side of man which participates in collective life. To use the language of Ferdinand Tönnies, capitalism has killed the spirit of *Gemeinschaft*, the community which lives in the human participation of its members and in its turn nourishes it, to put in its place the spirit of *Gesellschaft*, the society that is a sum of anonymous beings linked impersonally by monetary and formal relations, each without any authentic connection with the others, and therefore terribly alone. The adverb 'terribly' has been used expressly, because there is no doubt that solitude generates a sense of fear and insecurity. As we have noted at the outset that the discovery of the distinction between subject and object, the separation from nature, must have been an experience of trauma, to an even greater degree must the discovery of man's own individuality have been traumatic. The separation from the group, an experience full of terror and insecurity, has not only lastingly marked the deep layers of man's consciousness, but remains to this day a primary factor in human behaviour. It is no accident that it has been observed that already 'during the Renaissance the feeling of man's autonomy and of his responsibility for himself ... and the marked tendency towards self-affirmation in these relations, frequently went hand in hand with the feeling of loss of security and loss of stability; feelings such as these did not exist in the medieval ages.'[1] But at the point to which capitalism has today pushed individualism and the isolation of man, insecurity, instability, and fear connected with loss of bonds with the group, are able to reach the ultimate limits of madness. "I believe," writes Fromm (and we share his opinion) "that, individually and socially, man's greatest fear is that of complete isolation from his fellow men, of complete ostracism. Even fear of death is easier to bear. Society enforces its demands for repression by the threat of ostracism. If you do not deny the presence of certain experiences, you do not belong . . . you are in danger of becoming insane. (Insanity is, in fact, the illness characterised by total absence of relatedness to the world outside)."[2]

Depriving man of the communal and participatory aspect of his being, modern capitalism dehumanises him to such a point as to render him an object, a thing. But at the same time, by placing him in the modern socialised process of production, in the immense mechanism of accumulation and of capitalist development, it makes of him an almost insignificant cog in the gigantic machine that is large scale state monopoly capitalism, in which the individual man-cog is equally ignorant of his function and his aims. Deprived of the social side of his being, of scope for its participatory aspect, man also loses his individuality, his individual aspect, and he becomes an object in the power of external forces which altogether escape his control and thus dominate him completely. If it has indeed been the great merit of bourgeois society to arouse in herd-man consciousness of his own individuality, to free in such a way immense energies that have enormously contributed to the scientific, technical, economic, and overall development of society, it is nonetheless true that this parable ends, by condemning the man of today to solitude, to reification, to alienation, to desperation. On this score, Kafka is the most significant author of our time, prophet of a world which has killed even hope.

It is a great merit of Marx that, right from his earliest writings, he tackled these problems and indicated a solution to them. His formative years were in the epoch of the ascendent bourgeoisie and triumphant individualism: and he reacted from the beginning, vigorously asserting man's social character and insisting that it was impossible to concede the existence of pre-social men, of isolated men. "What is to be avoided above all is the reestablishing of 'society' as an abstraction vis-à-vis the individual. The individual is *the social being*. His life, even if it may not appear in the direct form of a *communal* life carried out together with others, is therefore an expression and confirmation of *social life.*"[3]

This is as much as to say that any manifestation of man's life is an expression of his participation in social life, or in other words that the participatory aspect exists *within* the consciousness of man, so that society itself is not the sum of isolated and separate individuals, united by external bonds, but in fact lives within the consciousness of each individual. The same concept was taken up again 13 years later in the introduction to the Critique of Political Economy: "But the epoch which produces this stand-point, namely that of the solitary individual, is precisely the epoch of the (as yet) most highly developed social (according to this standpoint, general) relations. Man is . . . in the most literal sense . . . not only a social animal but an animal that can be individualised only within society."[4] By this Marx does not mean to say that man is merely the result of the totality of social relations that come to bear on him, he does not mean to deny that the synthesis of these social relations makes a unique and individual synthesis, that the aspect of individuality is itself also essential to man. He recognises explicitly the presence of this individual aspect and rightly makes the point that man acquires his individuality in the course of history, in the course of the historical process, as we have already pointed out above. What he resolutely denies is that an 'isolated' individual can exist, since he sees man as a continuous dialectic between the social and the individual aspect of his being both of which are internal to his being, and both essential to the full unfolding of his personality.

Hence the violence of his polemic against a bourgeois society which always tends more and more to isolate man, putting the stress only on his individual character, breaking every form of *Gemeinschaft*, of community based on living participation, reducing everything to impersonal and objective relations, and thus immediately supressing every form of 'intermediate body,' leaving the individual face to face with the state, just as religion puts individuals face to face with God. Religious alienation and political alienation are the fruit of an analogous process: man objectifies, and projects outside of himself, his own forces; and attributes them to a distant subjectivity by which he allows himself to be dominated. The process of political alienation consists precisely in the isolation of man and in the deprivation of his participatory capacity, his social aspect. In this process the ensemble of social aspects of each man, an ensemble that actually constitutes society as a phenomenon that is internal to man, comes instead to be attributed to an extraneous entity, the state, which places itself above and against its constituent individuals as a dominant force, transforming men into abstract beings, mere phantasms, citizens equal one to the other. Such individuals are destined, therefore, ineluctably to lose, together with their social aspect, also their very individuality: characteristics which are simply reduced to the condition of equal cold and smooth billiard balls. "Hegel conceives the affair and the activities of the state abstractly on their own, and sees as their contrary particular individuality; but he forgets that the particular individuality is human and that the affairs and the activities of the state are human functions; he forgets that the essence of the 'particular personality' is not its beard, its blood, its physical abstraction but, to be sure, its *social quality.*"[5] "The perfected political state is by its nature the species-life of man in opposition to his material life . . . When the political state has achieved its true completion, man leads a double life, a heavenly one and an earthly one, not only in thought and consciousness but in *reality*, in

58

life. He has a life both in the *political community,* where he is valued as a communal being, and in civil society where he is active as a *private* individual, treats other men as means, degrades himself to a means and becomes the plaything of alien powers ... Man in the reality that is nearest to him, civil society, is a profane being. Here, where he counts for himself and others as a real individual he is an illusory phenomenon. In the state on the other hand, where man counts as a species-being, he is an imaginary participant in an imaginary sovereignty, he is robbed of his real life and filled with an unreal universality."[6] Translated from the philosophical language of the young Marx, the tenor of these words is that which we have been following up to this point: society and the bourgeois state (what Marx calls the true development of the political state) have brought about a separation between man's individual and his participatory or social aspects: while in his everyday life, in civil society, man's lot is only the private sphere of existence, so that he is not a true man: in political society, where man ought to live to the full, developing the participatory aspect of his existence, his lot is that of 'an imaginary member of a fantastic society,' which is to say that he does not really participate because he is deprived of his 'real individual life' which is precisely the ensemble of his social relations. As Marx later wrote in the *Grundrisse* "Their relationship with each other appears to individuals themselves as something extraneous and autonomous," which is precisely to say that human interrelationships, out of which the participatory capacities of man ought to be nourished, are taken away from man himself and concentrated in the hands of an abstract and distant power.

Marxist communism comes into being precisely as the will to overcome this separation of the two aspects — individual and social — whose dialectical synthesis constitutes the personality of man. To use Marx's expression in the *Manuscripts* of 1844, communism "is the true resolution of the strife between existence and essence," between private existence and social existence: it is, in other words, the reconciliation of man with himself, the end of the dissociation within him which today has carried humanity to extreme forms of dehumanisation and indeed to the threshold of madness. In an article of the same year Marx explains again that "a *social* revolution ... is a human protest against a dehumanised life, because it starts from the standpoint of the *single real individual,* because the collectivity, against whose separation from himself the individual reacts, is the true collectivity of man, the human essence."[7] To restore community to man and man to community, that is to restore man who has been dehumanised to himself again, to give him back his humanity, this is therefore the aim of the social revolution. But to make that revolution it is necessary that man should overcome the alienation of which he is a victim, should come to recognise that the forces by which he is dominated are his own forces which have become extraneous to his control, are his own relationships with other men which have been objectified, of which he has been deprived: this is the way of emancipation. "Only when real man, individual man, reassumes in himself the abstract citizen and, as an individual man in his own empirical life, in his own individual labour and his own individual relations has become a member of the *human species,* only when man has recognised and organised his 'forces propres' as *social* forces and so no longer separates the social force from himself, in the form of *political* force, only then is human emancipation completed."[8] Human emancipation is therefore the reconquest of the unity of man, the reconciliation of man with himself, a new synthesis of his individual and communal aspects which gives realisation to a higher personality.

These analyses of Marx, often involved and complex in form, were perhaps too much against the current of the epoch in which they were written, an epoch of capitalism in its ascendence and of the bourgeoisie triumphant, when the bourgeois ideologies, and hence also individualism, seemed to be a once for all, permanently valid discovery and an eternal idea. Today, capitalism, notwithstanding its continuous expansive force, is threatened by the gravest contradictions. It is only in the last few years that men have come to recognise, what Marx and Engels had already foreseen and denounced, the fact that capitalism also destroys nature and subverts the relationship between man and nature. This process is an attack on the conditions of existence of that type of man which emerged historically in a relationship with nature which has today been completely undermined by the work of spoliation and pollution. The condemnation of the Third World to a condition of exploitation, poverty, and subjection creates ever deeper problems that can only be resolved with the greatest of difficulty. But in the very heart of capitalism, and not only at its frontiers, the threat is greater every day, not only because of the continued growth of the number of those who are in rebellion against the economic consequences of exploitation, which can be modified: but also because of the rising revolt against the alienation, the dehumanisation, the destruction of the participatory quality of life, the solitude, the insecurity and the unbearable moral conditions under which people live.

To reason in terms of modern democracy and modern socialism means to cease repeating the old arguments about the relationship between state and citizen as opposed phenomenon, whose opposition can be resolved under forms of representative democracy or under the form of state ownership of the means of production. The matter at issue is not so much the defence of liberty as a sphere of the private autonomy of individuals against excessive intrusion by the state, nor of exalting the collective public control, against private property, of the means of production. Certainly this can be useful, and to be sure, necessary; but a true human emancipation will be attained only when men have found not outside of themselves but *within* themselves, a new equilibrium, a new harmony, between the specific individual aspect which capitalism has, at the same time, elevated and cast down, and the social aspect, gigantically developed in the forces of production, yet suffocated in man himself: when they shall feel anew, and in so feeling bring into being the reality, that liberty lies not only the defence of a private sphere of autonomy, but also living participation in collective life, and that the collectivity is not a sum of abstract individuals, personified in the state, but the ensemble of those reciprocal relations which have a living existence within us.

Is all this compatible with the development of modern technology, of modern industry, of the immense level of socialisation attained by the productive forces, with all the consequences that this implies? Or is the equilibrium of which we are talking conceivable only at the level of the Greek *polis* (and then only for the citizen, not for the slave) or of the village community, and is it today only a dream destined to remain unrealised? The reply to this question is, for us today, the main reply that socialists must give. Socialist humanism does not consist simply in setting claim to the rights of man against the oppression of the state, whether that be the bourgeois state or the socialist state. It consists in finding, *starting from today*, already within, but in conflict with, the society in which we live, new forms and manners of life in association with others, which entice man to a sense of participation, breaking the vicious circle of his isolation, and rupturing the processes which at present concentrate power in ever fewer and more remote hands. To rebuild society from the base up, dissolving all those patterns of behaviour which centuries of bourgeois civilisation have inculcated; to reassert man's control over himself, over his own life, over his own social relations, his own products; to restore to everyone a sense of his own responsibility towards himself and others, to create a society in the measure of man: this is the authentic revolutionary process which is destined to reduce capitalist society to its foundations, and this is the authentic socialist humanism.

FOOTNOTES

1 Bronislaw Baczko *Marx and the Idea of the Universality of Man:* in *Socialist Humanism* edited by Erich Fromm, Allen Lane, the Penquin Press, 1967, pp.167-8.
2 Erich Fromm, *op. cit.* p.220.
3 Karl Marx: *Economic & Philosophical Manuscripts of 1844,* trans. Milligan, Moscow FLPH, 1961, p.105.
4 *The Critique of Political Economy,* Lawrence and Wishart, 1971, p.189.

5 *Critique of Hegel's Philosophy of Rights:* ed. O'Malley, Cambridge University Press, 1970.

6 *On the Jewish Question:* in *Karl Marx — Early Texts,* translated and edited by David McLellan, Basil Blackwell, 1971, pp.93-4.

7 *The King of Prussia and Social Reform,* McLellan, *op. cit.* p.220.

8 O'Malley, *op. cit.*

CHAPTER V

The Socialism of Antonio Gramsci

V.G. Kiernan

Forty years ago, paralysed by the world slump, capitalism seemed to be on its last legs. Today it looks as large as life, and to nearly everyone twice as natural. It was saved from collapse in Europe, and given time to put its house in order, by fascism, which along with the War also helped to teach it the arts of regulation and of demagogy. This allowed it to evolve towards a new stage, of production for mass consumption, of motor-cars and television sets for all. But while rebuilding its economic basis, it has not succeeded in laying any new moral foundations, or has not tried to: a developed industrial system, which can hand out solid benefits here and now instead of post-dated cheques on Heaven, has less need of ideological supports. Our society is very much a body without a soul.

It has been easier for capitalism to dispense with ideas because socialism in the USSR, intent on catching up materially with the West, has let some of its own ideals fall into the background. And socialism everywhere, though its ultimate task is the liberation of the individual, has in common practice thought too woodenly in terms of "the broad masses", of class solidarity to the exclusion of anything else. Part of the difficulty it has found in recent years in appealing to younger minds, in any organized fashion, whether in communist or in capitalist countries, is that young people have come to insist on being viewed as individuals, not as ciphers in a multitude. Religions have always, when in good trim, known how to make a personal as well as collective approach to their flocks. In the affluent countries something like a dissolution of the mass has been taking place, even if this in itself healthy revulsion away from the *mass-man* has too often taken trivial forms, freakish costume or grotesque hairdressing – the same poor devices that women have always depended on for a sensation of identity, of having personalities of their own. Property has always conferred a similar sense of autonomy, largely illusory since it also imposes conformity to the system by which property-owning is maintained. It has been the cry of prosperous conservatives everywhere that socialism will put an end to all freedom of the self. When Harold Nicolson visited Italy in 1932, during his Mosleyite phase, to see fascism for himself, his comment was that 'it is certainly a socialist experiment in that it destroys individuality.'[1] The more suffocatingly overcrowded our little world grows, the more we shall all be scrambling for any means to escape being obliterated by the mass, until there is only the land of dreams and drugs left to escape into.

Capitalism nowadays can safely allow and indeed encourage the form of liberty that has come to be known as permissiveness. Something like this was happening in France before 1789, and can be recognised in other historical contexts where reconstruction of a whole social and political order has been overdue: individual license is the substitute for collective progress. But we have lately, quite abruptly, been brought up against the fact that reckless multiplication of the human species, combined with reckless use of the world's resources, has made industrialism as hitherto conceived, whether capitalist or socialist, not a solution but a blind alley or trap. It is clear that finding a way out will call not for an extension of liberty, in the crude sense of everyone being free to do as he pleases, or as he is conditioned to do by high-pressure salesmanship, but on the contrary for an extension of controls and rules, in some ways stricter than any ever known. Sundry cherished rights, including the businessman's right to plunder Nature, and the far older and equally sacred right of human beings to burden the earth with as many children as they choose, will have to be abandoned, and the entire economy reoriented. Capitalism has arrived at giving us something near to full employment, but a vast part of the work it provides has about as much social rationality as that offered by the National Workshops of 1848 in Paris – a stock gibe against "socialism" ever since, digging holes in the ground and filling them in again. What now has to be done can be accomplished, in any civilised way, only by socialism, or by capitalism under very strong socialist pressure. It will mean a struggle truly *revolutionary*, even if not in the old literal sense of barricades and sudden seizures of power. We have fascism as an ugly warning of the kind of solutions that impose themselves on a generation which shuts its eyes to the task of finding better ones. Europe did need some form of unification, and Hitler's New Order provided it in one form, by the same blood-and-iron methods that united Bismarck's Germany. It may be that men take more readily either to willing enslavement, as to fascism or war, or to anarchical libertarianism, than to a rational freedom midway between the extremes, which demands self-control.

Thus socialism, so far from having anywhere come to the end of its road, is today more than ever an urgent necessity. To talk of it is no idle discussion of Utopia, to pass the time, as for the courtly castaways on Prospero's island. It is more than ever incumbent on socialism to come forward as socialist humanism, as a humane, civilising force, as its original intention was always to be, freed from any association with the "Stalinist" habits which have done so much to discredit it. This cannot mean a simple return to liberalism; and whatever the shortcomings of socialism where it has held power, its achievements there have been great, and are not to be discarded or discounted. Nor are those of Marxist theory, inadequate and at times warped as its development has been. Classical Marxism however had a certainty of faith which belonged to a narrower Europe where modern technology was only in its cradle. It rested on the conviction that capitalism was destined by its own contradictions to speedy defeat. There can be no such confidence today: those contradictions are more glaring than ever, but overpopulation and exhaustion of resources suffer from no inner weaknesses, and cannot be self-defeating. If socialists are to be able to think of human survival as more than a bare possibility, it must be through belief in the human race, faith in the kingdom of Heaven which lies unrealised within mankind collectively.

Nothing strengthens this faith more than the example of individuals more highly gifted than the average, but eager to identify themselves with and work for the common destiny, like Bertrand Russell. Born into a social and political elite, Russell found his way into an intellectual elite, but he was all his life trying to find his way towards the people, and in spite of failures was little by little succeeding, because prepared to learn as well as to teach. Early a socialist, of Marxism he was often critical, but not ignorant and never contemptuous. Visiting Russia soon after the Revolution he had a long discussion with Lenin, and felt he had 'never met a personage so destitute of self-importance'.[2] The book he wrote about Bolshevik Russia was sceptical, though with moderation; it ended with the hope that communism would not emulate the savagery of capitalism, lately displayed in the Great War, but would prove able 'to heal the wounds which the old evil system has inflicted upon the human spirit'.[3]

As to this we can still only say, in the worlds of his Italian family motto, *Che sarà sarà*. About that same time an Italian socialist twenty years younger than Russell, but who was to die thirty years before him, was paying a lyrical tribute to Lenin and his party, as to a new race of men appearing on earth.[4] Antonio Gramsci, starting life very unlike Russell in a poverty-stricken village, evolved like him into an intellectual of the first rank. These two men so opposite in origin came out on to the same field of ideas, and devoted a great part of their lives to wrestling with the same problems. Not a few titles of books by Russell call up subjects that crop up frequently in Gramsci's writing – *On Education, especially in Early Childhood* (1926); *Power: a New Social Analysis* (1938); *Authority and the Individual* (1949); *Human Society in Ethics and Politics* (1954). Both men, though one was a pacifist and the other a communist party leader, stand out as contributors to the socialist humanism of which our world is so deeply in need.

Gramsci was a west-European, but from one of Europe's most antique corners. D.H. Lawrence was in Sardinia soon after the Great War, in search of the primitive and picturesque, and looked at labourers watching him with 'mediaeval faces, *rusé*, never really abandoning their defences for a moment, as a badger or a polecat never abandons its defences.'[5] Gramsci remembered an aunt who like many of her neighbours mistook the *Dona nobis hodie* ("Give us this day") of the Lord's Prayer for a "Donna Bisodia", a paragon of female virtue.[6] His family history was a chequered one. He had a dash of Spanish and Albanian blood, and it is an odd reflection that his grandfather was a Bourbon officer of gendarmes, his father — a petty official accused of peculation — at one time a convict like himself. He grew up familiar with standard Italian as well as the local patois: in spite of poverty there was something here to give him an early awareness of the gulf between the educated and the illiterate, between intellectual and ordinary people, which was to be one of his besetting problems. A scholarship gave him a college education at Turin, where he learned socialism at the same time, amid the excitements of work in a stirring labour movement and then of the Great War, in which his three brothers were called up, and of left-wing opposition to it.

He was in the first wave of those enthusiasts who founded — in Italy in 1921 — the parties of the Communist International, which with all their failures and shortcomings have been far the most remarkable parties in history, not least by virtue of their incalculable roll of martyrs. He was helping to organise factory councils at Turin, as counterparts of the Soviets, and to build an area leadership which he defended later on as not content with abstract theories but setting itself to deal with 'real men, formed in specific historical relations...'[7] In 1922 he was sent by the party to Moscow, where he could see the dying Lenin's followers at closer range. He was ill, and then in Vienna for a while, unable to return to Italy — now under Mussolini — until 1924, when he was elected to parliament and graduated to first place in the always much-divided Italian party. He and it, with nearly all communists of those post-war years, failed to see that Europe was not moving towards revolution, but sinking into reaction. The Great War had done more to exhaust or demoralise than to generate energy for change. By 1926 the renegade socialist Mussolini, at the head of his new Fascist movement, was effectively dictator. In that year Gramsci was arrested and given a long prison sentence, served in worse and worse health, most of the time at Turi in the far south, until late in 1933 — thanks to protests abroad about his treatment — he was removed to a succession of clinics, in one of which, in Rome, he died in April 1937.

Gramsci's prison achievement — a collection of letters which are now a recognised literary classic, and a series of notebooks filled with Marxist commentary on history, politics, society — is a unique memorial of how the revolutionary spirit can be preserved when hope of any near success has to be renounced. In gloomier moods he talked of the notebooks as only an occupation to pass away the leaden hours,[8] but it is clear that he really took them very seriously, even though he could have no assurance of anyone else ever being able to read them. Intellectually he was never a captive; his mind was always with the movement he had been part of, and with its vision of history, past and to come; like Hamlet in his nutshell he was "king of infinite space." And there may be times when to be a bodily prisoner is for such a man a lesser evil than to be free but unlistened to: in his cell he is at least free to believe that there are those outside who would listen if they could. Marx himself spent long periods of self-isolation at purely theoretical tasks; even Lenin could shut himself up in a library and write about empirio-criticism. They and many others had the benefit, as it was in some ways, of long spells of exile, rescuing them from the treadmill of organisational work. (Mao, by contrast, had no release from this until old age). Gramsci's destiny saved him at any rate from the most painful fate of communist leaders in his lifetime, which was to find themselves in power and at daggers drawn with one another.

Physically he was small, deformed, short-sighted, a chronic invalid even before his arrest; his body might have seemed prison enough for any human being, without need of stone walls, and one must wonder how long he could have endured the burden of political leadership if Mussolini had not relieved him of it. He filled his notebooks, page by page, like Browning's heroic grammarian who "Gave us the doctrine of the enclitic *De,* 'Dead from the waist down.' " In the earlier days this frail body still had a store of resilience. When he and his companions were on a long, painful railway journey, handcuffed to a chain, 'we had a sense of the perfection of the human mechanism, which can adapt itself to the most unnatural situations'.[9] To be accustomed to ill health is to be prepared in advance for loss of liberty, and hardship and privation were no novelties for Gramsci, with a boyhood of poverty and labour to look back on. He was proud of having known even then how to take responsibility for his own life.[10] Learning to live, he said, is harder than inventing philosophies of life.[11] He took pride also in a practical kind of common sense, an ability to face facts, to accept whatever he was reduced to and make the best of it. The vital need was to maintain strength of will and self-discipline, to go on working, never to surrender.[12] To be weak is to be miserable.

There were four years during which he never saw his face in a mirror, and when at last he did it was a shock.[13] Yet he was able to preserve his mental balance, with little company of other minds for a social mirror. He kept, as he says in various letters, his intellectual curiosity, his rooted habit of trying to analyse every thought or impression that came to him, and a faculty – of special value because his access to books was very limited – of extracting mental nourishment from even the most arid or trivial writings, as if born a desert plant. 'A political prisoner must know how to draw blood out of a turnip', he told a friend.[14] He was supported by a sense of humour, an appreciation of the ridiculous or incongruous in life, which could be aroused by very simple matters like the solemn arrest and incarceration of the trespassing pig at Ustica, the island of his pre-trial detention,[15] but which shaded into a fine irony of awareness and self-awareness. Four years later he confessed to his mother 'I don't laugh as heartily as I used to,' though he added 'I have not lost my taste for life; everything still interests me'.[16] In the later years it is in his letters to his small sons, far away in Moscow, whom he pined to be with — and to whom he could be no more than a name — that love of fun and drollery peep out again; as when he teases one of them for drawing pictures in which men walk on tip-toe on branches of trees or on top of animals' heads.[17]

Humour helped to keep him safe from egotistic self-absorption. Ustica, and then Naples, showed him types of men and women he had never encountered before. All varieties of mankind roused his interest. On a railway journey he was greatly intrigued both by an anarchist workman, under custody like himself, an 'ultra-individualist' who refused to be known by any other name than *The Unique,* and by a brigadier who was on the train and got into conversation with him, and proved to be full of wild philosphical fancies of his own.[18] In the Milan prison in 1927 he scrutinised observantly the daily round of its life — 'one is continually seeing new faces, each of them hiding a personality to be deciphered.'[19] Isolation deepened the feeling he had never lacked of human beings in their diverse qualities. He went on noting the reactions of his fellow prisoners, so far as he was in contact with them, and confessed that it sometimes horrified him to think of his own future when he saw the condition of many of them after five or ten years, their obsessions about their health, their wild hopes of a coming amnesty.[20] He saw a convict burst into tears one day when some other ration was issued instead of the regular soup. 'Hot soup had come to be for him his blood, his life. One understands why in the Lord's Prayer so much is made of our daily bread.'[21]

With all his dour stoicism Gramasci was sometimes very near the end of his resources. 'For more than a week I have not slept more than three-quarters of an hour a night,' he wrote in 1932.[22] An over-active mind was "fretting the pygmy body to decay." But it was another compensation that he could take the same absorbed interest in the inner world of his own experience as in the outer world from which he was exiled. Everyone ought to learn to psychoanalyse himself, was one of his maxims,[23] and as might be expected he was struck by the novel ideas of Freud, whom he blamed however for trying to make a philosophy out of a heap of empirical observations.[24] There were in Gramsci the makings of a remarkable psychologist, as there were also of a moralist; attributes in which the Marxist tradition, extroverted and sanguine, has been deficient.

In solitude he detected in himself feelings or states of consciousness long since left behind by his more logical self yet still emotionally persisting,[25] as they may be said to do in societies as well as in individuals. He was much drawn to child psychology, and to recollections of his own childhood, partly because his mind was often on his children, partly because, as he said, when one has no future to look forward to one falls back on memories of the past.[26] Even here the faculty of critical detachment was still awake; he watched himself as alertly as his jailers watched him, and was always making discoveries about his own reactions to life. At one time he had the experience of meeting some of his own prison thoughts in letters written by a nineteenth-century forerunner.[27]

He found in himself an impediment to emotional self-expression, which he thought of as a Sardinian trait.[28] In spite of it he experienced a need, sharpened by forced seclusion, for close relations with members of the strange human race to which he belonged. Prison virtually reduced his links with the outside to his relatives, and the family circle open to him was anything but an ideal one for helping to sustain him. His mother and sisters were uncomprehendingly Sardinian, though two brothers were able to give him some support; his wife was a sickly, neurotic foreigner in distant Russia. He had at times to reproach them for neglecting him, to try to make his mother understand the importance of letters to a prisoner,[29] as a lifeline to the world of the living. On his side his letters show a remarkable insight into his old mother's feelings, and he found more meaningful things to write to her than most men can to their parents, even when there is no intellectual gulf between them like the gulf which Gramsci's human sympathies were somehow able to bridge.

It was usually he, so much in need of comfort himself, who had to supply firmness and courage to others; into his patiently intense efforts to reach mutual comprehension with them must have gone much of the energy he was debarred from expending on the awakening of the people. The Julia Schucht whom he met and married in Moscow, a Russian born into an emigré family in Geneva, must have been at the best of times an elusive creature; and for so complex a being as Gramsci the process of falling in love with any woman must also have been complex and enigmatic. He was often conscious now of clouds of incomprehension or estrangement coming in the way of any real exchange of thoughts. 'We have never succeeded in starting a dialogue between us two,' he lamented in one letter, 'our letters are a set of "monologues" . . .'[30] As often he was experiencing vividly what for ordinary men and women is an unnoticed commonplace; far more marriages, it may be guessed, consist of pairs of monologues than of dialogues. It was characteristic of him to respond to this worsening dilemma rationally as well as emotionally, trying to look at his wife and their relationship with sober judgement as well as feeling; with the same dual vision he contemplated everything in his world, private or public. In November 1930, and again several years later, we see him reading her letters first emotionally, and then a second time with deliberate detachment.[31] Near the end of his life, when there was a question of her visiting Italy, he wrote unselfishly that if they met again after their ten years' separation it must be only as friends, free to decide afresh on their future.[32]

He was more regularly in touch with his wife's sister Tatiana, who lived in Italy, teaching science; she was able to visit him at times, and figures in the letters as his chief correspondent, and an intelligent, amiable, but feckless person ill-supplied with common sense, much resembling those women of the old Russian left-wing intelligentsia whose slipshod habits so irritated a man like Lenin. She exasperated Gramsci not seldom by pressing on him gifts or offers of service perfectly useless or impossible for him to accept, and he was stung into reproaching her for an inability to realise the harsh conditions under which he had to exist. At one moment he was deeply distressed by a fear that she was becoming entangled in anti-Semitic confusions; he sent her a penetrating commentary on the whole subject observing that questions of race or colour had never been stirred up in Italy, no-one in the north-west was shocked if a sailor brought home a black wife.[33] He struggled to get Tatiana to reform her ill-regulated mode of living, her carelessness over food. He preached to her the same virtues that he fostered in himself, self-discipline and constancy of will — qualities that Mussolini held up to the nation, in the guise of brute strength and will to domineer. History often exhibits the same things in heroic and in grotesque shape side by side, and socialism and fascism were the Jekyll and Hyde of the same Europe. In the end Tatiana rendered a magnificent service to make up for all the foolish ones she had tried Gramsci's patience with, by smuggling out of the clinic where he died the thirty-three notebooks where his ten years' thoughts were hidden.

Gramsci never gave way to any temptation to dramatise himself and his fate, to indulge in Promethean gestures, or to dream away the unalterabilities of either public or personal life. Another of fascist Italy's bizarre combinations is the spectacle of Gramsci, one of his country's great writers as well as thinkers, quietly at work in his cell, and Mussolini, pseudo-thinker and pseudo-artist, daily bellowing from his balcony and letting the world know of his nightly communings with his violin, his raptures of a minor Nero. Always repelled by crude undigested Marxism, Gramsci was at least equally so by the froth and flamboyance of 'Nietzschean charlatans in verbal revolt against all that exists', the 'fashionable titanism' of the Italy of D'Annunzio and Mussolini.[34] A thinker is formed by the mould of his society, but also by reaction against it; Marx took to realism in disgust at his pipe-puffing, philosophising Germany, Gramsci cultivated sobriety of language and conduct in protest against the gesticulatory rant whose appeal to the Italian temperament he must have been conscious of. Yet with all this restraint and moderation he had in him a strong infusion of the Romantic sensibility, the artistic temper as, among socialists of his day, Trotsky too had, with less of Gramsci's ability to keep it under control. He was an individual acutely conscious – prison can only have intensified this – of his own existence, his inner self and its separateness from others; a kind of consciousness that "monolithic" communism was setting itself to excommunicate. The fact of most of his letters being written to women may have done something, whether he thought they were being understood or not, towards turning the sensations of those crawling years into words still vividly alive. Women are always strangers, and strangers are easier to talk to. But his world was always bathed in the light of imagination. One facet of him was a keen feeling for nature; it shows in several of the letters from Ustica,[35] before he was shut away from nature's sounds and sights. Such a man could spin fine literature out of himself in his cell, without effort, and find things to say with a meaning for us all, since we are all, more or less rigorously, condemned to solitary confinement, or shut ourselves up self-condemned in our own cells.

A newcomer to Gramsci should begin by dipping into the letters, and getting to know him.[36] Either they by themselves or the notebooks would have been an astonishing achievement; in mood and manner, though the same themes can often be found in both, they are as far apart as *Alice in Wonderland* and Lewis Carroll's mathematical treatises. Matters of style were for Gramsci of serious importance. 'Literary expression reflects a corresponding mental life, an attitude that may be called "Goethean", one of serenity, of composure, of unshakable certainty.'[37] Another aphorism of his is that a style which satisfies good taste is the proof of harmony between what a man says and what he really feels;[38] we may recall the saying of another Marxist, Isaac Deutscher, that he made good style the first test of the truth of any political writing, from *Das Kapital* downwards.[39] In the notebooks the diction is severely dispassionate and grey. Here Gramsci was only jotting down fragmentary trains of thought as they arose, and he had need besides of some artificial disguises. Near the end, after a joke about professorial pedantry, he told his wife: 'Most of the time *I* am a pedant, against my will; I have manufactured a utility style, under pressure of circumstances, during these ten years of multiple censorship . . . a jailhouse mode of writing from which I don't know if I shall ever free myself after so many years of constraint.'[40] But pedantry, he added in a letter soon afterwards, is a lesser evil than sloppy superficiality.[41] Even in the notebooks there are scattered moments of the play of fancy, of thinking in images. Bukharin's habit, when writing against non-Marxist philosophers, of picking out insignificant ones to demolish reminds him of 'a man who cannot sleep because of the moonlight and who exerts himself to kill as many fireflies as he can

71

convinced that the light will wane or disappear.'[42] Marxism 'is beginning to exercise its own hegemony over traditional culture, but the latter, which is still robust and above all is more refined and finished, tries to react like conquered Greece, to stop the crude Roman conqueror from being victorious.'[43] It is easy to guess how Gramsci, restored to liberty, would have revelled in the process of licking his rough jottings into literary shape, as that other great writer Marx once told Engels he was doing.[44]

Gramsci's literary standards were formed by remarkably wide reading, poetry as well as prose. He was a devotee of the theatre; part of his political apprenticeship was served as dramatic critic of the Socialist paper *Avanti,* and he was one of Pirandello's earliest admirers.[45] Allusions to the drama are scattered through the letters: to Bernard Shaw, for instance, in connection with a question Gramsci raises of how far a playwright ought to seek to impose his conception of his characters, in every detail, on producers and actors.[46] One noble ambition of his was to learn to read English with ease.[47] We find him discussing or referring to Shakespeare and Kipling, Fenimore Cooper and Defoe and Jack London. In one suggestive passage he looks at Sherlock Holmes, exponent of a system of investigation based on external facts, as the heir of a Protestant bent of mind, Father Brown with his intuitive perceptions as a Catholic; and of the two he finds the latter more congenial.[48] In Russian literature he knew Pushkin's stories, paid tribute to Chekov as a foe to philistinism, and had an unbounded admiration for Tolstoy. As to Italian, he had earlier on written an essay on the evolution of the language, which he loved and felt in all its richness. Dante, the great political poet, was bound to appeal to him; in his dark days and nights many passages of the *Inferno* must have come back into his mind, and a conjecture about the meaning of the tenth canto occupied his mind at intervals for several years. In this canto Dante traverses the fiery place of punishment of the heretics, and meets among them Farinata, as indomitable yet 'as if he held Hell in great disdain.' Among contemporary Italian writers Gramsci does not seem to have known the work of Cesare Pavese, whose diary, begun in 1935, tells us much of the state of the arts under fascism. He too was a student at Turin, and the city was his favourite setting for novels.[49] His novel *The Political Prisoner*[50] portrays the year of banishment to a remote corner of Italy imposed on him in 1935, much like Gramsci's early detention at Ustica.

Queries and comments on cultural history are many in the prison writings, and it would be a profitable task to assemble them, just as Gramsci notes while criticising Bukharin that his references to aesthetics ought to be collected and analysed — adding that his view of Goethe's "Prometheus" was superficial.[51] Of music and painting, those two very Italian arts, Gramsci (although his wife was a musician) says much less. It may be a significant fact that most of the great Marxists from Marx onward have been attracted far more by the literary arts than by any of the others, where social content or message is far less readily conveyed or deciphered. Gramsci does at one point speak of music as today's most universal medium, through which a psychic condition can rapidly spread from one culture to another. He has in view the phenomenon of a debased, Americanised type of music and dancing, derived originally from the dances of West African tribesmen round their fetishes, filtering into Europe with results which must be, he points out, far-reaching.[52] They have gone on worsening since then, through the spread of jazz and all its derivatives, the whole gamut of what may be termed the *gibbering and twitching* art of our epoch. This can be recognised as a concomitant of industrialism, of a social environment dominated by inhuman machinery which men can only fraternise with or rise above by making even more noise, in similar mechanised or galvanic rhythms. Such noise evidently has an insidinous charm for blunted ears in socialist as well as capitalist countries. This is "popular" music, but "serious" composers too have displayed wonderful ingenuity at making orchestras reproduce the strident, endless, remorseless din of the machine-shop.

Gramsci could, especially in his earlier years, sound very much a traditionalist, eager to unlock for the disinherited the treasure of culture hidden in the vaults of class society. Now that we are all conservationists, socialists may well think it part of their mission to save these treasures from being left to rust, blighted like nature by capitalist materialism. The past has bequeathed to us 'elements which have eternal value, which cannot and must not perish,' he wrote in those hopeful early years, and he found in current neglect of them a symptom of bourgeois degeneration.[53] He and his friends started their paper *Ordine Nuovo* at Turin, he tells us, inspired by 'a vague passion' to help to spread culture among the working people, and their readers welcomed it because in its pages 'they found something of themselves, their own better selves.'[54] Every class as well as individual has a higher as well as lower self, which emerges when circumstances are propitious. Introducing a series of articles on Leonardo da Vinci, *Ordine Nuovo* declared that 'a Communist cultural review' must come to the aid of 'workers to whom the class struggle has given a new sense of dignity and liberty,' and who feel bitterly their ignorance of the poets and philosphers.[55] We may recall what Byron and Shelley – whose "Queen Mab" went through a score of editions and came to be known as "the Chartist's Bible"[56] – meant to toilers of the early industrial epoch in England, not yet completely cut off from the rural well-springs of poetry. Gramsci looked forward to seeing the leisure provided by the new eight-hour day being devoted to 'cultural work in common.'[57] Half a century later it must be confessed, nowhere more than in Britain, that capitalism has had one of its biggest and worst successes in the field of national leisure, that annual expanse of thousands of millions of hours; the "tired businessman" with his taste for facile, fatuous entertainment has been joined by too many tired working men.

Gramsci's own mind seems to have been painfully divided at times between veneration for Europe's artistic past, and an iconoclastic impulse to cast out all traditional culture, as tainted by its social origins, to make room for something new and more truly of the people. Revolutionary times and minds like his or Milton's have often felt ascetic promptings like these. Gramsci must besides have been disgusted by the spectacle of men like Pirandello and other writers he had admired coming to terms so readily with fascism. In the realm of philosophy he maintained that 'the beginnings of a new world, always hard and stony, are superior to the agonies of a declining world and to the swan-song which it brings forth.'[58] The same claim should be valid for the artistic "Waste Lands" of societies in their decadence as well, and if so the remedy might be to turn back to a healthier past in search of a fresh start. On the contrary, Gramsci held in some moods at least, during the first stages of working-class power 'Cultural policy will above all be negative, a critique of the past; it will be aimed at erasing from the memory and at destroying.'[59] This sternly puritan attitude has come into its own in the China of the Cultural Revolution, and been responsible for some certain losses and some as yet uncertain gains.

Gramsci's interests had the many-sidedness that has been a feature of the Marxist intellectual tradition, while academic thinking has retreated into smaller and smaller corners. It was never stronger than in Marx and Engels themselves, stimulated as the men of the Renaissance were by rapid social and scientific change. Gramsci belonged to another such time, and his mind roamed in many directions. He recognised the bearing of linguistic data on philosophy, and remarked: 'What the pragmatists wrote about this question merits re-examination.'[60] In church-ridden Italy he was bound to give a good deal of thought to religion, and he was an acute observer of it. By the time socialism entered the lists religion in the Catholic countries was trained and toughened to obstruct it by a century's dogged resistance to its earlier challenger, liberalism. Now this was merging with twentieth-century conservatism, and was tempted to join hands with the Church against social reform. Gramsci's early mental growth owed much to the intellectual movement of emancipation from the dead hand of theology which was led by Croce. He gave high credit to Croce for thus opening the way for 'a "religion of freedom",' meaning by this expression 'a faith in modern civilisation with no need of anything transcendental, of any revelations.'[61] He meant by it, in short, humanism. But with Croce and his liberal followers it was humanism without socialism, without an anchorage in the needs of mankind, and it was therefore fragile: many of them were relapsing into obscurantism, and Croce himself was prepared for a while to collaborate with fascism.

In those years, Gramsci wrote, the papacy was learning new tactics, 'manoeuvring brilliantly.'[62] He was however far from being a vulgar anti-clerical, such as Mussolini had once been before he struck his bargain with the Vatican over the prostrate mind of Italy. Gramsci liked H.G. Wells's *Outline of History* but found in it too much anti-clerical bias.[63] His own numerous comments on religion in history — one of the themes it is most to be regretted that he was never able to develop thoroughly, and a task Marxism has still not taken up — show a more discriminating approach. He could do justice, while defining the place of St. Francis in medieval Christendom, to his idealism, and to his poetic gists.[64] He thought of the Calvinist belief in predestination as the 'classical form' under which a creed may be translated into a rule of action.[65] All Gramsci's speculations took, like this, a historical shape, and history was with him the grand interest, embracing all the rest. He saw men and things in the setting of their growth, the past as inseparable from them as root from plant, or shadow from sun. His mind ran most often on the formative phases of his own nation, from the 16th century, where he pondered on the enigmatic figure of Machiavelli, to the 19th, with its movement for national unification and independence, whose shortcomings saddled the Italy which finally emerged with so many weaknesses.

Quite apart from his Marxism, it may be observed, this preoccupation with his country's modern history came more instinctively to Gramsci as an Italian, indeed as a continental European, than it does to Englishmen — of all European species the richest in history, as in poetry, and the most indifferent to both. Tocqueville pointed long ago to the Frenchman's preoccupation with his national annals, full of feuds and controversies still unsettled, by contrast with the Englishman's dismissal to oblivion of events that for him were over and done with, an account closed. In many a city from Paris to Athens the travelling Briton is surprised to find streets taking their names from dates of historical events; in their history-books he is surprised to find political movements labelled by the name of a month, like the "Thermidorian" at the end of the French Revolution, or the "Septembrist" in nineteenth-century Portugal. True, the foreigner remembering times gone by does so far oftener in a primitive spirit of partisanship than of sober enquiry, a bigotry carried so extravagantly far in northern Ireland. By comparison the Englishman is blissfully free of ancestral vendettas. But this is a negative advantage only. Socialism and humanism alike stand in need of a rational consciousness of the past, still silently at work in the present. Any country where ordinary folk could be got to think seriously about their past would have a better chance of a brighter future; fortunately for our governors, a serious concern with history is a slow outgrowth of culture, and does not come of its own accord to men and women, few of whom retain much recollection of things done or suffered in even their own bygone years. Marxism has had very limited success as yet in arousing such a concern. English Marxists have delved into the character and outcome of the English Revolution, and of British imperialism. But the civil broils of the 17th century are — it would seem — too remote in time, the empire too remote in latitude and longitude, to come home with any urgency to the man in the street.

Whatever historical topic he thought about, Gramsci was always concerned at the same time with Marxist historical theory, which he saw as being still at quite an early stage. Abstract logic of the old type had few adherents left, he wrote to Tatiana. 'The dialectic, on the other hand, that is to say the concretely historical mode of reasoning, has not yet arrived at textbook shape.'[66] As a Marxist he stands out by his high estimate — too high, in the view of some Marxists — of the part played in human affairs by ideas, and of the relative freedom of ideas, of the will, from the overlordship of material forces. Marxism as commonly understood he repudiated as a travesty, as doctrinaire in its erection of the mode of production into an 'unknown God' as any medieval theology.[67] In harmony with this conviction was his high estimate of the part played and to be played by intellectuals. One of his weightiest projects was a study of the evolution of the intelligentsia in Italy. Most architects of Marxist thought were born in the educated classes, and were forced as they came into active life to take note of heavy social clogs weighing down the movement and influence of ideas. Gramsci entered the world of the mind from outside, from the wilderness where at the age of eleven he was earning a daily kilogram of bread by ten hours' labour;[68] to him knowledge might well appear in an opposite light, as a potent, liberating force. His prime quest was always for the obscure frontier between freedom and necessity, the limit within which the human will could act as a free agent, 'as protagonist in a real and effective historical drama.'[69]

Gramsci continued to have faith in the ability of the human will to prevail against all humanity's problems and perils, because he remained untouched by anything like misanthropy, any rancour against his fellow-men. Never losing possession of himself, he never seems to have lost his respect for the human race and his confidence in its future. Yet evidently he regarded it as so far a very unfinished thing. Religion and conservatism have always wanted us to think of human nature as a fixed constant, with enough evil in its make-up to render any radical improvement in the human condition impracticable; though, rather inconsistently, they look on their own institutions — papacy, Tory party, British monarchy — as flawless. Marxism has been content to assert that men change in response to changes of social environment, which is doubtless true, but leaves it to be asked whether the alteration is in behaviour rather than in character, and is therefore superficial, impermanent. Here is another riddle of the Sphinx about which we must regret that Gramsci could not put together his thoughts more fully. He raised the question "What is Man?" and answered it by saying that man is what he is capable of becoming — 'man is a process.'[70] Nietzsche, one of Mussolini's and Hitler's mentors, had said the same, though he saw the process leading another way, towards an iron-fisted Superman. Between the most opposite philosophies of any epoch there are bound to be some parallels like this, and one can be seen as a distorted image of the other. Either of these two might draw evidence from times of war or revolution when the mass — like the individual in the excitement of 'liquor, love, or fights' — alters and expands most rapidly and unpredictably. It then not only undergoes a forced growth but recaptures dormant faculties or energies from the whole of its past, including its prehistoric and pre-human past, some of them healthy, others evil, so that the expansion or exaltation is always regressive as well as progressive.

In practical terms, Gramsci attached very great importance to education. He might be called an educationalist to his fingertips, for whom schoolroom-learning and politics, culture and the conduct of life, were all parts of one endeavour. It was not his way to make any of them look simple or effortless. He had come by his own education and self-education painfully; he understood it as a wrestling with knowledge, a gradual transformation of the whole man. He would have found something to agree with in the ancient saying that there is as much difference between lettered and unlettered as between living and dead. He wanted a 'unitary school,' 'a single type of formative school,'[71] which sounds much like our "comprehensive" model. Its curriculum should include 'the first nations of State and Society as basic elements of a new conception of the world.'[72] In schoolroom and society alike he was a believer in discipline and self-discipline, which he hoped would lead on at the higher stages to methods of group study, students pooling their resources, learning through mutual aid and mutual criticism.

Something like this has been making a welcome appearance of late in our own universities. But there is a useful lesson for our times, accustomed to think as casually of "expanding education" as of blowing up a paper bag, in Gramsci's insistence on the necessity of hard work, and of accuracy. Teaching has grown vague, pretentious, he writes: 'the pupil does not bother with concrete facts and fills his head with formulae and words which usually mean nothing to him.'[73] This tendency has gone on spreading since he wrote; in the English-speaking world one symptom of it is an almost universal inability of college students to write a page of their own language correctly. Gramsci's academic rigour recalls his refusal, before his imprisonment, to allow any of his journalistic work to be republished, because it did not satisfy his own standards.[74] As regards subject-matter, the traditionalist side of him is nowhere more happily expressed than in his defence of Latin and Greek, his stress on their immense value in 'the formation of character by means of the absorption and assimilation of the whole cultural past of modern European civilisation . . . the accusation of formalism and aridity is very unjust and inappropriate.'[75] Words to be inscribed in letters of gold above the door of every academy.

One aspect of education which meant much to Gramsci was its connection with the emancipation of women. Here too his Sardinia was a stony soil. At one place, we read in a report of the years before 1914, 'the girls' school has not even a window, and is lighted by some holes in the roof, through which, in bad weather, the rain falls abundantly on the pupils.'[76] Nevertheless, in his eyes any chance of education was to be snatched at, just as in jail any books were better than none. His own stoicism drew strength from memories of his mother's fortitude when she was left with seven young children to bring up,[77] and he wanted to see women helping themselves, not passively waiting for help. He was disgusted by news of a niece whom laziness and lack of 'ambition in the noble sense of the word' seemed to be dooming to no better fate than to suckle fools and chronicle small beer. 'She will share the lot of other Italian girls: to become what are called good mothers of families, that is if they can find some imbecile to marry them — which is not certain, because the imbeciles want brainless hens for wives, but hens with land in the sunshine and money in the savings-bank.'[78]

Pavese's novel *The Political Prisoner* has for second theme the alienation of men and women in Italy. But this has run through most of history, and reformers, Gramsci observed, have often been very conscious of it. 'It is worth noting that in "Utopias" the sexual question plays a large and often dominant part.'[79] One mission of fascism, he might have added, was to rivet the old fetters more firmly again. He noted the sex crisis caused by the absence of young men during the Great War and the shortage of them after it:[80] this indeed may be taken as one of the taproots of fascism, with the cult of virility, because it left the young "imbeciles" to posture before an admiring audience of surplus females. In Turin two-fifths of the workers were women, and they were to the fore in the labour movement. Gramsci saw as a vital need for them not only more independence but 'a new feminine personality,' 'a new way of conceiving themselves.'[81] He may sound like an earnest socialist schoolmaster, wanting his pupils to take life seriously, when he talks of monogamy as a requirement of the new industrial life, love 'shorn of the bright and dazzling colour of the romantic tinsel typical of the petit bourgeois and the Bohemian layabout.'[82] The new personality is still undiscovered, women everywhere are still in more or less need of liberation — though whether from men, or from themselves, may not always be clear. Romantic tinsel, along with its accompaniment of synthetic popular art, has spread further and wider, a consolation for the aridity of an industrialism more and more irrational and empty of social purpose. In this as in so many ways mature capitalism with its cornucopeia of cosmetics, stimulants, and tranquillisers has had a more insidious success than the older capitalism with its truncheons.

Many of Gramsci's opinions are thrown into relief by his reflections on contemporary America. He was ahead of his times in recognising that the material preponderance the USA was acquiring must have large consequences, good or ill, for Europe. Through its army of emigrants Italy, like Britain, had close ties with America, and a citizen of poor Italy was better able than haughty Britain to read the omens. Noting the pungent impression made on European readers by Sinclair Lewis's *Babbitt,* he considered that there was more to be said for the Babbitts of America than of Europe, adding: 'Anti-Americanism is even more comic than stupid'[83] — a sentiment we can still echo, with some effort, today. True, *Babbitt* as a novel he found mediocre. In the sphere of philosophy or the arts Gramsci, who may be called a good European as well as a good Italian, had no doubt of Europe's supremacy. Various non-European civilisations had been making contributions to the world's common stock, he remarked, but 'they have had a universal value only in so far as they have become constituent elements of European culture.'[84] America, with no intellectuals able to influence public opinion, 'is under the influence of Europe, and of European history', and, as late at least as the economic crash in 1929, still chewing over old European ideas, obsolete in their own homeland.[85] But in economic terms it was the reverse, and what struck Gramsci here, and again might well strike him as an Italian, was America's modernity compared with Europe's accumulation of parasitic or nonproductive classes, a dead load of useless passengers, 'pensioners of economic history,'[86] who in America with its time-honoured gospel of work were only just — in the form of idle-rich women — beginning to appear.[87] This tendency of archaic social groups to survive and multiply from epoch to epoch has been a feature of all old societies not periodically cleansed by revolution, and Gramsci was right to point out that the European imbalance was even more extreme in India and China and was the cause of 'the historical stagnation of those countries.'[88]

The second American phenomenon that interested Gramsci was what he called "Fordism," and envisaged as a callous but in its way forward-looking phase, heralding a new 'and undoubtedly *superior*' type of capitalism.[89] Evidently he had not fallen into the error of so many Marxists of his day of supposing that all the potentialities of capitalism were already exhausted. This new phase would he thought by its example accelerate industrial growth in Europe, to a point where socialism would be a nearer probability. On one side it was an attempt at a sort of 'planned economy,' such as every modern society must in some form or other construct.[90] We may recall that "rationalisation," made feasible by monopoly, was capitalism's magic password about that time, its answer to nationalisation: a substitute version of social planning, as fascism was also and more violently. On the other side "Fordism" in Gramsci's eyes stood for a kind of paternalism. It combined robust methods of labour control, and defiance of trade unions, with concern for its employees' moral welfare and physical well-being. In both respects it was a congener of the even more heavy-handedly patriarchal Japanese mill. Every pioneer like Ford needs a dash of idealism, and has to convince himself that what he is doing will redound to the benefit of mankind as well as himself. His sense of responsibility for his employees was like that felt by rulers in older Europe for their subjects – Shakespeare's duke, for instance, or Maria Theresa, each bent on curbing Viennese immorality – or by empire-building Victorians fervently resolved to teach or compel their tropical peoples to sew together figleaves, or buy them from Lancashire, and cover their nakedness.

There was a vein of the ascetic in Gramsci which made him find some merit in this. He took for granted, as we today cannot, both that industrialisation must precede socialism, and that it must bring socialism nearer. Its demands therefore had to be accepted, and the worker must adapt himself to them. 'We Europeans are still too Bohemian,' he wrote a propos of Ford's high wages and strict rules: ' . . . We are too romantic in an absurd fashion, and from not wanting to be petty bourgeois we fall into the most typical kind of petty bourgeois behaviour, which is just Bohemianism.'[91] It was not meddling puritanism alone, he wrote, that made employers like Ford take an interest in their workers' private lives: the new industrial life requires regulation.[92] Workers had to be protected against exhaustion by its methods of production, worsened by excess or irregularity in sex or drink.[93] Alcohol was a menace by itself to rational industrial patterns, and America needed prohibition, which was only thwarted by 'the opposition of marginal and still backward forces.'[94] But drink and dissipation were equally, in Gramsci's view, a hindrance to the socialist movement. He expected workers who learned to eschew them, and to adapt themselves to the new factory rhythms, to be able to perform their tasks mechanically, free meanwhile to think about getting rid of their employers.[95] He expected also that America's high profits and wages would crumble as the latest methods spread to other lands[96] – the prediction with which Jack London's hero frightened his audience of American businessmen thirty years earlier.[97] It underestimated the expansive capacity of the new capitalism. As this grew, austerity has given way to invitations to the workers to eat, drink and be merry, to take a modest share in bourgeois bliss. 'The vanguard of the proletariat is the middle class,' that life-long socialist R.H. Macintosh has wryly commented.[98] Organised labour in America has ranged itself firmly on the side of capitalism against all meddling outsiders, natives abroad or intellectuals at home. A critic of Gramsci might make use of all this to convict him of overrating ideal as against material forces.

America's rough vitality might well seem better at least than the pseudo-vitality of fascism, or the decay of an old order which fascism came to conceal, its loss of faith in its own household gods. In Europe, Gramsci wrote. belief in progress was being sapped by its former sponsors, unnerved by economic earthquakes. 'The old intellectual and moral leaders of society feel the ground slipping from under their feet ... their sermons have become precisely mere "sermons" ... the particular form of civilisation, culture and morality which they represented is decomposing, and they loudly proclaim the death of all civilisation, all culture, all morality; they call for repressive measures by the State ...'[99] All through his active years Gramsci was hoping for revolution to set Italy and Europe on a better road. But in prison if not earlier he was recognising that it would be far harder to bring about in the complex politics of the West than it had been in Russia. 'The superstructures of civil society are like the trench-systems of modern warfare.'[100] He remained faithful to the revolutionary ideal of a complete transformation of society and abolition of class division, instead of timid patching and propping. But he saw stretching ahead a long period of political struggle, during which the "trench-systems" and bastions of the old order would have to be reduced or outflanked one by one, with the help of what he was fond of calling "molecular change," silent renovation going on from moment to moment in the minds of men.

For this long-drawn task a political party of very high calibre, centralised but flexible, would be needed. Gramsci came to see that the new parties of the Third International — from some of whose tenets he was drifting away — still had much to learn about organisation and leadership. Lenin's model was copied, too faithfully, in spite of Lenin's warnings that the tasks facing other parties were quite different from those faced by the Bolsheviks in Russia. He and his party, he declared at the third congress of the International in 1921, speaking on Italian issues, did not want the others to imitate their tactics, as they were accused of wanting them to do. 'We demand the very opposite:' each party must find its own path. 'The revolution in Italy will proceed differently from the way it proceeded in Russia. It will start in a different way. How? Neither you nor we know.'[101] There was an obvious implication, though Lenin himself may not have been equally alive to this, that diverse situations called for diverse types of party. Gramsci's ideal was a form which would allow leadership, party, and working class to move forward in harmony with one another. It was for lack of such union, he held, that the Italian socialist leaders after the War shrank from the responsibility thrust on them by history.[102]

Since he frequently thought of politics in terms of military strategy it is not surprising that he thought at times of the party as an army. A party in good fettle is ready like a standing army to be thrown into action at the right moment.[103] He grew up in an era of great standing armies; in China the communist party had to be almost from the outset the nucleus of an army as well. Military analogies cannot but suggest blind obedience, and with it the 'unilateral "party" fanaticism,' or sectarianism, that Gramsci censures in one passage.[104] In another he appears to sanction it, by saying that the party 'revolutionises the whole system of intellectual and moral relations,' it regards as good or bad only what is good or bad for itself.[105] This is how Stalin's apologists talked of the dictatorship of the proletariat, meaning in effect that of their master. But Gramsci's chief emphasis is on the danger of authority hardening bureaucratically, the party being reduced to 'a simple, unthinking executive' of its leaders' plans.[106] Shortly before his arrest he was conveying to the Bolshevik party the misgivings of his Italian party about the struggle for power in the USSR, and reminding it that 'unity and discipline cannot be mechanically coercive . . .'[107] In prison he reflected on the inertias that hinder a party from regrouping swiftly in face of new challenges, 'the tendency to become mummified and anachronistic' that is strongest of all in its officialdom: this comes to consider itself a distinct entity, and in a crisis is apt to feel isolated, 'left as though suspended in mid-air.'[108]

In several passages Gramsci's highest conception of the party takes shape in the thought of its forming a bridge towards the society of the future, by making possible a new type of civic consciousness. Its spirit, the reverse of 'brutish' individualism, is the vital component of the 'State spirit' which progress requires.[109] In the voluntarily accepted discipline of the party 'necessity has already become freedom,' because its members have assimilated a code of conduct such as the State enforces on others. The party thus sets an example of 'the will to construct within the husk of political society a complex and well-articulated civil society.'[110] Gramsci clearly has in mind that by so doing it foreshadows the later withering away of the State, which can only take place as society grows mature enough to do without external constraints. All this picture contrasts sadly with the reality of Stalinism, where State and party were governed by the same coercive methods.

Gramsci's vision of the socialist party and its mission was coloured by his faith in the potency of ideas. Ideas need intellectuals to cultivate and spread them; but progressive intellectuals when few or isolated are helpless, whether in capitalist society or in a party and a country like Stalin's. Gramsci was much exercised about this problem of their isolation, the gulf between mental workers and others that had been one of the most fatal consequences of class division — and of the fact that ordinary men have never been encouraged by their governors to think, but have often been positively discouraged or forbidden. He speculated often, and did not always come to the same conclusion, about the relative nature of 'learned' and 'popular' thinking, the mental processes of the philosopher and the man in the street. Sometimes he seems to dig the moat between them very deep and broad. In another mood he seems to minimise the gap. It is only a difference of degree, he writes; all men are philosophers; the specialist thinks more rigorously, but he is 'much more similar to the rest of mankind than are other specialists.'[111] This may appear a hard saying, but a thinker whose subject is society or history may really be said to stand closer to mankind at large than a stockbroker or a designer of aeroplanes. In a similar vein Gramsci argues, with too much perhaps of the early Marxian optimism, that the test of any doctrine is its reception by the people, and that bogus teaching will sooner or later be rejected.[112] The truth is great, and will prevail, a cynic has said, when no-one cares any longer whether it prevails or not. Hence once more, a great deal of "molecular change" will be needed, but may not be impossible.

In all this Gramsci was trying to find the way to that combination of theory and practice which Marxism has always made its watchword. It was for his firm adherence to this principle that Regis Debray, studying him a generation later in his own prison at the other end of the world, gave him most praise, though critical of some of his theories and sceptical of some of his hopes.[113] Activity only becomes true action when tempered by understanding, cerebration only becomes real thinking when directed by significant social purposes. But any close approach to a fusion has seldom been achieved, and in this century of violence and unreason it has often seemed a mirage. Marxist parties have found it hard, though they have made praiseworthy efforts, to avoid segregating theory, repeating at stated times 'Let us think', as the preacher at fixed hours on Sunday says 'Let us pray.' Gramsci saw in the course of all progressive movements hitherto recurrent times of disjunction between intellectuals and others, of a damaging notion that *theory* is a superfluity, not seriously needed by practical men. For a remedy he looked towards a disappearance of the anonymous "masses," an increasing individuation of human beings each with their own response to ideas; though he did not forget that between individual and collective there can be no simple antithesis. In a random mob the 'mass man' falls below the ordinary human level, he wrote, but through membership of a rational organisation he may be lifted above this level: 'quantity becomes quality.'[114] The party he dreamed of would be the intelligentsia of the working-class movement, and nursery of intellectual talents, even of the highest order, recruited from the working class itself. Utopian as this may sound, the prospect of workingmen coming by knowledge has always been an uneasy one to their superiors. Some satirical Tory verses of 1825 on "The March of Intellect" complain of weaver and tailor, blacksmith and mason, talking learnedly about economics and science, and wind up –

'Oh! learning's a very fine thing!
It almost is treason to doubt it —
Yet many of whom I could sing,
Perhaps might as well be without it!'[115]

Only by a long process of gaining knowledge, as well as carrying on struggle, could the working class eventually win power to build socialism. It would then be able, in addition, to build socialism democratically. For democracy to be genuine 'It must mean that every "citizen" can "govern" and that society places him, even if only abstractly, in a general condition to achieve this.'[116] The old damaging specialisation of an administrative class, existing over against the people, must be got rid of. It was a specimen of what he called "fetishism," the conditioning of members of a State, a Church, a party, to think of this as something external to themselves, something over and above them.[117] Instead there should be a linking together of mental and manual work, legislative and executive power.[118] This was a good deal like Lenin's rough blueprint for State business broken down into very simple, limited operations that everyone could master — which has some likeness also to Ford's minute subdivision of factory operations. In administration, complexities of modern life have ruled it out except at the humblest parish-pump level. Even a society where all were well educated would stand in need of specialists. All the same, it could be wide-awake enough to criticise and control them. As Dr. Johnson said, we can all judge a carpenter's work though few of us could make a table.

Always realist as well as idealist, Gramsci never supposed that a socialist society could be created without recourse to some degree of compulsion. Its government would have to educate people to accept whatever necessities might arise, though not to accept artificial or unnecessary restrictions. Every new epoch in turn, he argued, had compelled men into submission to it, as industrialism was doing now, at first by sheer force. At such times, he added, it is not the toilers but the middle and a part of the upper classes that are most painfully affected.[119] These clearly have most to lose by the passing of an old order; but Gramsci may mean also that those among them who embrace the new order have to be the first to submit to its code, as the Puritans may be said to have done on behalf of their capitalist heirs. He was aware of how heavy the burden of change might be: he explains the spreading resort to psychoanalysis as a result of 'the increased moral coercion exercised by the apparatus of State and society on single individuals . . .'[120] Alcoholism and drug-addiction nowadays must owe a good deal to the same cause.

Since compulsion could not altogether be dispensed with, Gramsci's hope was to do away with dragooning as far as possible, persuasion and enlightenment. Sound ideas could not all come from the government; they must grow through frank discussion. Gramsci's approach excluded not only the steamroller of Stalinist thought-control, which he partially glimpsed, but the later Maoist habit of thinking at the top of a hundred million voices: China's recent Cultural Revolution had too much the aspect of a host of enthusiastic young ignoramuses being collected to shout down criticism which the regime was apparently unable, in the brief interlude of free speech and the "Hundred Flowers," to meet rationally. Marxist ideas are not and cannot be made obvious, because life is not simple, but they become more unintelligible when authority turns them into dogmas, stuffed animals in cages, and portrays history like a Derby race in the old paintings, all the galloping horses' legs stuck straight out before and behind.

Club and cudgel methods like Stalin's cannot in our day produce, on either side of the barricades, even effective soldiers, to say nothing of thinkers. Gramsci took for granted that only by intellectual independence and honesty, by free debate, could Marxism learn to prove itself against able opponents, instead of being content to impress 'crude uneducated people who are convinced in an "authoritarian" or "emotional" way.'[121] Correct views must be winnowed from false, and this could best be done by preliminary sifting and checking within learned bodies. 'It seems necessary that the hard work of research for new truths and for better, more coherent and clear formulation of the truths themselves should be left to the free initiative of individual scholars...'[122] This would leave intellectuals neither isolated from the mass nor submerged in it, keeping their own identity while growing and learning by association and interaction with it. For the people, it should mean a step by step graduation towards a not much lower level. There would then be no danger of free thought or taste straying back into the flowery desert of an obsolete class culture.

Socialism would in fact be building the ideal State which Burke dreamed of — 'a partnership in all science; a partnership in all art; a partnership in all virtue, and in every perfection'[123] — but which on the foundations of class society can be little better than a dream. One is reminded of the nineteenth-century English use of the word "Quality" when Gramsci writes that 'To back "quality" against quantity means simply this: to maintain intact specific conditions of social life in which some people are pure quantity and others quality.'[124] Ruling élites and leisured groups have always ruled mankind as much by persuading it to think them indispensable, as by force. In a genuinely educated society they could no longer do so. They have enjoyed culture by excluding others from it; their spokesmen have argued that there can be no alternative to this, since culture and leisure require so much money. Put in urbane language (if in awkward hexameters) this was the contention of Robert Bridges, the Laureate, in his "Epistle to a Socialist in London:" he must have more money than the commonalty because he wanted to buy books and Japanese prints — though he admitted that others with money preferred to spend it, in those early days of the motorcar, 'rattling along on a furious engine, in caoutchouc carapace, with a trail of damnable oilstench.' Modern technology has vastly weakened this argument: wealth, servants, etc, are no longer necessary for any genuine pursuit of culture, or even, for that matter, of driving about in a noisome death-trap. Their value sinks to an archaic one of social prestige; America has already largely outgrown any need of servants, and by so much has put itself ahead of Europe on the road to socialism.

Activities that may, very miscellaneously, be called "cultural" will deserve a growing place among us if only because the ideal of motorcars for all and two or three for snobs, that *summum bonum* of capitalist materialism, will have to be given up, since the planet Earth refuses to underwrite it. So will many other things. Bridges had better warrant for another point in the same poem, though it is far from refuting socialism as he fancied, about overpopulation. He cited an estimate of the old astronomer Herschel that if all couples in the four thousand years since Adam and Eve had left four children, their offspring would cover the whole earth and be piled up on top of one another to a height equal to a million times the diameter of Neptune's orbit. In the struggle now inescapably before us with the grand dilemma of the environment, we shall have to face many of the same problems that Gramsci thought of as confronting a socialist society. Among them will be the unavoidable use of compulsion against those who refuse to take part in the effort of salvation. The same Catholic Church which has been everywhere a vindictive enemy of socialism is a dogged enemy of plans to keep population within bounds. Gramsci always condemned the indifferent, procrastinating attitude of mind which takes refuge in the thought that whatever we do or do not do, life will go on. Seven years after his death Italy was deluged with war, the penalty it had to pay for its facile surrender to Mussolini. Indochina is deluged with war today because too many Americans have been indifferent. Once, indeed, Gramsci fell back on the consoling reflection that there is, after all, some truth in the thought that life will go on — 'it would be disastrous if there were not.'[125] There is far less truth in it today, when apathy will very literally mean disaster.

FOOTNOTES

1 H. Nicholson, *Diaries and Letters 1930-1939*, ed. N. Nicholson (1966), under 6 Jan. 1932.
2 *The Practice and Theory of Bolshevism* (1920), p.36.
3 *Ib.*, p.188.
4 Quoted by Palmiro Togliatti in his tribute to his old comrade, written in 1937 at the time of Gramsci's death, and later prefixed to the French anthology of his letters *(Lettres de la prison, Paris, 1952)*; see pp.32-3.

5 *Sea and Sardinia* (1923), p.87 (Penguin ed., 1944).
6 Letter to his sister Teresina, 16 Nov. 1931. Most of the letters cited below will be found in the French anthology, but I have compared passages quoted with the original, in the standard Italian edition (Turin, 1965).
7 See *Selections from the Prison Notebooks of Antonio Gramsci,* edited and translated by Q. Hoare and G.N. Smith 1971 — an admirable work, cited below as *Prison Notebooks* — p.198.
8 See e.g. a letter to his sister-in-law Tatiana, 21 Mar. 1932.
9 Letter to Tatiana, 19 Dec. 1926.
10 Letter to Tatiana, 3 Oct. 1932.
11 Letter to Tatiana, 18 May 1931.
12 To his sister Teresina, 4 May 1931; cf. a letter to his wife, 9 Feb. 1931.
13 To his wife, 24 Oct. 1932 and 25 Jan. 1936.
14 To Tatiana, 22 Apr. 1929.
15 To Tatiana, 15 Jan. 1927.
16 To his mother, 15 Dec. 1930.
17 To his son Giuliano, undated (No.423 in the Italian edition).
18 To Tatiana, 19 Feb. 1927.
19 To Tatiana, 23 May 1927.
20 To his wife, 19 Nov. 1928; to Tatiana, 31 Oct. 1932.
21 To Tatiana, 26 Dec. 1927.
22 To Tatiana, 29 Aug. 1932.
23 To Tatiana, 15 Feb. 1932.
24 To Tatiana, 20 Apr. 1931.
25 To his wife, 3 July 1929.
26 To his wife, 30 Dec. 1929 and 9 Feb. 1931.
27 To Tatiana, 13 Jan. 1930.
28 To his wife, 5 Jan. 1937.
29 To his mother, 24 Aug. 1931.
30 To his wife, 6 Oct. 1930.
31 To his wife, 4 Nov. 1930 and 5 Jan. 1937.
32 To his wife, 25 Jan. 1936.
33 To Tatiana, 5 Oct. 1931 and 12 Oct. 1931.
34 *Prison Notebooks,* p.369.
35 To Tatiana, 9 Dec. 1926; to his wife, 15 Jan. 1927.
36 Very regrettably, however, there is as yet no British edition of the letters.
37 To Tatiana, 25 Apr. 1932.
38 To his wife, 4 Nov. 1930.
39 Cf. my article in the memorial volume *Isaac Deutscher, the Man and his Work,* ed. D. Horowitz (1971), p.200.
40 To his wife, 24 Nov. 1936.
41 To his wife, 5 Jan. 1937.
42 See *The Modern Prince and other writings,* edited and translated by L. Marks (1957) — cited below as *Modern Prince* — p.98.
43 *Ib.,* p.117.
44 Letter of 13 Feb. 1866.
45 The volume *Letterature e vita nazionale* (1971), in the set of Gramsci's

works published by Editori Riuniti, Rome, includes a long series of dramatic criticisms.
46 To Tatiana, 21 Sep. 1931.
47 To Tatiana, 23 May 1927.
48 To Tatiana, 6 Oct. 1930.
49 *This Business of Living. A Diary: 1935-1950,* trans. A.E. Murch (1961).
50 *The Political Prisoner,* trans. W.J. Strachan (1966).
51 *Prison Notebooks,* p.471.
52 To Tatiana, 27 Feb. 1928.
53 *Modern Prince,* p.20.
54 *Ib.,* p.24.
55 *Ib.,* p.19.
56 K.N. Cameron, *The Young Shelley. Genesis of a Radical* (1957), p.274.
57 *Modern Prince,* p.21.
58 *Ib.,* p.75.
59 *Prison Notebooks,* p.263.
60 *Ib.,* p.348.
61 To Tatiana, 6 June 1932.
62 *Prison Notebooks,* pp. 61-2.
63 To his brother Carlo, 28 Sep. 1931.
64 To Tatiana, 10 Mar. 1930.
65 *Prison Notebooks,* pp.369-70.
66 To Tatiana, 25 Mar. 1929.
67 To Tatiana, 1 Dec. 1930.
68 To Tatiana, 3 Oct. 1932.
69 *Prison Notebooks,* p.130.
70 *Modern Prince,* p.76.
71 *Ib.,* pp.126 ff; cf. *Prison Notebooks,* p.40.
72 *Modern Prince,* p.130.
73 *Prison Notebooks,* p.36; cf. p.42.
74 To Tatiana, 7 Sep. 1931.
75 *Prison Notebooks,* p.37.
76 F.M. Underwood, *United Italy* (1912), p. 212.
77 To his sister Grazietta, 31 Oct. 1932.
78 To his mother, 1 Feb. 1932.
79 *Prison Notebooks,* p.294.
80 *Ib.,* p.299.
81 *Ib.,* p.296.
82 *Ib.,* p.304.
83 *Opere di Antonio Gramsci,* Vol.5 (Einaudi, Turin, 1953), pp. 352-4.
84 *Prison Notebooks,* p.416.
85 *Ib.,* pp.272, 286.
86 *Ib.,* p.281.
87 *Ib.,* pp. 305-6.
88 *Ib.,* p.285.
89 *Ib.,* pp.302-3.
90 *Ib.,* p.279.

91 To Tatiana, 20 Oct. 1930.
92 *Prison Notebooks*, pp. 296-7; cf. p.300.
93 *Ib.*, pp.303—4.
94 *Ib.*, p.279.
95 *Ib.*, pp.309-10.
96 *Ib.*, p.311.
97 Jack London, *The Iron Heel* (1907), Chap.IX.
98 In conversation with the writer, on 21 Apr. 1972.
99 *Prison Notebooks*, p.242.
100 *Ib.*, p.235, cf. the letter cited on p.lxvi.
101 *Selected Works*, Vol.X, ed. J. Fineberg (1938), pp.275-6.
102 *Prison Notebooks*, pp.96, 224.
103 *Ib.*, p.185.
104 *Ib.*, pp.266-7.
105 *Ib.*, p.133.
106 *Ib.*, p.155.
107 *Ib.*, p.lxxxv.
108 *Ib.*, p.211.
109 *Ib.*, p.147.
110 *Ib.*, p.268.
111 *Ib.*, p.347.
112 *Modern Prince*, p.73.
113 Regis Debray, 'Schema for a Study of Gramsci,' in *New Left Review*, no.59, Jan.—Feb. 1970, pp.49, 51.
114 *Opere*, Vol.5, p.149.
115 'Christopher North,' *Noctes Ambroisianae* (Edinburgh ed., 1892), Vol.1, pp.83-5 (1825).
116 *Prison Notebooks*, p.40.
117 *Opere*, Vol.5, p.157.
118 *Prison Notebooks*, p.186.
119 *Ib*, pp.298-9.
120 *Ib.*, p.280.
121 *Modern Prince*, pp.102-3.
122 *Ib.*, p.74.
123 Burke, *Reflections on the Revolution in France* (1790), p.93 (Everyman ed., 1910).
124 *Prison Notebooks*, pp.363-4.
125 *Ib.*, p.157.

CHAPTER VI

Violence and Human Self-Realisation

Mihailo Marković

Violence has always been present in human history both in individual behaviour and in social life, in both the "legitimate" form intended to preserve a given order and as a means to promote social change. What is new and sometimes indeed paradoxical in our century is the enormous discrepancy between the basic beliefs and theories, on the one hand, and the actual practices on the other.

One of the essential principles of Enlightenment, which underlies all contemporary civilization, is the belief that growth of human knowledge implies an increased ability to behave rationally, to predict events and to control blind natural and social forces. Even so, the less civilized and less rational world in earlier times never saw such outbursts of uncontrolled and irrational violence as those that took place in the two world wars, or in the ninety-seven local wars that, according to the Hungarian historian Istvan Kende, broke out in the period 1945-1970. Analogously, criminal forms of violence in individual behaviour do not tend to wither away with the coming of a higher level of comfort and education; contrary to expectations, data on delinquency appear to show an alarming correlation between violent crime and the level of material development.

Liberal bourgeois governments which for more than two centuries have adhered to the ideological principle of "ruling by consent," and which have never before had such excellent opportunities to produce this consent through the manipulations of powerful mass media, have recently manifested a frightening readiness for indiscriminate violent suppression of radical liberation movements.

On the other hand, while the right to violent revolution is still professed and preached but hardly ever used in the practice of Western Communist Parties, violence still plays a surprisingly important and sometimes even an increasing role in the internal affairs of post-capitalist countries many decades after the revolution. Socialism did not develop as a new way of life characterised primarily by fraternal relations among men and by the withering away of the power structures. Violent repression of heresy and

91

dissent has become part of everyday life in these countries — the theory of the necessary intensification of class struggle in the process of development of socialism, far from explaining anything, is logically absurd: socialism by definition means the transition period in which men evolve towards a non-violent, classless society.

The awareness of the fact that successful violent revolutions naturally give rise to authoritarian regimes has led to an historically extremely important attempt, in the early sixties, to create new types of mass movements which would explore the possibilities of attaining social power without the use of violence. This New Left shook the globe, and in France in 1968 it was on the verge of full victory without firing one single bullet. Had the workers' strike committees been integrated into a global national network of self-managing bodies, and had they organised production, they would have had a good chance to survive and to build up a new collectivist society. Failure to take these final, indispensable steps led to defeat and a widespread feeling of frustration. As a consequence, the New Left regressed to old patterns of organisation, ideology, and strategy. Instead of developing a variety of specific strategies and methods of struggle appropriate for the concrete historical conditions in a given society, most Leftist activities reverted in the last few years to the old idea of revolution as a violent seizure of political power — which in fact may only be the first step, and then only in some social situations. However, what is new in this old idea is the tendency to replace *instrumental* violence by *expressive* violence. It is one thing to kill the tyrant in order to stop mass suffering and to open the way to freedom and human dignity. It is another matter to believe with Sartre that one "whose only wealth is blind hatred" becomes human only "by this mad fury, by this bitterness and spleen," or by his "ever-present desire to kill us."[1] Once violence becomes a value in itself it turns against those who use it: after killing their oppressors men continue to kill each other. Such a reversal of means and ends renders the whole process of liberation a typical Hegelian *false infinity:* endless repetition of the same contradiction.[2]

When the phenomenon of violence is considered *in its own terms* the question arises whether it is the manifestation of an invariable universal structure of human beings or whether we are dealing with a disposition of human behaviour that is the product of specific historical conditions.

On the other hand, when violence is considered as a means to promote social change the obvious question is: under what conditions is violence an adequate or even a necessary means to create a better, more humane society?

Both these approaches presuppose a fundamental conception of human nature and a distinction between its actual and potential dimension. Humanity is not only what appears in actual, overt behaviour but also what subsists in a latent form in human individuals and comes into existence when appropriate conditions are given. This latent pattern of human capacities and dispositions need not be grasped as an eternal form and even less as a paradigm of a perfect harmony. The whole history may be viewed as a process of the emergence of humanity, of creating human potentialities and actualising them. Human *self-realisation* constitutes, then, the ultimate criterion of evaluation of all and various sorts of behaviour and social change.

The concept of self-realisation plays the central role in philosophical anthropology but it is also indispensable in humanist psychology. Abraham Maslow, for example, holds that *"all* basic needs (e.g., the need for food, safety, love, etc.) may be considered to be simply steps along the path to general self-actualisation, under which all basic needs can be subsumed." He continues: "... It looks as if there *were* a single ultimate value for mankind, a far goal toward which all men strive. This is called variously by different authors: self-actualisation, self-realisation, integration, psychological health, individuation, autonomy, creativity, productivity, but they all agree that this amounts to realising the potentialities of the person, that is to say, becoming fully human, everything that the person can become."[3]

The reason why the concept of self-realisation can be almost universally accepted as an ultimate criterion of evaluation is that it is very abstract and that, in fact, it represents only a very general and neutral theoretical framework which can be filled with very different images of man. If man is construed as an essentially aggressive being, then acting in a violent way would have to be interpreted as a mode of his self-realisation. On the other hand, if one takes the needs for peace and cooperation to be defining characteristics of man, violence would be considered a pathological phenomenon.

Various concepts of human nature may be ordered within a conceptual continuum, taking the degree of importance attributed to aggressivity and violence as the principle of ordering. One of the poles of this argument would be constituted by authors like Machiavelli and Hobbes.

Machiavelli in his *Prince* holds that men in general are "ungrateful, fickle, false, cowards, and covetous" therefore a prince ought not to mind the reproach of cruelty because "it is much safer to be feared then love." For example "the wonderful deeds" of Hannibal were due to his "inhuman cruelty." It is not possible to rule only by the law, it is also necessary to have recourse to the method of force, which is "proper to beasts." The prince "ought to have no other aim or thought, nor select anything else for his study than war and its rules and discipline."[4]

According to Hobbes the basic feature of man in his natural condition is the desire for power. Man is essentially egoistic and interested in satisfying his own appetites. As men have equal abilities and equal hopes to attain their ends "they become enemies and endeavour to destroy or subdue one another." "Hereby is manifest," continues Hobbes, "that during the time men live without a common power to keep them all in awe, they are in that condition which is called war, and such war is of every man against every man." As a consequence there is "continual fear and danger of violent death."[5]

From such premises it follows that self-realisation is bad for men and that constraints to men's freedom are necessary if violence and universal insecurity are to be overcome, which leads Hobbes to the idea that the best type of society ("commonwealth") is an absolute monarchy. A strong state is indispensable to curb evil human nature.

At the opposite pole of our theoretical continuum there is an over-optimistic utopian conception of man as essentially a free, peaceloving, social, creative being. We find it in all revolutionary thought, even in the thought of one of the most severe critics of utopian socialism, Karl Marx. In his mature works this utopian view of human essence is only a tacit value assumption of his critical scientific theory, but in his early writings it has been formulated in its pure form. For example, in his *Economic and Philosophical Manuscripts* he says: "*Communism* is the *positive* abolition of *private property*, of *human self-alienation*, and thus, the real appropriation of *human* nature, through and for man. It is therefore the return of man as a social, that is, really human being . . ."[6] In his *Notes of 1844*, speaking about free human production, he makes a projection of ideal human activity in a society without private property: this activity would involve full affirmation of one's individuality and at the same time would satisfy the need of another human being.[7] In the *Holy Family* Marx examines the implications of the materialist theories of the original good-ness of man and explains his conception of freedom: If man is "not negatively free to avoid this or that event but is positively free to express his true individuality, then rather than punish individuals for their crimes we should destroy the social conditions which engender crime, and give to each individual the scope which he needs in society in order to develop his life."[8]

From this point of view aggressiveness and violence are not the con-stitutive characteristics of human nature but temporary products of un-favourable historical conditions. Change of these conditions, removal of certain institutions (such as private property, professional division of labour, the state, the market, etc.), would allow man to be what he potentially *is* and would automatically do away with violence. If man is formed by circumstances, these circumstances must be humanly formed.[9] One should not put barriers to human self-realisation but remove them all. The task seems to be relatively simple and essentially negative.

There is no doubt that the practical implications of these two ex-tremely opposed views about the nature of human self-realisation and the place of violence in it are vastly different. If freedom necessarily gives rise to wolfish fighting and eruptions of violence, then any weakening of the existing social order involves great risks. But if, on the other hand, violence and alternation are precisely the consequence of that order, then practical commitment to break that order goes together with an enormous self-confidence and with an almost unlimited faith in the future.

In spite of these profound differences both extreme views have some common features. Both reduce the possibilities of self-determination and self-creation in history, both assume a fixed, a historical, reified conception of human nature, a conception that hypostatises either past forms of human selfishness, aggressiveness, and brutality or ideal future possibilities. Man has no future from the former, conservative point of view: he can only stay in the civilized, comfortable and secure present, or else return into a natural condition ("state of nature") with all its constant fear and insecurity. From the radical, utopian point of view man has a future but cannot choose among its alternative possibilities and create himself afresh. It is determined in an eschatological way. History has a purpose and an ultimate goal which is independent of the will of human individuals; they can only bring it to consciousness and accelerate its realisation.

If there were no other possible approach to the problem of human nature, in addition to both the examined extremes, it would seem as if we are faced with the following dilemma with respect to the problem of violence.

Either violence is an inevitable, essential, ever present lurking tendency of human behaviour and must constantly and for ever be repressed by external authority and force; or else violence is a merely superficial phenomenon without deep roots in the very make-up of human beings, a product of specific historical institutions, that is bound to disappear as soon as these institutions can be eliminated.

If we accept the former alternative we have to renounce any hope of an essentially more democratic, peaceful, and humane world. The process of liberation cannot proceed beyond a certain limit, the time will never come when human conflicts will be resolved in non-violent ways. All historical progress may be construed only in quantitative terms of growth, expansion, and increase of comfort.

But if we accept the latter alternative our hopes and expectations are so great that time and again we fail to grasp the recurrence of violence even when the specific institutions that were considered its causes, are removed. Inevitable frustration assumes sometimes tragic forms and leads to long periods of alienation and passivity.

This dilemma is obviously false. It is possible to build up a theory of human nature that is more realistic, embracing evil as its component, and still allowing the chance of unlimited historical progress. The basic assumption here would be that human nature is a structure of conflicting latent dispositions that evolve in time and may be manifested, suppressed, or modified in various ways in appropriate historical conditions. Previous history provides ample evidence about these conflicting tendencies; craving for freedom but also escape from responsibility; a striving for inter-group and international collaboration and solidarity but also class, national, and racial egoism; a need for creativity, but also powerful destructive drives; a readiness for self-sacrifice in certain conditions, but also a strong lust for personal power and domination in some others; a profound need for love, but also an incomprehensible, irrational need to inflict pain and suffering on both the hated and beloved ones. These features are the crystallisation of past history but they do not constitute a fixed static entity. Some of them tend to disappear, although they were characteristic of man during several historical epochs (for example, patriarchal loyalty to the older generation); some new features arise (such as the compulsory acquisitiveness of a *homo consumens*). These in turn become questionable for coming generations.

Analogously to the dynamic psychology which throws light on the mechanism of individual psychic processes, a dynamic anthropology might give us insight into the evolution of man in history. We might learn which are the basic conflicting human capacities, needs, and practical dispositions, what is their biochemical basis, and how their actualisation depends on economic, political, and cultural conditions.

With respect to the problem of violence our libraries are piled high with books which tell us how similar animals are to us.[10] This literature is a great source of joy to all conservatives who use the opportunity to jump to the conclusion that since we are animals and are so aggressive, all visions of a more peaceful and rational world are naive illusions. Methodologically this is the same kind of error as the one attributed by Sartre[11] to dogmatic "lazy" Marxists, who reduce complex and unique cultural phenomena to their general and abstract class description. "Valéry is a bourgeois writer but not every bourgeois writer is Valéry." Man is an animal but not every animal is a man. Instead of reducing human violence and belligerence to animal aggressiveness it is necessary to explain how their various characteristic forms emerged in specific historical conditions. It is good to know the biological background against which human history takes place. But it is even better to be aware of the fact that this background has been transcended. It is very important to know the genetic patterns that constitute the material basis of human behavioural dispositions; a far more advanced level of biochemistry would allow us to realise certain limits of men that are still only a matter of guesswork. But there can be little doubt that within these limits there lies a very large range of possibilities. Actual social conditions determine which of these will be realised.

As a matter of fact man has a number of creative potential capacities (for problem solving, for introduction of new elements into known, recurrent contexts, for construction of symbols and meaningful communication, and so on) that may have been manifested in earlier stages of life and are later blocked by unfavourable conditions of life and work in industrial society. Compulsory acquivistiveness may be a substitute for these arrested modes of behaviour, and violence may be a reaction to unfulfilled needs for affection and social recognition which produce a general feeling of insecurity and inferiority.

If such dispositions may be reactions to socially structured situations, if they may be substitutes for socially arrested and thwarted needs, if they may be actualised in different, socially more or less acceptable forms, depending on social conditions, then human self-realisation is not a strictly deterministic process and involves an element of human self-creation.

The problem of violence as a mode of self-realisation consequently takes the following form: *What do we intend to do* with deeply rooted human tendencies to aggressive, violent behaviour? Do we want to preserve the social conditions in which these tendencies will continue to take on most egoistic and vicious forms? Or are we ready to mobilise our forces to create new social conditions in which aggressive dispositions would be manifested in modified, relatively harmless, socially acceptable forms (in games, sports, arts, verbal disputes, work, love, etc).

Intuitively we know that all other conditions being equal, any sane human being would prefer the latter alternative. But because all other conditions are not equal and because this alternative may involve sacrificing important interests, many individuals would prefer the preservation of the *status quo* and would therefore be inclined to challenge the basic assumption of this alternative, namely, that violence in itself is bad. And indeed why should hostility and violence be worse than gentleness, sobriety, or peacefulness?

There are several possible ways to handle questions of this sort and to try to justify one among existing alternatives.

First is the criterion of logical consistency: a property of man and human behaviour is "good" to the extent to which it satisfies the concept of man.[12] And a particular definition of man is acceptable if, among other things, it is in basic agreement with actual usage of the term "man" in ordinary language.

In the given case "violence" is not one of the defining characteristics of the concept *man*, therefore one who acts violently is not a good specimen of human species. Naturally one may give his own, new definition of man that includes violence as an essential feature of human nature. Then he violates the principle that a good definition of an already existing concept must be only an explanation, preserving the sound core of its meaning in ordinary language. Or, in other words, he takes as an essential characteristic of man something that is not generally believed to be a specific feature of man.

To be sure, a consideration of this kind does not prove or disprove anything. However, the price that one may have to pay in order to defend this position is to introduce queer concepts and to break the link with the logic implicit in ordinary language.

The second approach is historical in a double sense.

On the one hand, it is possible to show what, throughout history, were the respective consequences of violence and peace. This makes sense if one is ready to agree that life is better than death, and that creation and happiness are better than destruction and suffering.

On the other hand, the history of philosophy and of culture shows a very high degree of agreement among recognised great thinkers in the past about certain fundamental values, such as freedom, equality, peace, justice, truth, beauty. This agreement again does not prove anything but indicates the universal human character of certain norms of human life that are incompatible with expressive violence.

A third approach is characteristic of a critical philosophical anthropology. Value considerations, including the problem of a hierarchy of values, are derived from a theory of man, of his potential capacities and genuine needs. This theory obviously contains not only an indicative but also a normative component. The former is implicit, for example, in the theoretical justification of the view that there are universal latent dispositions (like the capacity to use symbols and to communicate), that these get actualised at a certain stage of growth under favourable social conditions (i.e., any young child is able to learn a language provided there is enough interaction with a normal social surrounding), that these potentialities may be wasted and extinguished when appropriate conditions are lacking (for example, a number of adolescents found in a jungle were no longer able to learn to speak).

The latter, normative component is implicit in the very selection of basic human capacities (creativity but not destructivity, problem-solving but not problem-evading, participation within a community but not escape from community bonds, etc.). It is also implicit in the very distinction between true, genuine needs and false, artificial needs. This normative component, in the first place, expresses the general practical orientation of the author (in the sense of Fichte's *dictum* that the character of a philosophy depends on what kind of man the philosopher is). But if a philosophical theory claims to be more than a personal statement it must seek some kind of objective validation and refer to some kind of general commonsense. Now in a similar way in which empirical validation consists in the claim that all normal qualified individuals could observe some data under certain specified conditions, and logical validation ultimately refers to the expectation that all persons who know a language will use certain expressions in a certain way, so the validation of normative attitudes refers to the expectation that, other conditions being equal, all normal developed human individuals would have structurally similar affective needs and preferences in certain crucial existential situations: of deprivation and suffering, or of group activity, sexual attraction, etc. This expectation will not be fulfilled in some cases but this holds also for the expectation that all individuals will see the same things or use words in the same way; there is a difference in degree but not in essence. In this sense we may have good reasons to state that violence in itself is repulsive and evil, although taken as an instrument it may be considered a necessary evil. Experiencing violence, as such, as attractive, is as abnormal as being unable to distinguish colours or to draw correct inferences.

Contemporary humanist psychology offers another, *fourth* approach to the problem of validation of normative attitudes. Its results coincide very much with previous considerations. Its starting point is the distinction between psychologically healthy and psychologically sick individuals. The essential methodological point is that health and sickness here may be defined *operationally* and not with the help of higher-level abstract concepts. By studying neurotic and mildly troubled persons Carl Rogers came to the conclusion that pathological symptoms are the consequence of blocking a drive toward self-realisation which the individual normally has.[13] Abraham Maslow, on the other hand, studied healthy, self-actualised persons, and this allowed him to replace the normative question, "What *should be* human values?" with the factual question: "What *are* the values of the best human beings?" The concept of *best human beings* or of *full humanness* or of a *healthy, self-actualising human being* Maslow defines by a set of objectively describable measurable characteristics such as: clearer perception of reality, more openness to experience, increased integration of the personality, increased spontaneity, a firm identity, increased objectivity, recovery of creativeness, ability to fuse concreteness and abstractness, democratic character structure, ability to love, etc.[14] Maslow claims that there are clinical techniques available for studying corresponding subjective reactions, such as the feelings of zest in living, of happiness, of serenity, of confidence in one's ability to handle stresses, anxieties and problems, etc. Self-actualisation so defined does not exclude decisiveness, justified anger and indignation, self-affirmation, etc. However it is incompatible with hostility, cruelty, and destructiveness, and with corresponding subjective feelings of fear, anxiety, despair, boredom, intrinsic guilt, aimlessness, emptiness, or lack of identity. These are signs of psychological sickness, of self-betrayal, of fixation, of regression. What is characteristic of all pathological mental states is the falling apart of the unity of the person, of the *homeostasis* of the organism as a whole. "Then", says Maslow, "what he wants to do may be bad for him; even if he does it he may not enjoy it; even if he enjoys it, he may simultaneously disapprove of it, so that the enjoyment is itself poisoned or may disappear quickly. What he enjoys at first he may not enjoy later. His impulses, desires and enjoyments then become a poor guide to living. He must accordingly mistrust and fear the impulses and the enjoyments which lead him astray, and so he is caught in conflict, dissociation, indecision; in a word he is caught in civil war."[15]

This analysis seems to fit well the date about both the behaviour of violent persons and their introspective descriptions. It gives also good grounds for a negative answer to the question put in the beginning: aggressive, violent behaviour is not a mode of human self-realisation. Even at best, when it is the expression of a justified revolt and a necessary means to remove some impediment to self-realisation at a larger social scale, it leads to internal conflicts, to a discrepancy between the motive which has been approved, and the act itself which may be utterly repulsive.[16] Acting in this way one remains caught within the sphere of necessity and one is aware of it. Activity that involves instrumental violence is still very far from truly human *praxis*, which is not only approved for its implications but is also desired, needed, and enjoyed as an end in itself, as an intrinsic value. When violence is desired for its own sake it is a symptom of a pathological self-disintegration and self-destruction, which when transformed into an ideology, invariably has tragic consequences for mankind.[17] All those scholars who derive anthropology from zoology and who tend to praise violence as a manifestation of the life force and even of human creativity, pave the way to such an ideology.

If violence is not a mode of self-realisation is it not a means to it?

The answers to this question reveal the following paradoxes: Many of those who believe that violence is an inherent tendency in human nature reject violence as an instrument of social change. On the other hand those radicals who believe that man is essentially non-violent tend to affirm violence as a necessary or even sole means of social change.

The former attitude is characteristic of most present-day liberals. They eliminate from the classical liberalist doctrine some universally valid, revolutionary thoughts about the right of people to rebel against usurpation and tyranny. Locke, Rousseau, Jefferson, and other ideologues of the revolutionary bourgeoisie held that people are fully justified in using force in order to overthrow a government which violates the social contract and rules for its own rather than its people's interest.[18] According to Locke when the legislature or the prince betrays the trust of the people and works or plans to destroy the liberty or the property of the people, and to submit them to arbitrary power, the rulers forfeit the power given to them and thus cause the dissolution of government. By removing the legislature the tyrants remove the basis of their own authority and relapse into a state of war. If a rebellion breaks out because a prince destroys the liberties of the subjects it is the fault of the prince, not the subjects, just as when an honest man resists a bandit the resulting bloodshed must be blamed on the bandit. If honest men never resisted this would only produce more banditry.[19]

Rousseau also holds that peace under despotism is not desirable: "One can live peacefully enough in a dungeon, but such peace will hardly of itself ensure one's happiness. The Greeks imprisoned in the cave of Cyclops lived peacefully while awaiting their turn to be devoured."[20] When a government rules only by force then it is better for the people to "shake off its yoke" than to obey. If force itself makes right then a stronger force could reverse this right: so people are justified in using force to reestablish their freedom.[21]

The same attitude pervades all writings of Jefferson, in the first place *The Declaration if Independence.* "Whenever any form of government becomes destructive of these ends, it is the right of the people to alter or to abolish it, and to institute new government . . . . Prudence, indeed, will dictate that governments long established should not be changed for light and transient causes . . . But when a long train of abuses and usurpations, pursuing invariably the same object, evinces a design to reduce them under absolute Despotism, it is their right, it is their duty, to throw off such government, and to provide new guards for their future security."[22]

Even an unjustified rebellion is productive of good according to Jefferson: "It prevents degeneracy of government and nourishes a general attention to the public affairs. I hold that a little rebellion now and then is a good thing and is necessary in the political world as storms in the physical."[23] The way Jefferson comments on Shay's Rebellion must sound like sheer madness to many contemporary liberals: "God forbid we should ever be twenty years without such a rebellion. The people cannot be all and always well informed. The part which is wrong will be discontented in proportion to the importance of the facts they misconceive. If they remain quiet under such misconceptions, it is a lethargy, the forerunner of death to the public liberty . . . What country can preserve its liberty if its rulers are not warned from time to time that this people preserve the spirit of resistance. Let them take arms . . . The tree of liberty must be refreshed from time to time with the blood of patriots and tyrants. It is its natural manure . . ."[24]

This was the language of revolutionaries. Their theoretical achievements constitute still the ideological foundation of liberal bourgeois society. But the ideologues of that society have long ago switched to an unconditional, unqualified condemnation of revolution. They forget of course that the social order they advocate and tend to preserve has itself been born through violent revolution. And while they demand that the people use only peaceful means, they seem to overlook the fact that the whole system is based on enormous amounts of built-in, institutionalised "structural" violence.[25] In contrast to direct, physical violence that hits individuals in a dramatic, immediately observable way, structural violence affects large masses of people indirectly, slowly, invisibly through the system and its legal institutions. The number of people who die from starvation, pollution, carelessness, etc. is certainly no less than the number of those who are killed by bullets. That is why A.J. Muste had to say "In a world built on violence one must be a revolutionary before one can be a pacifist."[26] Merleau-Ponty has seen well the conservative and hypocritical side of the unilateral condemnation of revolutionary violence: "In advocating non-violence one reinforces established violence of a system of production which makes misery and war inevitable."[27] The only way to rehabilitate the principle of non-violence and to get rid of its apologetic, cynical interpretations is to apply it consistently, to extend its use so as to embrace also "established", "structural" violence. But then it becomes too revolutionary to be accepted by most liberals and too "soft" to be met with enthusiasm by most Marxists.

This leads us to the discussion of the other previously mentioned paradox: the belief that man is essentially a non-violent being goes together with the conviction that man will restore himself as a man only through an interlude of a violent revolution. It is clear from the whole preceding discussion why Marx and his followers insisted on the need to use violence in order to reopen the blocked road of historical progress and eventually reach a higher-level society in which all forms of structural violence would wither away, while direct violence would lose any ground in human relations. They faced tremendous power in the hands of the defenders of the *status quo*. Being the historically legitimate heirs of the bourgeois revolutionaries, they proceeded with the development of revolutionary theory, where Rousseau and Jefferson, Saint-Simon, Fichte, and the young Hegel had stopped. They rejected the myth of the social contract and the traditional substitution of the state-people relation for the class struggle. Once it was revealed that the real opponents were the ruling and the oppressed classes it also became clear then that the question of revolution does not arise only when the government *becomes* unjust and *begins* to rule contrary to the people's interests: revolution is legitimate *all the time* because the state rule is never just and never serves the interests of the oppressed bulk of the people.

However, from the fact that the proletariat has the right to use force against its oppressor it does not follow either that the use of force is in all situations the most efficient and necessary means to a qualitative change of the old society, nor that it is in principle possible for a non-violent new society to emerge after a prolonged period of increased violence.

Marx and Engels had their doubts. They allowed the possibility of a peaceful proletarian revolution in the most advanced countries.[28] And they were not unaware that "in the play of violence there is the risk of permanent involvement."[29] However they believed that proletarian violence as a means of liberation has a quite specific nature and will tend to recede in time. And they had a good reason for that belief: the working class really has no interest in installing itself as a new ruling class: rather its interest lies in abolishing itself as a class and in gradually introducing a new democratic, non-violent social organisation. They overlooked only one thing: that in certain historical conditions the victorious workers' vanguard may alienate itself from the rest of the class, seize all the levers of economic and political power, and establish its own sectioned rule. The socialist revolutionaries became conscious of this nightmare only when it already became true.[30]

The essential problem of contemporary Marxism is therefore: how to secure that the use of violence would really recede after the revolution, how to create a movement that would be strong enough to seize political power and to enforce necessary structural changes, without becoming bureaucratic and returning to the old forms of direct and structural violence.

There is also another possibility. If, according to Marx, a non-violent revolution was possible in Great Britain and Holland in the Nineteenth century, why should it not be a better solution, at least in some societies, in the last quarter of the twentieth century?

Thus it follows that unqualified condemnation and affirmation of instrumental violence has to be replaced by a concrete historical analysis of various types of situations. Strategies of revolutionary action would have to vary according to the type of situation, depending especially on the character of the existing centre of power.

In the simplest possible case we might take only two parameters into account: the strength of the centre of power (government, state) and its readiness to introduce reforms. We should distinguish, *first*, between a strong stable centre of power that still enjoys a support of the considerable part of the population and has a strong military and police force at its disposal, and a centre of power that is unstable, corrupt, with a demoralised army and with little public support. *Secondly*, we should distinguish between a centre of power that is rational, liberal, open to gradual progress, ready to introduce reforms within the framework of the given system, and one that is adamant, conservative, unwilling to make any consessions.

In this simple model with four types of situations, only in one case, of a weak and hard conservative regime, may violent revolution be the only possible means to further development with a good chance of success. While the centre of power is still strong, a movement that uses violence is doomed and would only provide an increase of repression, whereas in the case of a weak, reformist centre of power a violent revolution might be successful but is not necessary since its goals might be reached through a series of well-directed changes of the system constituting as a whole a structural transformation of the given society. And this is what a social revolution essentially is; its defining characteristics are not the use of violence or physical destruction or abrupt character of change, but the change of structure, the superseding of the old social order, the removal of those institutions that blocked further progress (which has to be more ultimately evaluated in terms of human self-realisation rather than of mere material growth).

In any judgment about the desirability and necessity of the use of violence in a certain situation the following principles should be taken into account if this judgment is to be both just and realistic:

(1) *Other conditions being equal, non-violence is preferable to violence*, and for the following reasons:

(a) Violence produces unpredictable amounts of human suffering and material damage;

(b) In many cases the use of violence does not offer any chance of success. A centre of power that is sufficiently strong in military terms will easily crush any opposition that uses violence. (Revolutions in Russia, Yugoslavia, China, and Cuba succeeded under conditions of defeat and disintegration of the forces hostile to the new regime). "Red terror" used by anarchists never produced any result whatsoever: it alienates a considerable part of the population;

(c) the use of violence provokes such a fear and anger among middle classes that under certain conditions (such as general economic instability, profound demoralisation, frustration with existing "permissive" regime) it might trigger a shift toward the extreme right on a mass scale;

(d) even if carefully prepared and used only at a favourable moment, with minimum bloodshed and destruction, the use of violence as a means to seize political power requires a certain type of political organisation (clandestine, centralistic, authoritarian, strictly hierarchical, with a strong sense of historical mission, highly intolerant toward all other organisations outside of its control) that, in case of victory, tends to be transformed into a bureaucratic elite.

(2) When other conditions are not equal, the undesirable *consequences of direct violence used by revolutionary forces should be compared with the undesirable consequences of indirect, structural violence inherent in the old system.* Critics of revolutionary violence usually take an entirely anti-historical position. They either analyse a revolutionary process in itself, without comparison with other alternative possibilities of the same society. Or else they compare a post-revolutionary situation in all its backwardness, destruction and loss of the best human lives (caused often through foreign intervention) with the situation in other much more developed countries. Obviously the only methodologically sound approach would be to compare developments of countries with different systems and similar starting positions (for example China and India), or to compare

the actual situation with other projected historical possibilities of the same society (for example, China now under Mao with what China would have likely now been under Chang).

(3) After traumatic experiences with fascism even the most ardent adherents of the principle of unconditional, unqualified non-violence find themselves in difficulties when they have to answer questions such as: Is it justified to use violence against these who strive to build up a society based on sheer violence? Would it have been justified to suppress Hitler's movement by force before it had come to power? The area in which an answer is to be found lies between an emphatic refusal to use violence under any circumstances and Saint-Just's maxim: "No freedom for the enemies of freedom." The former answer cannot be satisfactory: it leaves us and coming generations at the mercy of pathological minorities. The latter is too indiscriminate: any regime may use it for drastically repressive measures; what is needed is only an appropriate interpretation of the concept of the "enemies of freedom." And still, there is a sound core in Saint-Just's maxim; this is the idea that one has the right to be free only if he recognises this right in others. When we generalise this idea we get the following principle: *No human rights for those who do not recognise their universal validity.*

These three principles imply the following general conditions under which violence in social life might be transcended and a rational alternative to an apocalyptic vision of the future as a series of violent revolutions and wars would be offered. (1) The existing centres of alienated power would have to develop such a sense of history as to gradually renounce structural violence and open the process of radical democratisation and abolition of class distinctions. (2) The existing revolutionary organisations would have to renounce direct violence and to begin to develop strategies of non-violent struggle for social change.

The meeting of both conditions is not very probable. But it is not impossible if we all realise what the other alternatives are.

FOOTNOTES

1 J.P. Sartre. *Preface* to Frantz Fanon, *The Wretched of the Earth* (New York, 1963), p.17.
2 Hegel, *Encyclopaedie der philosophischen Wissenschaften, Die Wissenschaft für Logik*, p.104.
3 Abraham H. Maslow, *Toward a Psychology of Being*, 2nd ed. (New York, 1968), p.153.
4 Niccolò Machiavelli, *The Prince* (1513), Everyman's Library (New York).
5 Thomas Hobbes, *Leviathan*, Part I, ch. 13; "Of the natural conditions of mankind as concerning their felicity and misery."

6 *Marx-Engels Gesamtausgabe*, 3 p. 114, translated by T.B. Bottomore in E. Fromm, *Marx's Concept of Man* (New York, 1961), p.127.

7 *Writings of the Young Marx on Philosophy and Society*, translated by Easton and Guddat (New York, 1967), p.281.

8 MEGA 1/3, p.308.

9 *Loc. cit.*

10 According to Hannah Arendt "Anthropomorphism and theomorphism are but two sides of the same error." *On Violence* (New York, 1969), p.60.

11 J.P. Sartre, *Critique de la raison dialectique*, "Quéstions de Méthode," (Paris, 1960).

12 Cf. Robert Hartman, "The Science of Value" in Abraham Maslow (ed.), *New Knowledge in Human Values* (New York, 1959).

13 Rogers, *Psychotherapy and Personality Change* (Chicago, 1954); *A Therapist's View of Personal Goals* (Pendle Hill, 1960); *On Becoming a Person* (Boston, 1971).

14 Abraham Maslow, *Toward a Psychology of Being* (New York, 1968), p.157.

15 *Ibid.*, p.159.

16 Jules Humbert-Droz, who was a secretary of the Comintern in 1921, reports in an interview to *Le Monde* how Lenin detested the use of violence although he realised that it was a question of life and death. He recommended to a head of "Tcheka," Dr. Kedrow: "When you will be able to sentence someone to death without horror — resign. The political police is a terrible necessity; it should never become a profession." *(Le Monde*, February 18, 1970), p.11.

17 The atrocities of fascism are practical consequences of the following views expounded by Hitler in his various speeches and articles in the Twenties: "From all the innumerable creatures a complete species rises and becomes the master of the rest. Such a one is man — the most brutal, the most resolute creature on earth. He knows nothing but the extermination of his enemies in the world" *(Völkischer Beobachter*, Nov. 23, 1927). "Whatever goal man has reached is due to his originality plus his brutality ... All life is bound up in three theses: Struggle is the father of all things, virtue lies in blood, leadership is primary and decisive" *(Ibid.*, April 7, 1928). "In the power of the sword lies the vital strength of a nation." *(Ibid.*, May 4, 1928). One is either the hammer or the anvil. We confess that it is our purpose to prepare German people again for the role of the hammer" *(Ibid.*, March 17, 1929).

18 Already Martin Luther, during the struggle of Protestant princes against the Emperor, took the position that Christians had the right to fight in self-defence, and that the authority of the ruler should be respected only so long as he was just. If the ruler disregards the higher law and becomes a tyrant, the subjects are freed from their allegiance and have the right to revolt.

19 John Locke, *Two Treatises of Government*, Bk.II, ch. 19.

20 J.J. Rousseau, *The Social Contract*, Bk I, ch. 4.

21 *Ibid.*, ch. 1, 3.
22 *Social and Political Philosophy*, ed. by Somerville and Santoni (New York, 1963), p.240.
23 Letter to James Madison, January 30, 1781, *op. cit.*, p.258.
24 Letter to Colonel Smith, Nov. 13, 1787, *Op. cit.*, pp.259-60.
25 The concept "structural violence" was explored by Johan Gatung in "Violence, Peace and Peace Research," *Journal of Peace Research* (1969), pp.167-91.
26 A.J. Muste, "Pacifism and Class War," *The Essays of A.J. Muste* (Indianapolis, 1967), pp.175-85.
27 Maurice Merleau-Ponty, *Humanism and Terror* (Boston, 1969), p.XVIII.
28 See Marx's speech at Amsterdam 1872 quoted in M. Steklov, *History of the First International* (New York, 1928), p.240; Marx, "Konspekt der Debatten über das Sozialistengesetz," 1878 (in Marx-Engels, *Briefe an Bebel, Liebknecht, Kautsky und Andere*. Verlag Genossenschaft Auslandischer Arbeiter in der USSR (Moscow, 1933), p.516; Engels, *Critique of the Social Democratic Draft Programme*, 1851, sec. II.

CHAPTER VII

The Prospects for Socialist Humanism

A.J. Liehm

Ever since, with due acknowledgement to Hellas, the Renaissance brought it forth, it has been the fate of humanism to suffer one defeat after another. And yet it has always risen eternal from the ashes of hope, and new standard bearers have repeatedly come forward to lead the way, and always to victory. For, with the wisdom that comes of failure, we are now supremely confident that, at last, we know how to reach the humanist goal, to establish the rule of man and a way of life that will give free rein to his talents and his potentialities. Nor will the inevitable future defeat deter the succeeding generation of humanists. With the tears not yet dry, and the wrath not yet stilled against those whose pursuit of their self-interest or their ideal has again shattered the dream, they will call us once more to do battle for man's emancipation, for justice and the triumph of the human purpose.

It may well be that in this unflagging will and longing, in the hope and the dream, in the enduring resolve, we have the true embodiment of humanism. Perhaps it is the eternal non-fulfilment, the reaching for the stars, that lend the enduring quality to the humanist ideal, the ideal which will never permit the community of man, or any of its parts, to be content with what has been achieved. The Camus rebel in us is ever picking up torch and banner and, having borne them no more than a step forward, he always finds others of his ilk ready to take them from the helpless or exhausted hand.

And what is more, there is that quality in each of us which, all past experience notwithstanding, prevents us from accepting — even for a moment — the Sisyphean myth. In the knowledge of all that has been, we nevertheless cannot resist the temptation to fulfil our human role by striving to so live that we measure up to the aims we have set before us; moreover, time and again we give in to the temptation to share with others our response to the issue posed by our own experience. Nor can we resist the seductive thought that our own experience is something very special, without precedent, and that by analysing and generalising it we shall come up with the answers pointing to the ultimate triumph of humanism or, at the very least, to a long and maybe decisive step towards that goal.

This is the feeling that we, who were active participants in the decade leading up to the Prague Spring of 1968, in the eight months beginning with January of that year, in those six glorious days of national resistance at the end of August, the last four months of the year and the first five of 1969, share in one way or another. For some it is a feeling that all further effort is useless, a resignation, not of the ideals, but of the struggle to realise them. For others it is a mood acquiescence, acceptance of the status quo and, hence, of attitudes that are poles asunder from any ideals of humanism. Lastly, there are those — and I am one of them — whose first thought is to resist, who reject the nonchalance of the world in taking for granted yet another defeat of humanism. From this resistance, from this rejection, springs yet again the irrepressible urge to assimilate the experience, to single out what is unique in it and to transmit that uniqueness to others.

From the defeats suffered by the nineteenth-century radical movements in Europe and from the powerlessness of liberalism to avert the bloody consequences of these defeats and, at times, from its complicity and even identification with the victors, sprang that contempt for liberal or bourgeois humanism with which we in Western Europe are familiar. From the inability of the triumphant Bolshevik revolution in Russia to launch forthwith a frontal attack on the consequences of a thousand years of backwardness, obscurantism and Tsarism, sprang its offensive against the weakest of its opponents, Russian liberalism and all the movements or, rather, groups and splinter-groupings which had, in one way or another, absorbed the ideas of liberalism and humanism emanating from the West.

Any identity between these two different rejections of the liberal form of humanism is purely superficial and is, at the most, of theoretical interest. In reality they involved entirely different confrontations. The radical opponents and critics of liberal humanism in Western Europe were concerned, from the outset, with traditions, concepts and an ideal which had evolved over the centuries and which, undoubtedly, represented a step forward compared with all that had gone before. The ideal of socialist humanism, therefore, found itself confronted from the moment of its first enunciation with a whole body of accumulated experience, with the result that, again and again, it had to define itself not as a rejection of liberal humanism but as its positive transcendence. The prospect of a more just society, the curbing or elimination of the selfishness exemplified by private ownership of the means of production, the ending of the exploitation of human labour — these aims have always, at every point, had to be measured against the undeniable benefits that came with the liberal society. And so socialist humanism has been obliged, at every turn, to counter the allegation that, for the sake of humanising the lot of the non-privileged majority, it is willing to forget, or even take away, the values that liberal humanism had already brought to everybody.

The 'socialist humanism' inaugurated by the Russian revolution is not, on the other hand, in contact with an existing liberal tradition with which it is obliged to compete, nor does it have to measure up to the relative benefits of a past era of liberal humanism. On the contrary, its situation is not unlike that of the 'socialist humanists,' or the earlier western radicals, when their criticism of liberal humanism was first voiced. It was fairly easy to identify Russian liberalism with a last attempt to salvage Tsarism and the autocracy, for it was open to the charge of complicity with uncontrolled power and despotism and with seeking to extend the privileges of a tiny section of society to another not much larger. Moreover, the poverty of the deprived majority was such that any move to alleviate their plight could readily be regarded as the be-all and the end-all of socialist humanism. As for the meaning attributed to the word humanism after the revolution, it was soon equated with the moral postulates of the old society: paternalism, patriotism, belief in transcendentalism and the virtue of patient suffering and sacrifice, the subjection of individuality to the state and its officers. Liberalism and liberal humanism were anathematised, to be extirpated by fire and sword; while the old traditions (lacking, in Russia, the influence of the Renaissance and the Enlightenment), which should by rights have clashed in historical conflict with the liberal ideals, were rescued and were, to a remarkable degree, integrated into the new society.

This duality and the accompanying dual content of 'socialist humanism' passed unnoticed for a long time. Or, at least, no definition was accorded to them. In the meantime, the two aspects had diverged so much that the one was forced to deny the other. Whenever, in the West, any broader alliance was formed between the communists and other movements, socialist or liberal, the Soviet reader was never given the chance to learn how 'socialist humanism' was defined in the joint documents (from the Popular Front of the 1930s to the agreement between the French communists and socialists in the early '70s). On the other hand, the communist press in the West has carefully guarded the 'secret' about the Soviet version of socialist humanism from which even the worker and his organisations, with their rights deriving from the liberal era, had been eliminated. (The situation was confounded when the Soviet-type 'socialist humanism' became official in a number of countries which were, at least to some extent, linked with the West-European traditions of humanism and liberalism.) Not to mention the obvious truth that the material situation of the underprivileged majority in these countries bore no comparison with the plight of the rural and urban poor in Russia of the twenties.

With the exception of Bulgaria, and to some extent Rumania, liberalism and liberal humanism represented the most progressive historical traditions in Eastern Europe. In Poland and Hungary, moreover, they were directly linked with resistance to Russian domination, or with memories of the treatment meted out by Tsarist Russia in its role as an ally of the reactionary Austro-Hungarian monachy. Here, too, socialist humanism should have signified the positive transcendence and development of the liberal tradition, not its suppression. This, however, the Stalinist-type 'socialist humanism' could not do, nor could it even venture a step in that direction. For any other interpretation would have shaken the ideological monolith in all the non-Russian areas of the USSR, which were especially sensitive in the postwar years to any such impulses.

In countries like Poland and Hungary, where it had never really taken root, classical liberalism and its interpretation of humanism enjoyed, paradoxically, considerable prestige and remained the great hope for the future. In Czechoslovakia, on the other hand, the liberal tradition had prevailed ever since the latter third of the last century, and the spokesmen for liberal humanism had included men such as T.G. Masaryk, founder of the Czechoslovak Republic. For this very reason, however, there was a strong movement here which, bearing in mind the successive experiences of economic crisis in the 1930s, of Munich, of the so-called Second Republic following the Munich debacle, and of the Nazi occupation, pressed for the positive replacement of liberal humanism by a socialist type of humanism fully in accord with the traditions of the prewar radical Left in Western Europe. The Soviet part of Germany, being an occupied, defeated country, lacked even the semblance of choice and therefore played, at this stage, an insignificant role. Yugoslavia, on the contrary, where the liberal tradition was also weak and limited, soon arrived at an identification of 'socialist humanism' with the national, patriotic idea, which, under pressure from Stalin, ultimately caused Yugoslavia to seek new ways whereby, in a backward country, socialism could join hands with humanism. The multinational character of the Yugoslav State both facilitated and complicated the search and will probably prove the touchstone of success in the future.

In the event, postwar developments in the world having transformed Eastern, and parts of Central, Europe into something in the nature of an extensive and pretty heterogeneous Soviet protectorate, there was no choice. Either the uniform Soviet ideology — complete with its concept of humanism — would be extended by all possible means to the new areas, or the proximity of widely different traditions would affect the fringe areas of the USSR, causing grave problems, especially in the Ukraine and in the Baltic republics. Consequently, the Stalinist 'socialist humanism' had to be grafted on to an utterly different realm of ideas, and the results were not long in making themselves felt.

The moment the ideological pressure had eased after Stalin's death, the instability of the whole set-up began to appear. First, where the liberal tradition had been completely submerged by the years of Hitler rule and military occupation — in Berlin. It may be that here, particularly, the need was most keenly felt to test whether the traditions of the German working-class movement were still alive, whether its militancy had not been entirely sapped. The German workers were answered by tanks. But memories of the war were too fresh, mistrust of Germans too strong, even among the Left, for the first episode in the struggle over the interpretation of socialist humanism to leave any real scars on the minds of its West-European advocates.

In Poland the explosion was more violent and its consequences more far-reaching. Here, for the first time, clearly and openly stated — the Polish press and cultural scene of those days have not yet been analysed as they deserve to be — was evidence that socialist humanism in the Stalinist guise had not only failed to transcend the liberal ideology, but was actually making it more attractive as an alternative. The new leaders in Warsaw and Moscow drew the necessary conclusion; they tacitly adopted two dominant features of the liberal idea in their political practice — tolerance towards the second, non-established religion (in this case, the traditional Catholicism of Poland), and the concept of the nation as the vehicle and instrument of progress. This worked for some fifteen years, up to December 1970, when the massacre in the northern Polish ports sparked off another crisis, hoisted a new leadership into the saddle and faced it with the danger always implicit in a situation where institutional, democratic linkages between rulers and ruled are lacking. The third dominant idea of classical liberalism, the recognition of the relationship between rulers and ruled, was now urgently knocking at the door.

The Hungarian revolution of 1956, for its part, drew its inspiration to the full from the liberal revolution of 1848. It demonstrated that the ideas of that earlier revolution, crushed in its day with the aid of Russian troops, had not been erased from the national consciousness during the intervening century or more, neither by the Austro-Hungarian settlement nor by the fascist rule of Horthy, nor yet had they been superseded by the 'socialist humanism' of the Stalin era. It was clearly revealed that they remain an unfulfilled dream and a popular goal. Having suppressed the revolt and, evidently under compulsion, carried out the bloody reckoning with its spokesmen, the new leadership was careful to take these feelings into account. Gradually they established what may be termed an enlightened, tolerant absolutism, including, compared with the other countries of Eastern Europe — Rumania excepted — a novel feature in the shape of a kind of silent agreement between people and government in face of the new and, at present, unalterable geopolitical situation. In contrast to Poland, however, a new element had emerged in Hungary during the autumn of 1956. Not only did the workers in Budapest's biggest industrial concern, the Csepel Works, side with the revolution, they also set up their own organs of workers' self-management. Here, for the first time in the Soviet bloc, was posed the question of direct ownership of a socialist enterprise by its employees, not by the state. And again for the first time, it became clear that what really worried the men who identified socialism with state ownership of the means of production were not 'hang-overs from bourgeois liberalism,' but rather the moves towards transcending these ideas through direct worker participation in management, without intervention by the state.

In their response to the relaxation of the Stalinist grip, Rumania and Bulgaria, the two East-European countries almost completely lacking any profound experience of liberal humanism, were not susceptible to temptation in this direction. Rumania reverted to her tradition of subordinating everything to the interests of the state which, in her complicated geopolitical situation, signified a policy of manoeuvring and alliance aimed at maintaining and strengthening her independence. Bulgaria, owing her independence to Russia, made a virtue of the old allegiance at a time when such sentiments were, everywhere else, on the wane. In Czechoslovakia, however, the picture was entirely different.

In that country, in 1956, there was neither an economic crisis such as gripped Poland and Hungary, nor was there a tradition of animosity towards Russia which could act as a catalyst as in the neighbouring countries. True, an attempt was made to regenerate the ideas of liberal humanism and to pose the question whether the Stalin 'socialist humanism' was the genuine article. While this attempt was nipped in the bud, the questions re-emerged in the early sixties, coinciding with the onset of an economic crisis. And now they were there to stay, being posed with increasing urgency until the political crisis in the autumn of 1967 which precipitated the changes of January 1968.

And again in the forefront were found problems which firmly fit into the category of 'liberal humanism.' In Hungary, the rehabilitation of Rajk had already triggered off the events of 1956. But it was in Czechoslovakia that the issue of the rehabilitation of the victims of the show trials of the 1950s emerged as the key question. It was here that, in 1963 and again in 1968, two documents appeared disclosing almost the whole story of the preparation and conduct of Stalin's witch hunt. At first the concern was restricted to the issue of rehabilitation for the communist victims of the fake trials, but soon justice for all was demanded. The validity of the so-called "class justice" practised in the late 1940s and early 1950s was questioned, and demands for reform of the judicial system, with legal safe-guards for the individual, grew increasingly insistent. Here, too, came the first attacks on the all-powerful state-as-owner which, like the omnipotent lord in feudal times, can physically destroy anyone who in the most innocuous manner dares to encroach on its sacred property.

Ultimately the state backed down somewhat, giving the individual at least some measure of protection against arbitrary actions and reducing the harshness of penalties for 'damaging state property.' The second vital issue of the 'sixties was the relationship between the two nations within the Czechoslovak Republic. Despite the initial promises, the two-nation state had been moulded on the Soviet pattern as a state of one ruling nation. Step by step, Slovakia was relegated to the position of a province. Consequently, it was first in Slovak eyes that the national question appeared as a 'question of humanism,' entirely in the spirit of Masaryk or Mazzini, to acquire, at the moment of indirect and then direct confrontation with the dominating great power, the same significance for the Czechs. The principles of genuine self-determination, genuine national sovereignty, became one of the main issues of the day. In the insistence that these principles are intrinsic to 'socialism with a human face' (the name that, in 1968, the Czechoslovak essay on 'socialist humanism' gave itself) one observes features of the national-emancipation movement of the nineteenth century.

The economic reform, planned — but never implemented — to stem the growing economic decline, did not, up to the end of the 1968 Spring, propose any fundamental changes in the existing property relations. The brunt of the attack was directed against bureaucratic centralism and the endeavour was to revive the market as a counter-force. For the time being the reform passed over the problem that operating on the market would be enterprises belonging, in effect, to a single owner, so that this would involve something of a game at markets, a simulated market. An important aspect of the proposal was the admission that the market (conceived in a form somewhat akin to the Keynesian concept) would be an undoubted advantage compared with the so-called socialist planning as practised hitherto, which had been exposed as an instrument of the centralised, militarised, industrialisation policy pursued by Stalin's Russia.

The special political role which, in the absence of a national aristocracy, had fallen to Czech culture in the late eighteenth and throughout the nineteenth centuries was also very evident during the 1960s. In common with their liberal-humanist predecessors, the representatives of Czech culture now set themselves the task of awakening the national and social awareness of the people, of breaking out of isolation, of opening a window to Europe, linking Czech culture with world culture and overcoming the provincial outlook of Czech and Slovak cultural thinking. A parallel, though unspoken, process was the erosion of the reactionary Slavo-phile element that had been injected anew into the culture of the late 1940s and early 1950s. (Again, it is interesting to note that the 19th-century Czech liberals, from Havlíček to Masaryk, had fought this weapon from the arsenal of Tsarist expansionism).

For the most part, in its further course the 'Czechoslovak Spring' simply carried forward the process of restoring 'liberal humanism' and its structure within the system of state, or state-controlled, ownership in the economy and one-party rule in government. The demands voiced and gradually put into effect ranged from the ending of censorship, through democratisation of education, religious tolerance (in this case, tolerance on the part of the communist ideology towards the religious ideology), freedom of travel, restoration of the status of the trade unions and other public organisations, to the substantial reforms within the ruling party itself and in its organs of power – the armed forces and the police.

With this, however, the initial dynamism of the Spring was exhausted. Within the framework of the existing system there had been, in effect, a renewal of the liberal structure. 'Socialism with a human face' was, at the moment, simply 'liberal humanism' within the given system, that is, with one-party rule and an over-whelming preponderance of state ownership in the economic field. The majority of people in public life were, at the time, unaware of the paradox implicit in this situation, but it forced them to act: The system put a brake on the functioning of, at least de facto of the revived liberal structure, and the latter, for its part, put in doubt the functioning of the system. There were only two alternatives: either the liberal reforms would break the bounds of the system in the direction of genuine socialism, or the system internationally would crush the reforms to restore the neo-Stalinist structure. (Theoretically, there was a third alternative, to crush the system in order to restore classical liberalism complete with private ownership and private profit. It is interesting that in Czechoslovakia, a country living for eight months without censorship or police interference with opinion, not a single attempt was evident, either in the press or elsewhere, to turn things in that direction. This may be taken as evidence that the liberal structure, while presupposing a plurality of ownership, does not necessarily include private ownership of the means of production).

Let us pause a while over this point. Socialist humanism, in its critique of liberal humanism, has often given the impression that what really mattered was purely to solve the basic issues of economic inequality, the exploitation of wage labour by private capital, the alienation of stemming from the worker's place in the work process and his ever-growing impoverishment. Leaving aside here the historical background to the theoretical premises for this view, we may take it as proved that the postwar societies in Eastern Europe, at various levels of production forces, and specifically in Czechoslovakia, have met these requirements in large measure. The egalitarianism which was for a long time a Czechoslovak speciality, has, indeed, not infrequently been regarded as a sign of the exceptional maturity of Czechoslovak 'socialism.' There was no unemployment, no poverty, job insecurity had become a thing of the past, and with the maximum recruitment of women and the majority of young people

116

over 16 into the work process, a fair standard of living had been attained. True, alienation had not been eliminated, but the pressure on the worker was less severe, for the most part the tempo of work had eased and, with working hours cut, and once the five-day working week had been adopted, his mode of life had changed. (Much of this also goes for the non-socialist societies of Western Europe or America, but that is beside the point here).

However, there were also two consequences which no one intent on studying the social development in a 'statised society' can ignore.

First, the overall improvement in conditions of life was not adequately matched by growth in production on a scale corresponding to that in the West. It was becoming clear that where the state exercises monopoly control over industry and over society in general, the workers and practically all wage and salary earners, including the inflated bureaucracy, are reduced, far more than in any previous type of society, to insignificant cogs in the production or social mechanism, without acquiring the power to exercise the slightest influence on affairs. The system of pressures which capitalist society has at its disposal — albeit in increasingly restricted measure — had been abolished and nothing had been put in its place. Theoretically, pressures and interest motives were supposed to be superseded by the initiative of the free worker. But the worker had been freed solely from insecurity in respect of his livelihood, and since this was his only freedom, it was for this alone that he was willing to commit himself and, if necessary, take risks and engage in open resistance. Indeed, herein lay the greatest danger for the economic reform programme. It was the defence of this one freedom, this sole interest, which demolished, in an unexpected outburst of popular anger, Gomulka's timid, bureaucratic attempt at some kind of economic reform recognising the actual state of living standards and production in Poland.

In all other respects the worker remains unfree, more so than ever before. He has no say whatever in the political functioning of the society, nor even in deciding policies in his locality, not to mention being excluded from participation in matters of production, conditions of employment or anything else at his place of work. The outcome is a kind of unspoken agreement, which on the worker's side might run something like this: I have handed over to you all my prerogatives and civil freedoms. In exchange I demand job security, a decent living standard, minimal expenditure of my labour power and adequate free time. This agreement, essential for the working of the state-monopoly society, is only seemingly advantageous for that society. The worker, the employee, has contributed a great deal, everything he had, his individual freedom. But his demands are equally great, and as demonstrated by Poland in 1970, the balance between the two sides is very delicate. The sole concern of the worker-employee is to maintain the balance, to its underlying economic conditions he is indifferent. In these circumstances, it is a hard matter indeed to mobilise his initiative. Socialist emulation is in Eastern Europe today a subject purely for newspaper editorials: only there is it an economic and political reality. The economic passivity of the population is, however, a drag on industrial development, mechanisation, modernisation and so on, and that undermines every attempt by the East-European countries to increase their scope for independent decision and binds them ever more firmly to the USSR. In the Soviet Union itself the balance in question rests on a generally low standard of living, on the vast size of the country, and on its wealth and inexhaustible natural resources. Any improvement in the living standard, any reduction in international tension, any wider opportunities for comparison with other countries, taken together with the growing, though still limited, voicing of liberal demands, can only tend to upset the balance. It is not surprising that the Soviet leadership hit back so hard (with the arrest of Pyotr Yakir) after the recent appearance of leaflets in which, for the first time, this balance was openly and explicitly attacked.

Any effective economic reform, if it is to have any hope of drawing on the worker's initiative, on his active participation and help, must first make him a party to shaping the overall political and economic course and, consequently, make him jointly responsible for any upsetting of the balance. Failing this, the state-monopoly society is doomed to stagnation for a duration which must be dependent primarily on the resources available to the USSR. A change in the existing state of affairs, on the other hand, inevitably and irreversibly signifies the end of state-monopoly society.

The second consequence is a return to the vision of society into the classical silent majority and active minority. The first accepts the existing state of affairs for one reason or another — either because they have some vested interest in it, or simply because they cannot or dare not do otherwise — that is, they accept the unspoken agreement and its accompanying balance. By degrees they adapt their way of life, they learn to live with it all and ultimately to profit by it. And since the ruling bureaucracy cannot resort to mass terror against the producers, the workers and the peasants, it uses innumerable undefined pressure devices which, in the end, add up to an extreme economic conservatism. The active minority, for their part, recruited from essentially the same social strata as the majority (although, as in every 'active minority,' they include a larger proportion of intellectuals and other people with more than average access to information), come by degrees to realise that the price of maintaining the existing balance is too high and that it is to blame for diverting the society from the original goal, transforming it into a colossus obsessed with but a single problem: how to maintain the status quo without undue upset. It is interesting to note the growing prominence within the active minority of the one-time radical upholders of 'socialist humanism' in its eastern guise, those who only after the triumph of their ideal have come to grasp the true value of the liberal freedoms and to discern the actual relationship between the two humanisms. And so, lastly, the desire for genuine citizenship, the human striving for self-fulfilment with real freedom of choice, the urge to break out of the new alienation, which is an alienation more total than the earlier kind, these are the driving forces of the centrifugal trend which, naturally, threatens to upset the existing balance. And because of the threat it offers, the trend meets with opposition from both sides. Consequently, everything depends on whether a part, at least, of the silent majority can be won over, can be convinced that their interests will be served not by the existing balance, the marasmus of the status quo, but by a new dynamism. And that was finally achieved during the first six months of the Czechoslovak Spring. Only then were the genuine prospects, the actual choice, revealed.

Czechoslovakia's economists who conceived and drafted the blue-print for economic reform avoided, as far as possible, during the 'sixties and also, during the first six months of the 1968 Spring, the problem of workers' self-management. And when there was no avoiding it, most economists opposed the idea. Their attitude is understandable in view of what has been said above. Silent-majority thinking prevailed in industry and there were well-founded fears that, in the given situation, workers' self-management could turn out to be yet another instrument making for conservatism and for maintaining the status quo in the economy.

Simultaneously, however, the active minority was exerting all its influence to change the thinking and to shake confidence in the virtues of the existing balance. Undoubtedly, a decisive part was played in this by the press and other media, now free from censorship. As all the other examples of 'restricted liberalism' in Eastern Europe have shown, without the help of the media, events can only lead to a spontaneous explosion which offers no prospect of a genuine political solution. The guardians of the status quo, however, were also devoting exceptional attention to the silent majority and their 'active spokesmen.' Within six months the trial of strength was decided. Now defeated, the defenders of the past, backed by all the help they could win abroad, prepared for a counter-offensive, relying on the positions they could command in the armed forces and among the police.

The time had then come for the economists who supported the Spring to revise their attitude to workers' councils in industry. If the system was to get off the ground at all, there had to be a resolve to break up the old system. If the alienation of the industrial worker, the farmer, and the white-collar worker, from the social mechanism, was to be ended, it was essential to abolish the state monopoly over public life and to establish a community of self-managing producers. If the people were to become the real driving force of social dynamism and no longer be merely the passive defenders of the 'delicate balance,' they had also to be the real wielders of economic and political power.

At this point workers' councils began to spring up like mushrooms after rain and to the amazement of many they ranked among the most active supporters of the new system, of the political and economic reforms, of the new social dynamism. And it was these councils that, at this time, were the main targets of attack by those who later occupied Czechoslovakia and found in the workers' councils, and in the enterprises managed by them, the most determined and obdurate opponents of the policy of putting back the clock and 'normalising' the country.

It was also the emergence and spread of the workers' councils that posed, for the first time in concrete terms, the question of the political system. Throughout the Spring there had been many arguments and heart-searchings on this matter. Obviously, to maintain a single, and therefore ruling, party on the condition that it undergo reform was a purely temporary solution. A return to some form of political pluralism looked increasingly likely. Yet any return to the earlier set-up of political parties, if only on the pattern existing around 1948, would clearly be out of place in the now entirely different situation. Advocates of some kind of corporative pluralism gravitated towards the old fascist designs. The political clubs that were making their appearance tended to be more directed towards regional and municipal self-government, and however valuable they might be in general, they were not the answer to the problem of finding a new system. Only when the workers' councils, or enterprise self-management, arrived on the scene was there at least an indication of where the answer might lie.

The political initiative sparked off by this development called attention to the circumstance that under the Stalinist system state ownership and a monolithic political bureaucracy are simply two sides of the same coin. Party and state are merged, with the party, in the last resort, becoming the owner of the state and of everything belonging to the state. With the break-up of the monolith of state ownership and its replacement by self-management and gradually by group ownership, the political monopoly is *de facto* abolished, plurality of ownership is introduced and the foundation laid for a new political pluralism which, of course, had not time during the Czechoslovak Spring to assume a definite form. In the brief space allowed, however, workers' self-management in an industrially advanced country with a tradition of democracy gave every promise of offering the practical means by which to advance from classical liberalism and liberal humanism in a positive way in the direction of socialism — a humanistic socialism capable of overcoming the underlying alienation in the economic sphere.

In the evolution from a movement to reform the system of society into a movement to change that system, that is, into an essentially revolutionary movement, we have the kernel of the lesson that the Czechoslovak Spring carries for the future. We may sum up as follows: the state monopoly over society cannot solve the problem of the alienation of the working man in modern society. Only the circumstances are changed, the emphasis is shifted, the alienation becomes total and the system, instead of liberating the creative initiative and energy of the masses, instead of giving free rein to the creative powers of every individual, reduces everything to security of livelihood in exchange for the dropping of all other demands by the 'liberated' worker. Therefore, there is no transcendence of 'liberal humanism,' but rather a reversion to paternalism, to a system where political power derives from the centre of property-holding: this time, however, not in an agrarian, but in an industrial society. That is the reason for the great appeal, the 'rehabilitation,' of liberal humanism and its postulates within the state-monopoly society. Times having changed, however, to advance liberal demands and to implement them in no way implies turning the clock back (it should not be forgotton that liberal humanism has never been transcended under the state monopoly, it was simply decreed out of existence, forbidden, denied) on the contrary, it marks the beginning of a new phase. Revival of the liberal freedom (albeit, in the Czechoslovakia of 1968, merely the *de facto* existence of such freedoms): freedom of the press, speech, assembly, movement, organisation, inviolability of the person and so on, simply prepares the ground for the formulation of political and economic demands and programmes, for the growth of an active minority and for erosion of the silent majority. Then, and only then, are the conditions present – and it is the creation of these conditions that the old system tries everywhere to prevent – for the political and social revolution which will aim to expropriate the state. Only with the elimination of state ownership – with the exception of some areas of economic activity, namely, transport, services and some enterprises in certain branches of industry, which will be strictly defined by law and the subject to public control – and the establishment of group ownership, will the way be open to democratic socialism and the appearance of the new socialist citizen. Conditions will then emerge for him to overcome his alienation in the economic and social process and to devote himself to achieving 'socialist humanism' – that is, a humanism integrating in itself the benefits of the liberal humanism in order to extend it by adding new benefits. It goes without saying that we shall then see the beginning of a new series of victories and defeats.

The question of ownership – and hence also of state monopoly and self-management – is, therefore, the key question in considering the prospects and opportunities for socialist humanism. No wonder that it holds pride of place in the debates conducted on the Left in Europe and elsewhere. And in Central and Eastern Europe, too, this will be the inescapable, central issue for the future. The identification of state ownership with socialism (and with one-party rule as its inseparable accompaniment) has tied the hands of those who, in this part of the world, stand for genuine socialist humanism. With the taboo lifted and with the setting of aims going beyond the mere, though essential, renewal of human rights and liberal freedoms, a new dynamism will be imparted to the movements for change in these countries, enabling them — let us hope in cooperation with similar movements in other parts of the world — to arrive by degrees at a more precise definition of socialist humanism as they envisage it, and of its prospects.

CHAPTER VIII

Commodities, Computers and Mystification

Stephen Bodington

Bertrand Russell wrote of John Stuart Mill "What he achieved depended more on his moral elevation and his just estimate of the ends of life than upon any purely intellectual merits."[1] Something like this, but with a much deeper sense, might be said of Bertrand Russell himself. Current orthodoxy is ready to praise the great philosopher or the great mathematician in Bertrand Russell, but the real point is that he was a great man, that he lived greatly. For most humans the problem is to find opportunity to use the qualities that are in them. The testing problem for Bertrand Russell was of a quite opposite sort. His quality showed itself in the manner of life he adopted in face of enticing opportunities offering prestige, distinction, congenial practical and intellectual activity. Early in life he was under pressure to take up a political career in which his own abilities, combined with advantages of tradition and influence, would have opened almost any position to him. Alternatively, he could have become a very important figure in the academic establishment. Or – the most appealing seduction of them all – he could have deafened his ears to the turmoils and miseries of the world and sought fulfilment and satisfaction in the intellectual beauties of mathematics. On his eightieth birthday he wrote "I set out with a more or less religious belief in a platonic eternal world, in which mathematics shone with a beauty like that of the last Cantos of the Paradiso." He also records how G.H. Hardy (whose tongue, I think, often maligned his heart) told him that the beauty of an irrefutable proof gave him such delight that he could not regret the conclusion of the proof even if this were the immediate death of Bertrand Russell himself. To this Bertrand Russell replied that he well understood his feelings.

The temptation of forgetting the world in 'job satisfaction' is very great when the opportunity of totally satisfying work is to hand. I sometimes think that Bertrand Russell's coolness towards the philosophies of Epicurus and Lucretius is connected with his determination not to be snared by this temptation. He seemed to regard the philosophy of Epicurus – in my view, wrongly – as a philosophy aiming at spiritual peace at the cost of compassion. Epicurus's disciple Lucretius at least had one over-riding purpose in common with Russell. Both were enemies of mystification as an instrument of human oppression. Do not these words of Lucretius breathe also something of Russell's spirit?

> *"Humana ante oculos foede cum vita iaceret*
> *in terris oppressa gravi sub religione*
> *quae caput a caeli regionibus ostendebat*
> *horribili super aspectu mortalibus instans,*
> *primum Graius hómo mortalis tollere contra*
> *est oculos ausus primusque obsistere contra,*
> *quem neque fama deum nec fulmina nec minitanti*
> *murmure compressit caelum, sed eo magis acrem*
> *irritat animi virtutem, effringere ut arta*
> *naturae primus portarum claustra cupiret.*
> *ergo vivida vis animi pervicit, et extra*
> *processit longe flammantia moenia mundi*
> *atque omne immensum peragravit mente animoque,*
> *unde refert nobis victor quid possit oriri,*
> *quid nequeat, finita potestas denique cuique*
> *quanam sit ratione atque alte terminus haerens.*
> *quare religio pedibus subiecta vicissim*
> *obteritur, nos exaequat victoria caelo.*[2]

Russell in the concluding paragraphs of *History of Western Philosophy* dealing with his own philosophical position writes: " . . . The human intellect is unable to find conclusive answers to many questions of profound importance to mankind, but they (the philosophers of logical analysis) refuse to believe there is some 'higher' way of knowing, by which we can discover truths hidden from science and the intellect." A few lines later he writes: "In the welter of conflicting fanaticisms, one of the few unifying forces is scientific truthfulness . . ."[3]

Bertrand Russell spent a great part of his life fighting alongside Marxists against war and oppression of man by man, for the liberation of mankind. However, at the level of theory there seems to be a great distance between Russell and Marxism. Various circumstances, which it is not possible here to explore, prevented Russell seeing Marx in a way that might have aroused a greater intellectual interest in what Marx was trying to do and trying to say. These circumstances may include the non-availability until fairly recently of some important writings of Marx, but more important were the fanaticisms perpetrated in the name of Marx coupled with Russell's rebound from his early intellectual love affair with Hegelian ideas. Russell was delighted to escape from the murky fog of Hegel's absolute idea. "This point of view", he wrote in 1956, "was temperamentally unpleasing to me. Like the philosophers of Ancient Greece, I prefer sharp outlines and definite separations such as the landscapes of Greece afford."[4] He took very unkindly to anything that smacked of

STEPHEN BODINGTON

Hegel in Marx. "Broadly speaking," he wrote in his History of Western Philosophy (page 754) "all the elements in Marx's philosophy which are derived from Hegel are unscientific, in the sense that there is no reason whatever to suppose them true." Actually the intention behind the whole of Marx's arduous intellectual work was the freeing of men's minds from the mystifications that made them a prey to their oppressors. "There were, in the past," wrote Bertrand Russell, "physical obstacles to human wellbeing. The only obstacles now are in the souls of men. Hatred, folly and mistaken beliefs alone stand between us and the millennium."[5] These words of Russell's are, in fact, a succinct statement of the central thesis to the scientific proof of which Marx dedicated the greater part of his intellectual labours. Marx, like Lucretius, saw men's minds bound by superstition, but this he saw also was not merely the superstition of false religious beliefs but also superstitions about the nature of the civil institutions and the civil society in which man lived. Men had created social and economic institutions which now stood terrifyingly above the heads of men crushing and destroying human lives as if they were natural forces outside of human control. What is more, the advance of science and industry, the very advances in control over nature, seemed to generate more and more destructive social forces. Marx saw, as Russell saw, that the physical obstacles to human wellbeing, which had existed in the past, were now surmountable. The problem was to discover how the consciousness of men comes to be formed and from this understanding to see how false consciousness, the 'folly and mistaken beliefs' that shackle men to oppressive institutions and war-making institutions, may be overcome. Marx, when still in his twenties, wrote in his Introduction to a Critique of Hegel's Philosophy of Law: "The struggle against religion is therefore indirectly the struggle against the world whose spiritual aroma is religion. Religious suffering is the expression of real suffering and at the same time the protest against real suffering. Religion is the sigh of the oppressed creature, the heart of a heartless world, as it is the spirit of spiritless conditions. It is the opium of the people . . . the criticism of religion is thus in embryo a criticism of the veil of tears whose halo is religion."[6]

Marx was trying to answer questions 'factually' in a double sense; that is the understanding of a problem requires analysis of the historical actuality, the specific factual circumstances in which it arises and at the same time solutions to problems must take off from actual social processes from socio-economic developments that are in actuality taking place. Blueprints for salvation cannot be parachuted in from outer space. Marx writing in 1847 spoke of socialists and communists as the theoreticians of the proletarian class. So long as the struggle of the proletariat with the bourgeoisie had not yet assumed a political character and so long as productive forces were not sufficiently developed, socialist theoreticians tended to be merely utopians who 'improvise systems and go in search of a regenerating science.' Marx went on to say "In the measure that history moves forward and with it the struggle of the proletariat assumes clearer outlines, they (that is socialist theoreticians) no longer need to seek science in their minds, they have only to take note of what is happening before their eyes and become its mouthpiece. So long as they look for science and merely make systems, so long as they are at the beginning of the struggle, they see in poverty nothing but poverty, without seeing in it the revolutionary, subversive side, which will overthrow the old society. From this moment, science which is a product of the historical movement, has associated itself consciously with it, has ceased to be doctrinaire and has become revolutionary."[7]

Let us try to apply logical analysis to the understanding of a contemporary problem. I shall take as my starting point a note that appeared in The New Scientist on 8th June 1972 on Solar Power. Fossil-fuel as a source of energy may well prove inadequate to the task of freeing the masses of the world from the oppressions of poverty. When the peoples of the world are free to develop they may not require to squander energy resources as wastefully as some industrial societies of the West, but even so, it is certain that mankind cannot afford to squander limited resources of fossil fuels and needs urgently to make use of new sources of energy. Energy from the sun is one of the most important such sources. Professor Manfred Altman of the National Centre for Energy Management and Power at the University of Pennsylvania believes that solar energy has not progressed because few people have taken it seriously. To harness solar energy "no technological or science break-throughs appear to be needed," states The New Scientist with the authority of Professor Altman. The article then goes on to say "Economic and commercial feasibility present the real difficulty." Statements such as this are made again and again without any analysis of their meaning being made. They serve accordingly as a mystification deterring men from the use of powers which they possess, but of which they are deprived of use by false consciousness. The scientists know how but 'for economic or commercial reasons' the use of this knowledge is not feasible. Once this pronouncement has been made, supported possibly by affirmations from reputed experts on 'economic and commercial feasibility,' people are asked to desist from pursuing what authoritative opinion has declared 'unfeasible.' To say that a project is commercially unfeasible presumably means that no entrepreneur is prepared to undertake it because he cannot see the project as yielding a profit. If this is what it means, it is clear that the statement implies a specific type of socio-economic institution, namely, an institution embodying economic categories such as private capital, money, market exchanges, etc. On such a definition the tests of commercial feasibility are very simple; in general what is commercially feasible will be undertaken and if a particular project is not undertaken this immediately suggests that it is not 'commercially feasible' and the only feasible action is to make information available to people with capital in the hope of persuading them to think again.

Presumably 'economic feasibility' is something different from commercial feasibility. In what way different? Again one must ask what economic institutions are assumed. One possible assumption is the same commodity, capital, money, market exchange system implied in the term 'commercial feasibility' discussed above. On this assumption economic feasibility to be different from commercial feasibility, must needs be regarded as undertaking of a project by public authority capable by some means of extracting resources from the commercial/market system. A state may tax. A local authority may collect rates. A financial authority may generate purchasing power in the form of credits. On this set of assumptions, the analysis of economic feasibility amounts to studying the impact of the activities undertaken by public authority on the market/commodity system. Discussion of economic feasibility, therefore, implies under all circumstances the assumption of some system of socio-economic relations. Such discussions can hardly be meaningful unless they investigate also the possibility of changing existing socio-economic relations in such a manner as to make the use of scientific and technical knowledge feasible as a means to meeting some desired social aim. In the vast majority of cases in which technical and scientific potentials are not exploited the obstacle is the institutional economic structure, that is the socio-economic relations prevailing, and not 'physical barriers.' 'Physical barriers' would, for example, be insufficient resources of energy, insufficient supplies of required materials plus the impossibility of making required materials, insufficient human beings to work on the project or insufficiency of skills and knowledge plus the impossibility of training, i.e. imparting required skills and knowledge by an educational process.

Once one has begun to pose the problem in this way, one begins to see that the efforts of the vast majority of economic experts are not devoted to the real problem of economic feasibility at all. They confine themselves to considering economic feasibility within the framework of very restrictive assumptions. The real economic problem is 'how can changes be effected in socio-economic relations and what changes need to be effected in order to deploy and develop the potential of science and technology and productive experience generally so as to apply available resources to social needs?' Because this problem does not appear as the central problem on the agenda of the economic experts, they declare unfeasible any solutions that imply transformed socio-economic relations. In so doing they become master mystifiers, magnifying as it were the already pre-existing mystifications in the 'common sense' of the man in the street. What is the basis of this great mystification? This is what Marx set out to discover. The motivation of his vast theoretical labours whose fruits were in the Grundisse, Capital, and many other writings that were to follow is quite clear in his and Engels' writings in the 1840s. "The phantoms formed in the human brain are also", writes Marx in the German Ideology,[8] "necessarily, sublimates of their material process, which is empirically verifiable and bound to material premises." Marx embarked on a very deep investigation of these material premises. His key in investigating the structure of modern society was the commodity, something produced for exchange and in its value expressing the social relations structuring capitalist society. Fully developed commodity production is capitalism and society is structured by class relationships defining the relationships of different categories of men and women to the process of social production. Obviously, we cannot here pursue Marx's full analysis but one can fairly readily begin to see how it is that the economic system becomes, as it were, external to the individuals whose activities cause it to function. The buying and selling of labour power, the buying and selling of commodities effects the links of man to man in the vast process of social production. Men no longer consciously co-ordinate their several activities in the process of determining and meeting their needs. The thing they have produced, the commodity, goes to the market and through the market dictates the course of the economic processes. The great mystification of modern society results from the commodity becoming a law unto itself. Society is dominated by the belief that no other form of economic organisation is feasible. This elementary notion of the thing produced for exchange appears in many forms. Its most complete and perfect abstraction is money, its domain is the market place, its expression as social power is capital. But each of these manifestations is implicit in the commodity, the thing produced for exchange as the basic cell out of which the body of modern economic institutions, the structure of socio-economic relations, is built. "A commodity is" writes Marx,[9] "a mysterious thing, simply because in it the social character of men's labour appears to them as an objective character stamped upon the product of that labour, because the relation of the producers to the sum total of their own labour is presented to them as a social relation, existing not between themselves, but between the products of their labour." Marx goes on to contrast the mystified forms assumed by the productive processes in a commodity economy with other forms of production in which resources are directly used to meet needs. However, actual societies preceding the development of commodity production were primitive and technologically backward. They also were class societies veiled by ideological mystifications. "The life process of society", Marx goes on, "which is based on the process of material production, does not strip off its mystical veil until it is treated as production by freely associated men, and is consciously regulated by them in accordance with a settled plan. This, however, demands for society a certain material ground work or set of conditions of existence which in their turn are the spontaneous product of a long and painful process of develop ment." The long process involves the development of material conditions, means of production etc., scientific knowledge and techniques and also a social consciousness capable of piercing through the mystifications of the commodity society. This is just where we are now. It is no longer possible to find acceptable solutions within the framework of the commodity institutions. Yet policies are framed in terms of the language and ideas of the commodity society. Criteria are expressed in terms of money, market ability, profitability, etc. Problems are framed in terms that imply there are no alternative patterns of socio-economic relations that are feasible. Yet the inadequacy of the market/money analyses are again and again declaring themselves. The Upper Clyde Shipbuilders and the economy of Clydeside is a case in point. Redundancies associated with modernisation, e.g. dockers' jobs and containerisation, is another. Issue after issue reveals the inadequacies of the market system; these include, for example, integrated fuel policy, rational transportation and integration of modes of travel, pollution, waste recovery, protection of scarce resources and so forth. The myth is that the market is the only rational way of allocating resources. The reality is that the market system is totally geared to the realisation of profits and squanders resources doubly: first, it fails to use capacities for creative work as evidenced by mass unemployment in the industrialised countries and the less recordable unemployment, the absence of work opportunities in the stagnating rural economies bound by the invisible ties of the international market and the domination of finance capital. At the same time the insatiable thirst for accumulation of capital that the competition of a commodity exchange system generates, leads to blind plundering of natural resources dictated solely by the profit rationality of the present. Elementary human demands inevitably challenge the market/commodity system. Yet these demands continue to be discussed in the holy verbiage of the market myth. Take for example the wage claims of the miners or the rail men. The demands of the workers are elementary and simple. "A modern technology can provide us with a tolerable standard of living; we demand such a standard; we shall not work unless tolerable living and working conditions are accorded to us." In the last analysis the continuance of social production must over-ride the rituals of the market. Action outside the market must be taken to meet the demands that the power and the united consciousness of the workers press against the resisting policies of the capitalist state. The developing mass movements and the new demands and new forms of action that are being adopted reveal the development of a new social consciousness and a crumbling of the false consciousness that accepted the market system as in the nature of things.

It falls to socialist theory to become the mouthpiece of the movements that are developing. The social logic implicit in these movements needs to be explicit. The inability of capitalist policies to meet popular expectations needs to be met by workers' organisations making more than economic demands, more, that is, than the demands that can be made on capital within the market system. The implicit demands of the mass movements need to become explicity demands for taking control of productive resources away from capital in order that they may be organised for the direct satisfaction of social needs against the principle of market regulation. The slogan 'Plan against Market' begins to transform the economic struggle into a political struggle, substitutes for economic demands against capital a challenge to the social relations of the commodity system on which the power of capital is based. The economic and the political struggles are inextricably connected with a struggle for a new consciousness about social and economic relations. That the battle is about social consciousness also, was very clear in the case of Upper Clyde Shipbuilders. Here the Government's attack on the yards was launched in the name of economic viability in the competitive market. The counterattack launched in the name of the social audit challenged the ability of the market/ commodity criteria to measure social benefits against social costs.

Several recent examples have been quoted above suggesting that the conflict between planned production for use and exchange value production for profit lies at the root of the great social struggles developing in contemporary Britain. These are class struggles in the most basic sense; that is they are struggles against the capitalist way of organising social and economic life (based on the commodity, money, profit, the market and competition) for the proletarian or socialist way (based on social benefit and accountability, people themselves controlling use of resources, worker-controlled planning of production to meet social needs, in short, democracy in its literal sense of 'people-power'). Concretely the struggle for social change is the struggle to strengthen the advocates of the socialist way — which in turn means seeing through the mystifications and making stronger the institutional basis from which to fight for the socialist way. The particular forms assumed by the struggle for 'plan' against 'market', for 'the workers' and people's way' against 'the capitalist way' may be very varied and superficially different. The participants on either side may not themselves consciously identify the alignments to which their actions give expression; they act intuitively from a sense of justice; they do what they regard as right and wrong, possible or not possible, desirable or undesirable in very specific and from the point of view of political principle very complicated situations. Defenders of the status quo naturally make big claims for its virtues and many of those who are in fact struggling against the status quo are motivated by the failure of the existing order of society to live us to its promises. The truth of a social philosophy in the sense of what Marx called its 'this-sidedness', is established by its ability to do what it claims to do. Class struggle takes the form of presenting 'promises to pay' to the dominant class and demanding that they be met. A class is dominant by virtue of its control of institutions and also by virtue of its ideas, its social philosophy. Institutional and ideological control go hand in hand. Pressure by a subordinate class against a dominant class may be relieved by promises on the part of those who are dominant to produce results more acceptable to the dominated. If in fact promises are not met the social philosophy is impugned and the dominant class are faced with much deeper problems of trying to impose by force policies to which more and more people are hostile. The multiplicity of actions and interactions involved in social struggle make political analysis a complicated undertaking. Here it is possible to do no more than hint at some of the many elements taking simply one of the examples mentioned, namely, U.C.S., by way of illustration.

At its most superficial level the U.C.S. confrontation was between the philosophy of 'the right to work' on the one hand and the 'lame duck' philosophy on the other. The fight for the right to work evolved out of new forms of challenges to the authority of capital over recent years in Britain. First of all the A.E.I. Woolwich organised themselves in protest against closure, but without success. The virtue of this action was simply that the authority of capital, its right to do what it liked with the means of production that it owned, was challenged. A more militant, but still unsuccessful challenge was made by the workers in Merseyside when declared redundant by G.E.C. – English Electric. Institutionally these contestations changed little; but they caused men's ideas to change. Two years after the events on Merseyside, in Summer 1971, the Upper Clyde Shipbuilding workers refused to accept redundancy and decided to work on. The shop stewards' committee took over control of movement in and out of the yards and to a limited extent controlled employment. The workers had considerable support from management functioning now as production organisers and not as bailiffs for the owners of capital. Property rights in the ownership of capital were now represented by the liquidator. If work continued the value of the assets would be enhanced and expediency, accordingly, dictated a curious equilibrium in this confrontation between the workers' demand for work and the capitalist state's decision to put U.C.S. into liquidation.

Capitalist philosophy, as interpreted by the Heath government, found its expression in the 'lame duck policy' – this asserted that public funds should not be paid out in support of 'lame ducks', i.e. firms that could not stand on their own two feet and face the bracing breeze of market competition. It might be argued that this policy was a foolish one even from the point of view of capital since reduction in economic activity must also limit opportunities for profit taking. Against this it may be argued that a high level of economic activity means a high level of employment that puts the workers into a strong bargaining position. The threat of unemployment enhances the power of capital. If this is the real truth of the capitalist philosophy what has happened to all the Keynesian arguments about investment planning and full employment? Clearly the U.C.S. issue is not just one battle front in the class war but a complex of many fronts. The claims of Keynesian policies, the rights of capital and much else is at issue.

And after all was U.C.S. such a lame duck? The social philosophy of capital is plausible only so long as the market is regarded as a good instrument for allocation of economic resources. The case for allowing the capitalist to do what he likes with his capital rests entirely on the argument that this causes efficient and effective use of resources. But the whole recent history of U.C.S. has been one of production reorganisation accompanied by far-reaching concessions on the part of the workers to make the yard technically efficient. There had in fact been a marked increase in productivity. Yet the market and the money system was declaring in its own simple language, of which the alphabet is L.S.D., that U.C.S. was a failure. This coming hot on the troubles of Rolls-Royce — whose technical prowess is a household word — causes the public at large to become very puzzled about what the verdict of the market means. In the case of U.C.S. it was not possible even to establish whether the problem was simply one of ready cash, as a man building a house might need to borrow money to buy bricks before he could sell the finished article, or running at a loss. Inflation, worldwide money crises upset all the reckonings and at the end of it all, what does the market measure? In all this there is a rich quarry for excuses but the truth of a social philosophy in the last analysis is not defended by excuses. The argument of the U.C.S. workers is more cogent than all these excuses put together; it runs as follows: "A decent society should accord all its members congenial well-paid work; this is all we are demanding and we are not budging until our demands are met." U.C.S. workers were fighting for their own jobs, but they recognised from the outset that their jobs were an integral part of the prosperity of the Clydeside and the prosperity of the Clydeside an integral part of the Scottish economy. Alongside their work-in a new form of struggle found an embryonic expression outside the place of work. This was the 'social audit.' "The idea of the Social Audit ... is to compel public scrutiny of the social effects of management or government decisions, and to provide the work people and the general public with a means of expressing their opposition to harmful decisions. It is not the least of the achievements of the workers in the Clyde shipyards that they have made this demand their own and thus brought nearer the day when no authority can humiliate ordinary people without risking public exposure and condemnation."[10]

An enquiry along these lines was instituted by the Scottish T.U.C. and exposed the yawning gap that divides social interests from objectives aetermined by the capital/market philosophies.

After a long struggle – from June 1971 to June 1972 – it looks as though the workers' immediate objective – 'no redundancies' – has been won. A government which thought £6m too much to spend on saving U.C.S. in June 1971 are ready to pay £35m to Govan Shipbuilders to support them in running a part of the U.C.S. yard. They will, in addition, be giving support to an American firm which will build oil rigs in the remainder of the old U.C.S. yards. The workers fought back against the decision-making power of capital. Their weapons included defiance of the property rights of capital, albeit over a limited area, namely, movement of goods into the yard and the setting of men to work. They fought back by a campaign up and down the country which won moral and financial support. They fought back by campaigning in the local community. They became a symbol of resistance to unemployment. The struggle against unemployment took a new form in that dismissal from employment was being resisted and the campaign against unemployment was centred in the employed workers and the Trade Unions. Despite the action of the U.C.S. and other workers unemployment in the U.K. sailed up above the million mark. These battles are very far from solving the problem. A few jobs have been saved and morale has been raised in the workers' camp. But 'the right to work' is very far from having been won. Such a right, simple and reasonable as it is, is totally incompatible with the market-controlled commodity economy. A society in which everyone is able to do what they need and want to do for their own and others' welfare in a simple and direct way is not a capitalist society. It is not a commodity society. A commodity society is one in which people's work and needs are linked to those of others by exchange of goods on the market. This, in the fully developed version of the system, which is capitalism, takes place only insofar as exchanges are profitable. The exchange-money system gives no more than the right to buy if one has the means and to offer what one has for sale, including capacity to work. The exchange-money system gives no right to have one's offer to work accepted. The 'right to work' – if that then will be a meaningful expression – can be realised only in a differently organised system of socio-economic relations; one in which people directly control and use their economic resources as means of meeting their social and individual needs. The final de-mystification of capitalist society, the learning of the truths and falsehoods of the competing social philosophies can only be the long process of a whole people learning by experience the nature of the existing and the possibility of new socio-economic relations. It is in the arena of experience as well as of ideas that the truth, the this-sidedness of socialist economic philosophy, establishes itself. U.C.S. is but one of a long series of battles on many different fronts by which social truths come to be established and myths come to be destroyed.

It is the economic logic of the counterattack that needs to be worked out, and to become part of the consciousness of the people in struggle against the commodity system. This cannot be seen in terms of Keynesian economics which is precisely an argument for planning within the commodity system. Economic planning, to be effective as an instrument of struggle against capital, must be planning *against* the market system. It is not possible here to explore fully the implications of this distinction, but the need for the distinction derives very directly from the need to escape from the mystification of social relations determined by commodity exchange through the market, to social relations in which freely associated men consciously regulate the deployment of resources in satisfaction of social needs. Decade by decade new technological revolutions are transforming the material base of modern society. The inappropriateness of the market/profit system becomes more and more obvious, but the myth that equates productive relations to value relations mediated by money still strongly grips men's consciousness. There have always been certain areas outside the money system, as for example in the domestic economy of each household, which prepares food, raises garden crops, undertakes repairs and minor construction. Circumstances may well compel transportation as a free social service as medical care already is, to some extent, a free service. But all these non-market systems remain dominated by the market and finance capital as the purest expression of economic power in the commodity system. What, other than the inhibitions of consciousness, holds back popular movements, as militant as those for wages, aimed at taking away more and more areas from market control? One factor is, of course, the power of the owners of money, of finance capital. But the retention of such power is constantly reinforced by the difficulties of envisaging how it would be without money, without capital. The practical function of money in a commodity economy is that of defining in unambiguous terms how social relations are to be in the interconnected processes of social production, exchange, distribution and consumption. The information that articulates in a practical sense related economic activities is conveyed by money, through the various money and commodity markets. Freely associated men, if they are to direct their activities in production to meet such needs as they plan to meet, must freely convey and receive information concerning other associated activities. Such information flows are the preconditions of planning and also the preconditions of control by people themselves over their own activities. In short, information flows are the indispensable precondition of consciously controlled democratic economic activity. It is for this reason, amongst many others, that socialist theory cannot afford to neglect the significance of the computer revolution. "Computer revolution" is a shorthand way of describing the harnessing of the electron to the task of information processing. This is of gigantic significance since it implies the possibility of more and more automated production. This implies an over-all reduction of human time involved in production processes. However, it is equally important from the point of view of transforming social relations in production to see that the harnessing of the electron for information processing and communication makes it possible for each production unit and each community unit to sense, in a very precise way, its relationship to other social units in any part of the world, to be informed of needs and to inform others of needs. It makes possible also concise and effective conveying of technical information, the learning of new techniques and much else besides. The electronic revolution makes it possible to present information in a variety of forms adapted to individual temperaments and requirements that vary with circumstances. These will include messages in sound, in sight, in diagram, in moving pictures and many ways besides. Here again I am touching on a wide area that cannot be explored within the scope of this article, but we know enough of the new electronic techniques to envisage the new possibilities that alreay exist for co-ordinating human activities in new ways dispensing with the money measures which life within a market economy has accustomed us to regard as the only possible instrument of economic co-ordination.

At the outset of this essay I said that Russell would be remembered more for the kind of man he was than for the kind of theories that he produced. In his opposition to dogmatism he practised what he preached. He was constantly accepting correction to his ideas and constantly engaging in new social battles as his vision widened and as new issues confronted him. The monumental work of Principia Mathematica was undertaken, I believe, in the belief that an edifice of truth could be constructed on absolutely sure and solid foundations. As the work developed Russell came to realise that this was an impossibility. After completing Principia Mathematica he says that a staleness beset him whenever he tried to return to mathematical logic. "Although" he writes "I did not completely abandon logic and abstract philosophy, I became more and more absorbed in social questions and especially in the causes of war and the possible ways of preventing it."[11] At the time when Russell was heavily engaged in his work on mathematical logic I do not suppose that the thought of mechanising mental processes entered his mind for one moment. He was trying to lay foundations for philosophical and mathematical truth. Lobachevsky and Riemann in developing non-Euclidean geometries also possibly had no thought of the practical implications to which their work might lead and the functions it might serve as a mathematical tool in the hands of Einstein. I believe however that the real importance of Russell's work on mathematical logic lay similarly in directions that he had not foreseen. This is how things go in many developments of science and human knowledge. Today, however, I think there can be no doubt that the most far-reaching significance of mathematical logic arises in the field of

135

practice. Precise analysis of the processes involved in constructing logical and mathematical models intellectually, enables the electronic engineer to imitate these processes and reproduce them in minutely small machines in which communication is effected at speeds approximating to the speed of light. However unconsciously, I think that Russell's work on mathematical logic, which he himself in a certain sense felt to have failed, has, in actuality, made a most important contribution to developing the material base for the free society of the future for which, as a social and political man, he fought so arduously and courageously. But the condition for seeing that such work serves the good and not the bad cause is the winning of Russell's other battles for peace, freedom and workers' control. When man — and not the market — is in control, he will no longer need to fear his own wisdom. The electronic revolution can become the means of vastly multiplying and diffusing human knowledge. Knowledge, the saying goes, is power. The point is to see that the electronic revolution leads to 'people power' — for which the Greeks had a word 'demo-cracy' — and to see that this is possible is the final demystification.

FOOTNOTES

1 *Portraits From Memory*, 1956, p.114.
2 Translation:
When human life lay grovelling in all men's sight,
crushed to the earth under the dead weight of superstition
whose grim features lowered menacingly upon mortals
from the four quarters of the sky,
a man of Greece was first to raise mortal eyes in defiance,
first to stand erect and brave the challenge.
Fables of the Gods did not crush him,
nor the lightning flash and the growling menace of the sky.
Rather, they quickened his manhood,
so that he, first of all men,
longed to smash the constraining locks of nature's doors.
The vital vigour of his mind prevailed.
He ventured far out beyond the flaming ramparts of the world
and voyaged in mind throughout infinity.
Returning victorious, he proclaimed to us what can be and
   what can not;
how a limit is fixed to the power of everything
and an immovable frontier post.
Therefore superstition in its turn lies crushed beneath his feet,
and we by his triumph are lifted level with the skies."
Translation by R.E. Latham, *Penguin Classics*, p.29.

3 Cf p.789.
4 No.5 of his six autobiographical talks.
5 Autobiographical talk No.4.
6 Quoted from *Marx Before Marxism* by David McLellan, Penguin, p.187.
7 *The Poverty of Philosophy*, Lawrence & Wishart, p.141.
8 Lawrence & Wishart, 1965, p.37
9 *Capital*, Vol.I, Chapter 1, section 4.
10 Institute for Workers' Control Pamphlet No. 26 on *U.C.S: The Social Audit*, page 4.
11 Autobiographical talk No.4, entitled *From logic to politics*.

CHAPTER IX

Adult Education and the Liberal Tradition

Michael Barratt Brown

It has become the fashion amongst historians and political scientists to polarise opinions inside the Labour Party over many years into an official majority — ex-Liberal and meritocratic — and a radical minority of syndicalists and revolutionaries. It no doubt suits the platform at Labour Party conferences to categorise opposition to it as 'fundamentalist,' but in serious political analysis this is not good enough. It is an especially inadequate conceptual framework in which to examine educational policy.[1] For one thing it means lumping Russell, Tawney and Cole in with Will Thorne and the N.C.L.C. The pacifist tradition in the Labour Party, moreover, which drew upon the I.L.P. *and* the Liberals, and was represented at one time by both Russell *and* MacDonald, cannot be explained within such a framework. The fact is that there is a tradition in the Labour Movement in Britain, which Russell, Tawney and Cole stood for, that is democratic — opposed to meritocracy and paternalism alike — and liberal. What is the meaning of this liberal tradition with a small '1'?

When a group of mainly left-wing Labour Party lecturers in Universities, in Trade Unions, in the Workers' Educational Association, and in Local Authority Colleges formed a society of Industrial Tutors in 1968 they committed themselves "to advance the general education of men and women in industry and commerce ... in the spirit of the adult education liberal tradition." Whether it is because of, or despite, that commitment, the Society has flourished. The point is that this seemed to them a proper commitment. It was certainly not a cover for clandestine polemic. They are not the sort of people to conceal their political commitment. They would no doubt concur with William Morris's conviction that "Socialism would advance as education spreads," but accept with Tawney that they "never felt tempted to engage in propaganda," adding with him "that doubtless a very improper conceit persuaded (them) that the world, when enlightened, would agree with (them)."[2] The liberal tradition in this context is seen then as freeing men from the ignorance that permits them to be enslaved.

ADULT EDUCATION AND THE LIBERAL TRADITION

Tawney writing in 1914 quoted the statement to him of an educated man: "What! You teach history and economics to miners and engineers? Take care. You will make them discontented and disloyal to us", and Tawney went on to comment: "That division of mankind into those who are ends and those who are means, whether made by slaveholders or capitalists, is the ultimate and unforgivable wrong with which there can be no truce neither in education nor in any other department of life. To such wickedness only one answer is possible, *Ecrasez l'infame.* "[3] Yet more than fifty years after I have too often heard from educated men the same sentiments, as crudely expressed. It is not by chance that the liberal tradition is associated with the cause of adult education. For adults come for education precisely in order to be freed from the ignorance in which primary and even secondary education has left them.

Now the ignorance that enslaves is not just a question of lack of schooling. Even in 1914 Tawney was writing of the improvement in secondary education, the chance in time for every child to win a scholarship to the University, and while deploring the slow pace of this improvement, was insisting that it was "not simply equality of opportunity but universality of provision" that must be the aim. There is still in 1972 a long way to go in Britain before that aim can be said to have been realised. But more than this the implications of the aim of universality, which Tawney himself explored in his writings on Equality, involve the ultimate transformation of any society that is divided by class and status reinforced by different types of educational provision.[4] This is not the place to analyse the divisions, or stratifications one might say, of Public, Grammar, Technical and 'Modern' secondary education. The struggle for a comprehensive system has opened up this analysis, although it is far from having concluded it.

I do not simply mean here that I refuse to accept the dire warnings of the *Black Papers* about our educational system, viz. that more means worse, that the quality of the students deteriorates as the numbers increase. It is significant that there is no section in the *Black Papers*[5] dealing with Adult Education. For the experience of adult teaching, especially the teaching of the educationally underprivileged or, more truthfully, educationally stratified adults has for long demonstrated the great reserves of untapped talent in our society. Indeed this experience provides the most conclusive answer to the assertions made in the Black Papers. This is not, however, just a matter of adult education having caught a few bright people who had slipped through the educational net of the state system. The experience of adult classes is more profound than that and what I want to examine here are the implications of a divisive educational system for adult education today. For liberal does not only imply more – for more people and more generous helpings; it implies something about the quality of the education provided; in short that it liberates.

When Russell wrote about education he concerned himself hardly at all with its organisation. He considered its aims and its content. "The modern world" he wrote in 1926, "needs a different type (of intelligence, that is, in contrast to the virtues inculcated by Mathew Arnold's system — M.B.B.) with more imaginative sympathy, more intellectual suppleness, less belief in bull-dog courage and more belief in technical knowledge. The administrator of the future must be the servant of free citizens, not the benevolent ruler of admiring subjects."[6] So the great aim is an educated democracy and the content must be such as to dispel the fears and inhibitions, the prejudices and dogmas that have held men enslaved, and intentionally so, at the hands of their rulers for so long.

Liberal means anti-authoritarian, liberating both negatively from fear and prejudice and positively towards the development of the whole man and woman. Much of Russell's pioneering has become incorporated in modern educational thought, especially in relation to the needs of the youngest age groups, to punishment and discipline, to the frankness of sex education, and to the discovery method in science teaching; but it has all been incorporated within a wholly individualistic framework. The result is that while our children are probably very much nicer and more relaxed than we were or are, those with any social commitment are barely more numerous, and thus more rather than less exposed to the antisocial forces of private capital accumulation. Yet for Russell co-operation and social action were among the chief objectives of education. His judgement of Universities could be repeated today, "If pure learning is to survive it will have to be brought into relation with the life of the community as a whole, not only with the refined delights of a few gentlemen of leisure."[7]

Now there has for long been a real ambivalence in adult education as regards individual and social advance. On the one hand, the aim has been seen precisely as giving the educationally underprivileged a second chance, of studying in the evenings or on 'day release' and then of entering University or one of the Labour Colleges for a full time course. Social mobility through self improvement and the retraining of manual workers for non-manual occupations to keep up with the changing demands of the labour market are in this way accelerated; and the temptation for tutors to boast of the accomplishments of their best students is inevitable, however meritocratic the implications. Over against this there has always been, on the other hand, in adult education a concern for the advancement not only of individuals but of the working class. It is not for nothing that the W.E.A. is still called what it is — the Workers' Educational Association. The Statement of Policy appended to the constitution of the W.E.A. still reads that adult education is valued "not only as a means of developing individual character and capacity, but as a preparation for the exercise of social rights and responsibilities."

There has always been a certain tension that is not quite a question of individual or social advance at the heart of the very concept of liberal education. Liberal means originally what is becoming to a free man. "Fit for a gentleman" is the Oxford English dictionary definition, with the rider that this "meaning is now rare except in *liberal education,* i.e. directed to general enlargement of mind, not professional or technical." It is indeed the case that the liberal tradition has its origins in the earlier aristocratic tradition of the amateur scholar and of learning for its own sake. That *literae humaniores,* the study of the languages, history and philosophy of the ancient world, were thought by Dr. Arnold to be suitable training for the rulers of the British Empire should not be held against the Renaissance tradition of humanism. Rejecting divine authority for social institutions and fearing the threat of anarchy from the working classes, Arnold wanted to imbue his scholars with "the best which has been thought and said in the world."[8] What is best of human thought remains at the centre of liberal education, however perverted its employment by bourgeois law makers and imperial proconsuls or its enjoyment by a leisured class whose power and income were sustained by a mass of servants and workers kept largely in a state of blind ignorance.

It was inevitable perhaps that the reaction equally of the Fabian Socialist, Sidney Webb, and the Catholic Conservative, W.A.S. Hewins, against the British ruling classes, from which birth had excluded them, was to reject not only the genetic principle of selection of rulers but also the aristocratic tradition of education through the more humane letters. There is no doubt that this tradition stood in the way of both greater professionalism in scholarship and greater attention to technology. The connection between a meritocracy and more scientic studies was firmly established in the founding of the London School of Economics by Webb and Hewins. It was unfortunate that even one strand in Socialism and social action appeared in this way to be separated from the liberal tradition. No such separation occurred with Russell or with Tawney or Cole. Russell as a Mathematician put the "cultivation of the scientific spirit" alongside the "creation of an educated democracy." Tawney and Cole were social scientists, and also historians who were concerned in Cole's words "not merely with 'diffusing' more widely a culture of which a few are already in possession, but rather with that of devising a new mental training appropriate to the needs of the new society."[9]

It is one of the ironies of British economic development that just when science and industry today more than ever need inter-disciplinary breadth and generalisation of experience, the new technical education in Britain should have begun to spread more widely — just those ideas of professional specialisation and technocracy that were so strong in Germany at the beginning of the Century. It is these ideas that were built into the L.S.E. by Webb and Hewins 60 years ago and it is against them, as much as against the authoritarian rule of governors and senates, that the students are now in revolt.

If adult education is not then concerned only with the diffusion of an aristocratic tradition, what answer to the meritocrats does it have? *Literae humaniores* is obviously as dead as the Dodo and modern greats — its Oxford successor — evidently dying. There is always a danger of woolly eclecticism in the open-ended amplitude of liberalism — of being, like the Liberal Party, all things to all men. It is, however, far from necessary that a liberal approach should lack vigour or that teachers in the liberal tradition should lack social and political commitment. What is being insisted on here is not a particular set of philosophical principles but the right of a student to think for himself and to be given *all* the tools and materials with which to work. One group of University students in a recent staff-student seminar on teaching methods were delighted to find a lecturer in *adult* education among them until he began to speak of the liberal tradition. They wanted something more positive than that. It seems to me that the risk has to be taken by all teachers, including socialists, that the students will not like being made to think, will prefer pre-digested pabulum or will not agree with their teachers as Tawney hoped they might. It is still the teacher's 'Socratic Oath' that his task is to help his students to think for themselves.

The missing element in the liberal tradition of the past has been in the area of social action and social responsibility. The emphasis on individual humanity and responses was appropriate for an aristocratic, not a democratic society. In building a democracy, as Russell, Tawney and Cole all insisted, universality in education is of the essence and with it a commitment to a new kind of society. But liberal studies cannot be grafted on to illiberal studies; the liberal approach must inform the whole. The requirement of the Department of Education that Technical Colleges should include in all their curricula some liberal studies reveals the strength of the Mathew Arnold tradition; but such spatch cocking of elements of 'culture' on to a technocratic commitment is neither viable nor particularly liberal.

It is not insignificant that the centres of revolt at both Hornsey and Guildford were the liberal studies departments. There is at least one Polytechnic where the Liberal Studies Department has nailed to its door the notice "Department of anti-Management Studies." "Most teachers of liberal studies in Technical and Art Colleges see their task as helping to straighten out some of the 'twisted products' of the educational system."[10]

This is where the profound connection between adult education and the liberal tradition is made. Adults have already suffered from a divisive educational system. They are already citizens. Their interest in education where it is not only personal self-improvement is a social one. They are in Tawney's words to some extent seized by the secret of democratic organisation "to build from within instead of borrowing from without . . . to develop their own genius, their own education, their own culture."[11]

The experience of adult classes over 50 years has confirmed the aspirations of the founding fathers in two respects at least. In the first place, it has revealed that it is by no means always, or even generally, the most quick-witted student who develops furthest in understanding. Our society and our educational system today put an enormous premium on speed; but as the computers take over the task of memorising and analysing, the need of society in the future will be increasingly for judgement and that combination of knowledge and experience that provides wisdom. Secondly, the adult education experience has shown that the class run on democratic lines in seminar and discussion group can reach deeper into problems and create more abiding devotion to learning than the more authoritarian methods of instruction have achieved. The disputation remains the best method of reaching for the truth, but it tends to be shunned by those who prefer to establish and to hand on a consensus.

In a period when freedom of speech is almost suffocated by the consensus politics of the democracies as much as by the edicts of the dictatorships, the socratic requirement of teachers, and of teachers of adults in particular becomes the overriding one — that they expose all ideas, including their own, to challenge and argument and assist their students in making the challenge effective. This is not at all to be unserious or dilettante. But if it is not to counterpose an academic scepticism to the practical conviction that must inform everyday actions, then such teachers must once more orient their teaching towards the problems of social action. This commandement flows naturally from the nature of education; it is literally a drawing out. To live with oneself one does not need to be educated. But to be human one must live with others, and that requires education — social education.

If, finally, social action is the object of education, and above all of adult education, then the two have to be more closely involved together. In an important sense the W.E.A. drew strength in the past from its association with the Labour Party and the Trade Unions. It can still do so, but funds from national Trade Union centres will not take the place of a living movement growing from below. If it is to survive, the W.E.A. has to become more effectively rooted in local communities. Its branches and classes must, therefore, study local problems, not only local history and archaeology, local art and architecture, geology and geography — all these are important — but local sociology, politics, industry and economics, using published statistics and reports and making their own surveys. It could become the centre of those forms of public participation which the Skeffington Report on People and Planning so admirably outlines.[12]

In this work local groups will need the help of the Universities, and the Extramural Departments could take the lead as major centres of research and local knowledge in each region. W.E.A. branches will need to associate closely with the adult education centres of the Local Authorities, which are themselves moving in the direction of community education for all ages around the comprehensive school campus. They will have to develop a style of work of their own, however, which is highly professional in its marshalling of evidence and information, but profoundly humane in submitting the findings to the widest democratic discussion. The pressures and possibilities of the new technology do not require our withdrawal to the olympian slopes of academic speculation but rather a deep involvement with our fellows in discovering to what use we want to put the new techniques and ensuring that they are in fact put to such uses when they are discovered.

Teachers in the last resort are not trainers or propagandists let alone hypnotists but liberators — that is the liberal message — that they can help men and women to become free. It is then, in Russell's words: "Not we, but the free men and women whom we shall create, who must see the new world, first in their hopes, and then at last in the full splendour of reality".[13]

FOOTNOTES

1 See R. Barker, *Education and Politics 1900 - 1951 — A Study of the Labour Party*, which precisely adopts this framework.
2 R.H. Tawney, "The W.E.A. and Adult Education" in *The Radical Tradition* p.90.
3 R.H. Tawney "An Experiment in Democratic Education," *ibid.*, p.72.
4 R.H. Tawney, *Equality*, especially Chapter III.
5 C.B. Cox and A.E. Dyson — *Fight for Education — A Black Paper* and *Black Paper Two — Crisis in Education*.
6 Bertrand Russell, *On Education*, p.44.
7 *Ibid.*, pp.237-8 and see also *Education and the Social Order, Passim*
8 M. Arnold, *Culture and Anarchy* (Murray) p.viii. quoted in R. Williams *Culture and Society*.
9 G.D.H. Cole "The Aims of Education" in *Essays in Social Theory*, p.48.
10 D. Page, *The Hornsey Affair*.
11 R.H. Tawney, *op.cit.* p.76.
12 Report of a Committee on Public Participation in Planning, H.M.S.O. 1969.
13 B. Russell, *op.cit.* p.248.

CHAPTER X

Heresy, Ancient and Modern

Vladimir Dedijer and Jean-Paul Sartre

In April 1969, Fadil Hadžić, the Yugoslav film director, on behalf of the Jadran Film Company, proposed to his countryman, the historian, Vladimir Dedijer, that they should work together on a film, based on Dedijer's writings, to be called *The Land of Heresy.* The scenario that they prepared covered the history of Yugoslavia from the medieval dualistic heretics, the Bogomils, to the young students of today. The scenario envisaged interviews with Jean-Paul Sartre, Rossana Rossandra, Leo Valiani, and Ole Wivel.

Jean-Paul Sartre came to Yugoslavia in July 1969. A dialogue between Sartre and Dedijer was filmed at the Bogomil necropolis of Radimlje in Herzegovina, and also at nearby Stolac. The thirty-minute discussion covered not only the medieval heretics (a comparison between the Bogomils and the French Albigensians) and their attack on the social and economic power structures of the time, but also the contradictions in contemporary capitalist and socialist societies. Special emphasis was given to student dissent, the war in Vietnam and the work of Bertrand Russell's war crimes tribunal (Sartre and Dedijer had been members).

The film was never finished, despite the wishes of all the participants and the director Hadžić himself.

The document which follows is the transcript of the Sartre-Dedijer conversation.

* * *

Dedijer: Here we are at the Bogomil necropolis of Radimlje in my native Herzegovina. The Bogomils held a Neo-Manicheanian heresy having strong links with the Pattaerens, the Cathars and the Albigensians in Italy, France and Germany. Unlike that of the Albigensians, the history of the Bogomils has not yet been fully explored. Like other dualistic Neo-Manicheanians, the Bogomils rejected the materialistic aspects of the Christian Church. and its greed. Their movement had a strong anti-institutional character. For more than three centuries they defied the

147

Popes and the various crusades which were organised against them. To that extent they were luckier than the Albigensians in your own France. In 1203 a Papal Legate arrived in Bilino Polje, some fifty miles north from this place, and accepted a renunciation of the Bogomils' ideas by some members of the sect. He left some Roman Catholic monks to "heal the people from this dangerous heresy," but some years later the Pope established that even his monks were under the influence of the malignant dualistic teachings. In the 1230's the Pope organised a crusade against the Bogomils, led by Hungarian armies which penetrated into these lands, ravaging all around in the name of pure religion. They imposed the Roman Catholic Bishopric of Bosnia, which started building cathedrals, but never had time to finish them. As soon as the bulk of the Hungarian army withdrew, the Bogomils drove out the Bishops, stopping work on "the church of Satan" as they called the Roman church. Many historians believe that the real effect of the Crusades was, like the initial effect of the Albigensian Crusade, to unite the native population (heretics and Catholics) against the invader.

Sartre: To what extent did the Bogomils influence heretical thinking in the later centuries?

Dedijer: Historical sources indicate that the Bogomils existed in Bosnia and Herzegovina until those two countries fell under Turkish rule, this is to say around 1460s. The extent of their later influence is a controversial issue. Some historians, like the Austrian Gruber, maintain that the Bogomil impact was felt, in a certain sense, right through from the 15th century up to the 19th and even the 20th century. I have not been able to find any historical documents which could prove this bold thesis, although I would like to see it proved. Yet, if we look at the social psychology of the peasantry of Herzegovina, Bosnia and Montenegro, if we study their folk philosophy, their folk poetry, which remained alive up to 20th century, because the tribal forms of life here were preserved, as if in a deep freeze, from medieval times up to modern times, we can see a certain restlessness, a kind of idea of permanent revolt. The Yugoslav writer Ivo Andric described it as the *nemiri od vijeka,* disturbances through the centuries. No doubt it is true that the material conditions of the peasantry in this area kept this idea of permanent rebellion very much alive. There existed a feudal system, and a rather oppressive one at that, and the peasantry tried many times, in desperate uprisings, to get rid of it. This feudal system was finally abolished only in the 1920s, and even in the 19th century there were over twenty peasant uprisings in the area . . . But turning to the case of the Albigensians, do you think that they influenced the heretics of later centuries in France?

Sartre: Absolutely. They left a mark on Hugenots, without doubt.

Dedijer: Coming back to what we might call functional Bogomilism, it seems to me that the conditions of life and struggle of the people of this area kept some of the dualistic teachings very much alive . . . Take the idea that the whole material world is a product of Satan, take the relationship between death and real life . . . Mass, violent death has been a fact of life here right through the centuries and up to modern times . . . What were the losses of population in rebellions, and wars in the past no one knows exactly, but in World War I, the South Slavs lost 1,900,000 out of 11,000,000 inhabitants, and in World War II 1,700,000 out of 13,000,000 inhabitants . . . Therefore it is true to say that the land is, for most of us, just a vale of tears . . . The Bogomil teaching about the necessity of struggle against the evil world and its mighty institutions no doubt had its impact on later generations . . . Hope became the mightiest weapon of the subjugated peasants . . . They endured genocides through the centuries, but this mass, violent death brought them together with people all around the world who were also afflicted by such deaths, particularly in the period of imperialism. If we go to the nearby town of Stolac, and talk with people, and ask them why are they on the side of the Vietnamese in the present war, you will see very plainly that the main cause is exactly this experience of mass, violent death. It cut our people here to. the very marrow of their bones, through generations. It has also been hitting the Vietnamese on an even bigger scale . . . But let us see how this relates to the Russell Tribunal's deliberations on the question of genocide during the last decades of imperialism . . .

Sartre: During the First World War intentional genocide made its appearance only sporadically. War was primarily a question of crushing the military power of a country, even if the ultimate aim was to destroy its economy. But, in cases where it was no longer possible to distinguish clearly between civilians and soldiers, it was rare — for that very reason — for the civilian population to be made into a special target, apart from the occurrence of some terror raids. Moreover, the belligerent nations — those who were conducting the war, at least — were all industrial powers, which involved, at the outset, a certain balance between them. In the face of possible mass extermination, each could invoke its own power of persuasion, which is to say its ability to retaliate, which accounts for the fact that in the midst of the slaughter a kind of discretion was preserved . . . But the structure of colonial wars changed after the end of World War II. The nature of the struggle was determined in advance: the colonists were superior in arms, the colonised in numbers . . . Entire genocide was then revealed as the absolute foundation of anti-guerrilla strategy. And, in certain circumstances, it even appeared to be the ultimate objective either in the immediate future or as an act of escalation. It is precisely this situation which arose in the Vietnam war . . .

. . .At one and the same time we have two kinds of totalities: the army and imperialism itself; both of which make use of their extraordinary powers of destruction, and make no distinction between combatants or non-combatants, or the entire population which sustains and supports the forces of resistance and liberation. In these circumstances, we have to face a situation which is leading unremittingly to genocide: but the contradiction inherent in capitalism is that, in general, it does not follow genocide right through to its conclusion, since it cannot destroy the men who supply the means of production and who, being hyper-exploited and under-paid, provide the basis for colonial, imperialist exploitation. But in the case of Vietnam the prime motives are, in essence, military (economic, certainly: but only indirectly). The idea is simply one of creating a cordon around communist China. A perfect demonstration of a reign of terror is given here to other peoples, because the rising of the population is complete; while there is no other motive governing the conduct of the United States than suppression, since its investments in Vietnam are small, and there is no reason to spare any forces of production which might add to the country's value as a colony. Consequently, the war quickly moved towards genocide and we are still, despite the negotiations, in the realm of genocide. What we have been saying for the past two years is still true today. If, moreover, the day comes when peace is established, it will be because the internal situation of the United States — and the courage of the Vietnamese — is such that the Americans will be unable to pursue their attempt to its conclusion, and the contradictions inherent in capitalism and imperialism will reappear. But up till now their purpose has been constant and they have been perpetrating constant genocide.

Dedijer: I have thought a lot about the criticisms made of the Tribunal and, most of all, about the criticism that we wished to form ourselves into an international court of law. What do you think of this criticism?

Sartre: I simply think these people have not understood. Amongst those who make this criticism and who have not understood I would mention the recent example of Gunther Grass, who believes we consider ourselves so good, so superior to others, that we venture to act as judges. I much admire his writings but, from an intellectual point of view, he would do well to think along other lines, for these are entirely misleading. If we considered ourselves superior, we should, precisely because of this, lose all right to judge. On the contrary, it is because we believe we are just like other people that we have initiated this Tribunal, as the representatives of anyone and everyone. To tell the truth, this Tribunal is heretical in the sense that it cannot be an institution; it is a counter-institution. It is something which came into being at a given moment and which is bound to disappear at a later time and is, quite simply, an expression of the people, who happen to have arrived here once only, for a moment in time, in the guise of a certain number of individuals who form a part of the people. If our Tribunal had been an institution, like the one which the people who initiated the Nuremberg trials at one time wished to establish; if, to put it another way, the nations of the world had, at a given moment, undertaken the task of creating a tribunal to settle all instances of war crimes, what would have occurred? ... Such a tribunal is unthinkable under present international conditions. But all men can be judges. All right, why us? Quite simply, because we were the ones called together by Bertrand Russell, who had had the idea of doing so. But we believed we were doing something which was only of immediate value and could only be worth doing if the people, afterwards, advanced on our judgements and said, "yes, we are the judges now, we agree." We, then, judge so that others may judge our findings. And we wished to form this counter-institution in such a way that after having pronounced judgement, instead of establishing ourselves by a unanimous vote as a permanent Tribunal which would afterwards discuss any other instances of war crimes, we broke up — in other words, we may always dissolve ...

Dedijer: The withering away of the Tribunal ...

Sartre: Scuttled voluntarily, and if another tribunal must come into existence, why not somewhere else, by others, who happen at a given time to be mobilised by the state of affairs? Thus, to this extent, we are anti-institutional. We have, at the same time, if you wish, criticised the idea of an established Tribunal in the manner in which we have acted as an established Tribunal without being one, and we have given a judgement which, afterwards, has been taken up by the people; and we have, in a sense, acted contrary to international laws, while making use of these same laws. There are the laws which States have made to circumscribe dangers — the possibility of crimes between States. But they have formulated them with the very deliberate intention that none of the States who have elaborated them should ever fall foul of them. They made these laws after the fall of Hitler because, according to them, Hitler's actions had been excessive, but, in fact, what they were seeking above all was some way of securing themselves and they in no way wished their rules to be used against the signatories themselves. And what have we done? We have challenged this same law, by invoking it against the most powerful of the signatories — the United States. Thus, when the Tribunal disputes international law, we do so simply because it is a formal, bourgeois law, which serves to screen all possible kinds of crime. In doing this we have happened to demonstrate an example of the peoples themselves judging the actions of governments — their own governments.

Dedijer: Do you remember the criticism of our Tribunal made at the beginning by Charles de Gaulle?

Sartre: Yes, precisely. He had tasted a mouthful, as we say. His argument was that the Tribunal couldn't exercise the power and sovereignty it would have, had it been established by a State. Put differently, the State itself is an institution and any tribunal created by a State becomes as institution set up by an institution; the people count for nothing in it. What we wished to demonstrate, on the contrary, was a popular Tribunal assembling as such, in the name of the people. We weren't asked, certainly, but the fact that we turned back towards the masses shows that we were right to demonstrate the sovereignty of the people against the irrelevant sovereignty of the State — against that form of indirect democracy which, in the last analysis, is no democracy at all.

Dedijer: Yes, I think this approach had been lost from sight at that time, for even General de Gaulle, when he issued his proclamation on June 19th, 1940, was not on the side of the State . . .

Sartre: Exactly.

Dedijer: His was, without doubt, an act of rebellion.

Sartre: Yes!

Dedijer: This is the land of heresy, not only in the time of the Bogomils and Cathars but also before the World War. Look down there at the town of St. Lac. Over there lived a Bosnian, Mehmed Basic. In the opposite direction, about 10 to 12 kilometres away I think, is the village of Prenj where Mustafa Golubic lived — a very strong young Bosnian. The young people of his generation believed it was necessary to wage permanent revolution. They were against the Habsburg monarchy, but at the same time they were against parents, teachers. They wished to construct a completely new society. They were against all structures. Remember last year, after the "May events" in your country and the "June events" in mine, we spent a few remarkable days in Bohinj. Then we went to Bologna where we discussed the problems facing youth to-day, and in particular, the problem of the University. After that meeting, with 400 Bologna students, you wrote a text in which you set out your 'thesis' and this text was never published. It really is, for me, a historical document. And I am asking *you*, Sartre, this question: can you consider this thesis and say whether you think it still holds true? Is it still valid, or not? Do consider it . . . You will remember our discussions, and especially our recognition of the dangers of interfering in the affairs of young people, for fear of being accused of paternalism (that's me, with my weight of 110kg) or of 'jumping on the bandwagon' (that's you).

Sartre: I weigh 58kg . . .

Dedijer: So how do we avoid this danger? What do you think?

Sartre: Young people are increasingly being 'followed'. I find my remarks already somewhat outmoded. You remember our plans to organise, in Bologna or elsewhere, a meeting of students from different nations, all of them revolutionary students, in an attempt to see if, once gathered together, they found similar reasons for their attitudes. Now that ideas have become somewhat clearer, I think that it is no more the business of old people to serve as mediators between young people than it is to send young people to fight wars. I think that our idea of a meeting was far too academic. In fact, they must all unite. All the student movements must find unity. But I think that it will only happen through action, by challenging the status quo and fighting, and not through a quiet meeting where each will speak in turn. This was in fact proved in France, when, in May '68, an agreement was reached through action between various tendencies, which later again found many differences of opinion between themselves, once the action was over. It seems to me, unity must be achieved in the heat of action.

I do retain one idea: these young people are rebelling, not as a result of a passing fancy or out of capriciousness, but because their situation leads them precisely into a state of permanent revolution. What appears to me essential is the existence of a contradiction in our countries, at a time when monopoly capital is dominant. On the one hand, the capitalist firms are partly responsible for a relative increase in the standard of living in some places, and an increase in the number of students. This means that, after A-level, many people can get into further education which apparently leads to certain positions in society; but on the other hand, the same capitalist firms are incapable of offering suitable jobs to all those students whom they have encouraged to quality. As a result, we see the following contradiction: the universities are becoming increasingly selection-minded. For example, in France, 75% of the students who are, so to speak, elevated by our society, find themselves out of appropriate work, and fall back into the lower middle class or even sometimes the working-class, while all the time more and more individuals are encouraged to become candidates. This creates a sort of sub-proletariat of grammar-school leavers who learn that culture could be open to all, since they are all "called", but who also learn that culture has become an institution — in France, a monopoly institution, in which few are "chosen." The monopoly of learning is given to Professors, and this monopoly of learning implies a power which is linked to power in society at large. They have power to say: *you* will go a stage further in your studies. As for *you*, it's over, go back with those who haven't entered further education. And this power is not shared with the students. The students are only objects: they are not recruited at will, selected at will, they *receive* an education, a form of knowledge which is determined for them. It is either the old bourgeois humanism inherited from the nineteenth century: or, for people like Edgar Faure, it will be the acquisition of a technical knowledge which will prepare them to fulfil given jobs in industry, jobs of middle management, that is to say jobs making them into instruments of selection or slave driving: and the students don't want such jobs. Therefore, the students are trapped between two notions: on the one hand, they are the objects of culture — whatever they are taught leads to more selection. On the other hand, culture must be seen as mass culture — otherwise it ceases to exist. As a result, through their very situation, and besides, through the very bad material conditions resulting from all this, they are led to challenge, radically the form of culture that is granted them.

153

Dedijer: In our thesis, we have been talking about social and economic conditions in the so-called welfare state. There was a social-democrat thesis, but not only a social democratic one, about this. In my country, there are people who think that in such societies, all conflicts, all contradictions have a non-antagonistic character, and can be solved by "evolutionary" means. But we have seen, not only in France, but also in several other welfare states, antagonisms which cannot be solved simply by evolution, but must be solved by revolutionary acts and revolutionary conflicts. What do you think of such a thesis, which you have already formulated?

Sartre: This is what I was saying earlier: here is one of the cases where the contradiction really is antagonistic. This so-called welfare society in fact creates very large numbers of students, and at the same time, refuses them entry into it, so that precisely no solution can be found in reforming it, but only in questioning, in a total way, the bourgeois order which is responsible for this type of contradiction.

Dedijer: I asked this question because at that time, for example in France, it was temporarily easy, I think, for the student movement to develop. But if this thesis is true, if the socio-economic conditions have not yet been solved, it means that the situation can develop again, as it did in May, because the very conditions that caused the spontaneity of the revolt . . .

Sartre: remain exactly the same . . .

Dedijer: so we can have this conference and do other things, but here's a proof that, as the social conditions have not been solved, we can wait again, it may flare up again, in other situations.

Sartre: If not in France, it will be somewhere else, but the situation is the same.

Dedijer: Do you agree?

Sartre: Completely. All the more so because you may notice that the weak reformist attempt by Edgar Faure in France has already been completely chopped to bits. Faure has been thrown out of office, and we shall see that all the efforts he made in order to go in the direction you indicate of avoiding antagonistic contradictions, are going to be completely ruled out. We're already reconsidering on the question of latin, Vincennes will probably be suppressed next year, or at any rate, the most revolutionary students will be thrown out and we shall end up, in fact, with a situation similar to that we had before. In other words, reforms are impossible, both because they remain nowhere near adequate to meet the demands of the students while at the same time they involve too much to be acceptable in a reactionary society.

Dedijer: Good, thank you.

Sartre: I completely agree with you, I think that these socio-economic contradictions are not solved, and will not be solved, by reforms. Therefore, this opens up a revolutionary perspective, which is that cultural institutions as they exist in many states — in France for example — must be disrupted, and the structures depending upon them broken up. The proof is in Edgar Faure's reformism, which failed: to-day, all his efforts, which anyway didn't amount to much, have been completely diverted and destroyed. He has been replaced by a reactionary minister. In six months or a year from now, we'll find the old university restored with all its faults. And this proves one thing: Faure's reformism could not satisfy the students, since the real problems were much more fundamental — for example the financing of the University in a way that would allow access to higher education for all: these problems have not been solved. And the students find themselves in the same situation as before. Moreover, this weak reformism was already more than the reactionaries who are now in power could tolerate. As a result, from both sides, reformism fails, and this is why we are faced with the same situation. If the students, not only in France, but everywhere, are revolutionaries, if they have set out on the path of the "permanent revolution", — i.e. questioning the culture itself, the education itself, and the institutions granted to them, this is not out of a passing fancy, an idea just crossing their mind, suddenly, but because they find themselves in a situation which demands this total questioning. They are themselves, as students, as young men, as future men, totally invalidated by the institutions which pretend to be made for them. Consequently, the only solution open to them is revolution, and the only problem: with whom? since they are too weak to make it alone. This is the problem which does not directly concern us here: the relationship between the students and the working-class. So far, my dear Dedijer, we have discussed some contradictions of capitalism, and you know, better than I do, that Marx said that contradiction is the driving force of history. Can't we speak also of the contradictions of socialism, since socialism is also an evolutionary process? But what is socialism for you?

Dedijer: It's not only the exploitation and the development of productive forces, but also the fact of simultaneously raising all the relations between men to a higher and more human level. This is also the reason why man started the revolution against capitalism and its ills . . .

Sartre: Is this conception of socialism common in all the socialist countries?

Dedijer: The historical fact is that the idea of humanitarian socialism is embodied in the constitution of all the socialist countries. What remains to be established is the difference between words and facts, principles and practice . . . We have witnessed phenomena like genocide (for example the Tartar question in the USSR); the revolts in Eastern European countries in 1953, 1954, 1956; workers' strikes (for example in Yugoslavia); the student revolt in almost all socialist countries. And in the field of the relations between socialist states, the practice of secret diplomacy, economic blockades — like the blockade imposed by the USSR on China, threats of aggression and even open acts of aggression like the invasion of Czechoslovakia by the five countries of the Warsaw Pact. The most painful contradiction is the question of war, or rather the possibility of war between socialist countries. Marxism had taught us that modern war and armies were a historical phenomenon, and not the result of the unchangeable character of human nature; more precisely, war and armies are formed at the time of the division of society into classes, and the emergence of exploitation. Marxism considered war as the most atrocious phenomenon provoked by capitalism and imperialism and had led us to believe that wars would disappear if classes disappeared. We are now faced with a socialist system in which war becomes possible again: the armed intervention in Czechoslovakia as well as the confrontation between the USSR and China have struck a terrible blow against the very idea of socialism, especially amongst the younger generation, which has been increasingly looking towards the socialist model as a way of changing the old world and its violence. That is why the opening of a discussion on the origins of these contradictions in socialist societies is becoming urgent, and is not only an abstract analysis, or a piece of historical research, but the condition for a new revolutionary start, for the future of socialism itself. Hiding these problems leads nowhere, except that it makes them worse. It was obvious at the time of the most recent conference of some Communist Parties which met in Moscow: some of the decisions taken, and the modes of discussion, reveal the survival of the Stalinist conception, according to which there are no deep contradictions in the development of socialism. In a publication towards the end of his life, between 1950 and 1952, Stalin sustained the thesis that all problems in socialist societies can be solved by "gradualism" and "evolution," and that the transition from "quantity" to "quality" would be abrupt only in the non-socialist world. But mass revolts started breaking out in the socialist world before his entombed body was cold.

In the USSR, there was an attempt to explain them away by the theory of the "personality cult," a sort of subjectivism or neo-pragmatism ... what Plekhanov was already calling "subjective idealism." In fact, in such a conception, what is denied is that the contradictions to be found in socialism have any economic or social basis. Whereas I think that, on the contrary, we should start from there. If the material basis of the USSR and the socialist camp was as progressive as all that, it would not cause such awful results in the superstructure. It is necessary to re-examine completely the problem of the relationship between social being and social consciousness in the USSR and other socialist countries, and the totality of material problems and relations of production; to come back to the basic question, which is the formation and the distribution of the surplus value in the USSR and the socialist camp, and the resulting economic and social system. It is only by starting from these facts that the analysis of the Soviet system under Stalin is possible; although of course, it is necessary to consider not only the economic groundwork, but also social psychology, the problem of culture and values, the data of sociological, psychological and even psychoanalytical research, so as not to slip into a mechanical view of the relations between structure and superstructure.

As an historian, I am looking for the concrete aspects of social contradictions in socialist states, and in this light I have set out the following scheme for further study:

A) Introduction:
The theoretical problem of contradictions, as outlined by the various marxist or communist groups; the theoretical question of the law of value.

B) Description of Material Processes:
How is the surplus value distributed?
1. Mechanism of distribution between the State and other structures on the one hand, and the producers on the other; degree of participation by the producers in decisions inherent in the distribution of the surplus value and the control of the decision-making processes; distribution of wages.
2. Decision-making mechanisms concerning the distribution in the various structures of power (State, party, army, police, trades unions, technocratic groups etc.).
3. Productive and distributive structure (centralisation, market).
4. Distribution of the surplus-value between developed and under-developed areas in a Socialist State and between national groups within each socialist state.
5. Distribution of surplus-value among producers, according to the division of labour and the specific interest of the various groups of workers:
   a) manual and intellectual work
   b) skilled and unskilled work
   c) city and agricultural workers
6. Distribution of the surplus-value between male and female workers.
7. The same, according to generational divisions (technocratic models and the role assigned to young people).

C) Division of Work and Distribution of Surplus-value Among the Socialist States:
1. Theoretical principles concerning economic relations between socialist states.
2. Comparative study of the level of development in each socialist state, to check whether the distance between economically developed and under-developed socialist states increases or diminishes.

3. The USSR and Eastern Europe, during the Stalinist phase and afterwards (methods and principles of export trade, direct forms of exploitation, "mixed societies," "aid," etc.)
4. The USSR and China.
5. The European Socialist states and other Socialist states (Cuba, Vietnam, North Korea).

D) Relations Between Socialist States and Underdevelopment (aid, trade with third-world countries and "third-world socialism.")

E) Relations Between Socialist Countries and the World Capitalist Market:
1. Influence on productive structures.
2. Characteristics of "mixed enterprises" with capital from capitalist countries.
3. Influence of capitalist loans on socialist countries.

For me as a Marxist, the contradictions between the productive forces and the relations of production represent the fundamental contradiction which conditions the development of society in socialist countries. The crucial question is the distribution of surplus-value in the various socialist countries. I am absolutely certain that socialism, as a world system, has already defeated the capitalist system, and if these contradictions in the socialist countries are not solved, we shall certainly see the phenomenon of permanent revolt which no violence of any sort can stifle. This is the essential condition of progress... This is what I think, I don't know whether you agree. You are a more philosophical marxist than I am ...

Sartre: I think you are absolutely right, that if socialism is not a permanent revolution, that is to say, if it not constantly calling into question the institutions which it creates, in order to create better institutions, it will mark time and become state capitalism: and the real problem, in fact, is always the calling in question by the masses of institutions which, in general, are created, despite everything, by an elite outside the control of the majority.

Dedijer: And the basis of the heresy which holds sway to-day in socialist countries. Do you agree?

Sartre: Completely.

Dedijer: Thank you very much.

CHAPTER XI

Victims of Aggression

Gunther Anders

The belief that today's aggressors wish to crown their aggression with victories is naive. To win wars is no longer the aim of those who are eager to wage wars — at least not for those who make the prosperity of their country depend upon their armament industry. What American industry demands, in order to guarantee the continuation of its arms production, and, thereby, the continuation of the nation's prosperity, is to *have* wars. Wars are the basis of the industrialist's power. If this basis collapsed — and it would collapse through the victorious conclusion of a war — this power would be defeated. In other words: In the present stage of capitalism, *wars as such are victories*. Victories, in the old-fashioned sense of the word, would amount to defeats, since they would promote a situation in which the further production of weapons (the prerequisite of power and prosperity) would become superfluous. What the U.S. desires is the smooth continuity and escalation of the sale and consumption of armaments, a continuity and escalation just as regular and just as reliable as that of the sale and consumption of bread or gasoline. This means that what is desired is a war which will never end, which will survive and which cannot be killed. No wonder that those of our fellow men who criticize and try to subvert this situation are called and treated as subversives.

According to the basic lie of our epoch, the production of weapons is needed in order to prevent wars. The truth is, on the contrary, that wars are needed in order not to prevent the production of weapons. It is for this reason, in order to guarantee the production of weapons, that wars are being produced. Thus, they are a means of production.

Nothing is more dishonest than cowardice cloaked as justice or as fairness. Many who fear to be slandered or to be called "biased", have made it their scandalous principle never to mention an aggressor belonging to the so-called "Free World" without simultaneously discrediting his victim, too. Whoever says something against a President Nixon pretends to be morally obliged immediately to add something against a Chou En-lai, and thereby to prove how objective and how just he is. In a way this cowardly tactic

159

amounts to acting as if we believed in the existence of a universal "equilibrium of guilt" or of a "balance of infamies" — a simply ludicrous belief which would imply, for instance, that as many American women and children are being slaughtered by Vietnamese napalm bombs as Vietnamese women and children are being slaughtered by American napalm bombs. And this is not only nonsense but outright hypocrisy and fraud. I am afraid that this fraud in our European and American peace movements will eventually cause their moral ruin. He who applies the same yardstick to the murderers and to the victims is taking sides: for by accusing both of the same violence, he is excusing the aggressors. Let's leave this task to the murderers themselves.

If we confine ourselves — and this danger exists in the anti-atomic movement — to fighting against nuclear weapons, we prove that we have not mastered the ABC of our epoch. There are those who believe that the B and C (the bacteriological and chemical) weapons or the new mechanical gadgets, such as the "lazy dog", which are being "tested" and developed in Vietnam today, will not provoke the final catastrophe of mankind, at least not as directly as the atomic weapons, and that, for this reason, they are less dangerous. This argument leads to a frightful self-delusion. If these new weapons are so often belittled as being "only comparatively dangerous" or "only conventional," or if they are even being welcomed as "human," this has become possible only because today's blackmail of total nuclear destruction has become the yardstick with which the magnitude of other weapons is being measured. In other words: the production and the daily testing and usage of the new weapons in Vietnam are taking place under the protection of atomic blackmail. This is indeed a "shield" — though not in the sense in which the manufacturers and managers of public opinion like to use this word today. For it is not peace or mankind which is being shielded by the nuclear deterrent, but rather the production of those means of destruction the effect of which is not total; and it is not only the atomic weapons themselves which we have to fight but just as energetically the production of other types of arms.

On July 3, 1966, two American jets tried to support some units of the U.S. 1st Infantry Division which were engaged in battle with the Viet Cong. However, the napalm bombs missed their mark and fell upon the American soldiers twenty of whom, screaming, their clothes ablaze, died in the mud. What should we say? Should we perhaps exclaim: "How ghastly that such accidents are possible!"? Wouldn't this imply that it might have been less frightful — even not frightful at all — if the American pilots had aimed more precisely so that only Vietnamese would have burned to death? This would be infamous. However, it would be no less infamous to welcome this "mishap" and to stress that at last the aggressors now had had the chance to experience what they are doing to others. And no less infamous to say: "Now maybe they will learn that this misfortune was not an exception; that they are always hitting *themselves,* even when they believe they have hit the mark and have struck only the enemy." These arguments, however, true they may be, are no less vulgar than the words of those who regret that the wrong people were burned to death. After all, these American soldiers are victims too; even those who may enjoy their bloody work and who may be proud of it, since others drilled them to enjoy this sort of pleasure and this sort of pride. Even worse than the other responses was that which General DePuy of the 1st Infantry Division made after this terrible misfortune had struck his unit. In a tone which he meant to sound dauntless, but which, in reality, only betrayed his utter emotional illiteracy, he stated: "We are not angry at the Air Force." In order to stress the harmlessness of this "mishap," he commented that, after all, "this was an error of only about 50 meters." Apparently General DePuy felt and wished to convey that the accident would actually have been appalling if the bombs would have missed their mark by 100 meters — that to err is human, human even when through an error B goes up in flames instead of A; that, after all, in the game played in Vietnam such human errors cannot be excluded; that it would be inhuman to expect that every bomb could hit its target; that it would be unfair to demand such inhuman achievements, even in the war against the Viet Cong. In his words, which are obscene, although he may have meant them as words of consolation: "It's the chances of the game." Game indeed.

As an ingenuous gesture — "we have nothing to hide" — the Americans have repeatedly not only admitted but even emphasized that they have accidentally bombed wrong villages in Vietnam. Nothing is more deceitful than such an exhibition of veracity. For by stressing their error in having bombed this or that village, they are implying that their bombing of other Vietnamese villages has been and will be legitimate. Whenever a criminal volunteers a confession, we have to ask which untrue supposition he thereby tries to make us believe to be valid.

Those — and amongst them are even chancellors and presidents — who like to compare the number of war deaths with the number of traffic deaths, and who then triumphantly proclaim that the number of victims on the highway in the United States is greater than the number of American boys who have fallen in Vietnam, are simply frauds.

Even if their figures should be correct — what do they prove? After all, the number of sex murders is also smaller than that of traffic deaths, but does this say anything in favour of sex murders? Those who make use of such comparisons have no other aim but to lead us to the false conclusion that if we demand the abolition of napalm or lazy dogs (not to speak of atom bombs) we should — or rather, we are even obliged to — demand the abolition of our cars as well. Secretly speculating on our fear of expropriation, they seem to ask us: "And what would you say if we would ask you to give up your cars?"

Unfortunately, it cannot be denied that time and again this pseudo-argument has been successful. When hearing this comparison, most people seem to forget the simple fact that napalm and lazy dogs (not to speak of atom bombs) are manufactured for no other purpose than to kill people — while cars, so I am told, are being produced to transport people, although occasionally they may happen to lead fatal accidents. And even if it were true (and presumably it is) that there are criminal car producers who, by methodically planning obsolescence of their products, are indirectly planning and committing murder — why should this fact excuse those who are planning and committing murder directly through their production of deadly weapons and genocidal wars?

Of course, it is true — and again and again we must point to the fact — that the Americans are using weapons and gadgets (such as napalm bombs and the lazy dogs) which are banned by international law, and that they are destroying temples, hospitals and schools. And yet, as long as we confine ourselves to protesting against these crimes, we create the utterly false and misleading impression that we wouldn't object to the American aggression in Vietnam if, instead of napalm, only "conventional weapons" were used; if, instead of temples and churches, only "conventional buildings" were destroyed; if, instead of the sick and children, only "conventional people" were liquidated. Under no circumstances should we allow or make ourselves guilty of causing such a misunderstanding. Once and for all we have to state: The real crime is not that the American government is waging its aggressive war with *this* weapon instead of *that* weapon, but that it is waging an *aggressive war;* and not that it is destroying *this* type of house instead of *that* type of house, but that it is destroying *houses;* and not that it is liquidating *this* human being instead of *that* human being, but that it is liquidating *human beings.* What counts is the attack as such. The atrocities to which one commonly points are only crimes of a second degree. Only *crimes within a crime.*

*   *   *

On July 22, 1966 the New York *Times* published, without comment, a report about the launching of a Polaris submarine, the *Will Rogers,* in Groton, Connecticut ... and its christening by Mrs. Hubert Humphrey. Despite its brevity, this item contains five disgusting, even obscene, elements.

It is obscene

that a vessel, the underwater rockets of which are supposed to commit genocide, was given a name just as if it were any ordinary banana boat or passenger ship;

that this act of naming an instrument of genocide was called "christening";

that no more suitable name could be found than that of a humourist;

that this act of "christening" an instrument of genocide with the name of a humorist was imposed upon a woman; and finally

that this woman — no less than the wife of the Vice-President — apparently carried out this request without any inhibitions.

As far as we are concerned, we can only hope that those millions who may be killed by this instrument will feel consoled by the knowledge that it is not to a tragedian, but to a comedian, and not to a missile "christened" by a man, but to one "christened" by a woman, that they have fallen victim.

*   *   *

... We would lose face if we once again stopped bombing North Vietnam ... Official Cliche

I cannot remember that anyone really possessing a real face has ever argued that, because he "couldn't afford to lose his face," he was forced to undertake this or that — generally something very bloody — or that he, unfortunately, couldn't get out of this or that — generally very bloody undertaking. Whoever possesses a face can rest assured that it will stick to him, that he won't lose it, either in his own eyes or in those of others; it is much easier to lose his hands or his feet. The figure of speech is used exclusively by those who are not only faceless, but so egocentric that it doesn't enter their minds to try to visualise what (if at all) they look like in the eyes of others. If they did, they would, to their never-ending amazement, have to recognise that it has never occurred to anyone to acknowledge as faces those amorphous spots that they themselves, when looking into the mirror, never tire to admire; and that, therefore, all of their bloody efforts, which supposedly serve the purpose of face-saving, are nothing but a waste of time.

No matter whether they ever had a face which they could lose, what counts are the following questions and answers:

1. Whose eyes are murderers thinking of when they fear losing face in the eyes of others by not continuing their bloody work?

Answer: Only the eyes of other murderers.

2. What do they imply and impute by issuing their declaration officially and publicly?

Answer: They imply and impute that by renouncing their bloody job they would lose face in the eyes of everybody; thus in our eyes too – thus that their way of death is our way of life.

3. Are they entitled to thus disgrace us?

Answer: This question can be answered only by our actions.

*   *   *

News item from Saigon: *During the last week in October U.S. bombers mistakenly attacked the South Vietnamese village of Du Duc thereby killing forty-eight civilians and wounding fifty-five.* (Needless to add that the Americans immediately flew medications to the surviving victims and that representatives of the South Vietnamese government promptly expressed their gratitude for this helpfulness.)

When the director of the Molussian Mafia, Mr. Fu, saw that his third attempt to blackmail the merchant Bim had failed, he decided to apply measures which were customary in such cases: to do away with the oldest son of this unreasonable man. Of course this action didn't cause any difficulties, and when, on the following morning, the specialist reported to the director about the business dealings completed during the night, he could also, amongst others, relate the decease of young Bam. "What?" screamed Mr. Fu to the surprise of his specialist, "the son of Mr. Bam?" "According to instructions," the specialist replied. "Instructions! Instructions! That's murder! I said Bim, not Bam." Wherupon the employee, remarking that one corpse doesn't exclude another, got up and strolled away.

If and how Mr. Fu has punished his specialist for his negligence is unknown to us. But we do know that he was unable to forget the older Bam, who had been thrown into such grief through an effort of the firm. With the promptness which is known only to the truly virtuous heart, Mr. Fu immediately sent a message of his most profound condolence to the bereaved Mr. Bam, and even let this message be followed by an autographed portrait of himself. It is certainly a consoling testimony to the urbanity of Molussia that the old gentleman Bam, despite his unspeakable pain, showed himself worthy of Mr. Fu's humane gesture, and that he not only expressed his gratitude for the unexpected present, but even gave it a place of honour on the wall of his desolate home.

GUNTHER ANDERS

"For five days now," announced the well-known chief of the Molussian Mafia, Mr. Fu, who temporarily had confined himself to slaughtering only the inhabitants of the Southern part of the city, "for five days now I have most puritanically abstained from shedding blood in the Northern suburbs." And after ten days, he bragged in a similar way, and after fifteen his words were even more boastful. "Truly," he concluded his third proclamation – and the ring of his voice was as ominous as that of all moralists who are about to lose their patience – "truly, if there are still people in the Northern part of our city who refuse to trust me and who fail to recognise the unmistakable signs of my peacefulness, I'm warning them for the last time. They will have no right to complain about the consequences of their stubbornness."

And not only did his Mafia Brethren applaud, but also the Most Honorable Gentlemen: the members of the city council, since they too despised nothing more than violence and loved nothing more dearly than peace.

*   *   *

"Join with people!" runs the second commandment. "Understand their life, use phrases from their language, honour their customs and laws!" And the third commandment: "Treat women with politeness and respect!" And the ninth: "Reflect honor upon yourself and the U.S.A."

Urbane recommendations for the use of Fulbright students sent to European universities? Nothing of the sort, but rather rules belonging to the official code of behaviour handed out to American G.I.'s stationed in Vietnam.

"Use their language!" Of course it is idiotic to expect from American boys, many of whom are not even able to speak their own language correctly, that they should, immediately upon arriving in Saigon or in jungle villages which they are supposed to destroy, attain linguistic genius and overnight toss off Vietnamese proverbs or local expressions. But how harmless is this idiocy compared to the hypocrisy on which the other commandments are based!

How should boys who are being sent over in order to violate the population;

who are told to poison rice fields;

who are encouraged to pose as brothel masters of cities;

who, working as torture specialists, are tape-recording the screams of the interrogated and (long live Social Psychology!) "evaluating" these tapes–

165

how should these poor boys carry out such tasks "with politeness and respect?" And in a way which "reflects honour upon themselves and the United States?"

Some months ago in Auschwitz I walked between the mountains of hair, of eye glasses, of suitcases, of brushes, of artificial limbs; between the mountains of those dead objects which, used to being dead anyway, have survived their murdered owners. I know what the Nazis perpetrated in Auschwitz, but I fear that, compared to those American hypocrites, who have formulated and handed out the Vietnam maxims, these Nazis were — horrible to say — men of honour. Never did I hear that employees in the concentration camps were being told to handle their victims with kid gloves or treat them with respect. Never that any S.S. man or anyone else working in a crematorium was ordered to gain the confidence of those to be liquidated by using their native language, never that anyone had to lure the Jews into the gas chambers in Yiddish. Not that. However dreadfully the word "love your enemies" has been destroyed in Auschwitz, even more dreadful are those who, although ordering or executing the bloody handiwork, dare to pretend to fulfil this gospel commandment and are even impudent enough to offer themselves as its missionaries.

CHAPTER XII

The View From the South

Keith Buchanan

At a time when the world scene is seemingly dominated by an increasing trend towards larger units and towards an increasing external uniformity, it is well to be reminded that, in Walter Goldschmidt's words, "the worlds of different peoples have different shapes."[1] This observation is true at two levels. In a more literal sense what we may term the "contours of existence" — the degree of wealth, the extent of development of resources, the availability of and access to services — vary greatly between various peoples, including various classes within the same nation. Fig. (1), which shows in diagram form the variations between the major blocs, gives us a rough measure of the great contrasts in "shape" between the worlds of different peoples. And at a deeper level the observation underlines that the way the world is perceived differs greatly from one people (or social stratum) to another, that the shape of the world as perceived from Hanoi or Havana, from Beirut or Bogota, is very different from that perceived by folk in Washington, Moscow or London. And within a single society, say that of the U.S.A., the contours of existence of the Black American and his perception of the world are very different from those of the White American.

At the global level the most striking contrast is between the shape of the world as seen by the nations of the White North and the nations of what Richard Hensman[2] terms the Tricontinental South — which is another, and perhaps less ambiguous, term for what the French have termed the Third World, for what the UN, hopefully or hypocritically, terms "the developing nations." I shall be concerned in this essay not only with the shape of the present world but also with some of the major changes which are altering this shape and, by inference, with some of the broad outlines of the world that seems to be emerging. And in my comments my emphasis will be on how the world order, and the socio-economic trends within this world order, appear to us in the Tricontinental South. And if I use the collective pronoun here I do so deliberately. A sizeable segment of my working life (between one-quarter and one-fifth) has been spent within the dependent societies of the South;

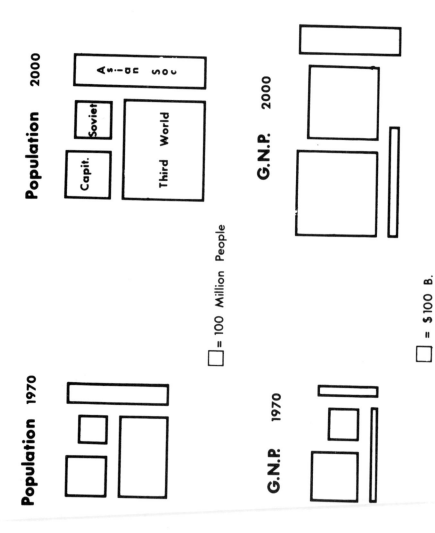

Figure 1.
The "Four Worlds" 1970 to 2000
Note that the continuing stagnation of the Third World (the Tricontinental South) means a growing economic gap between the peoples of the South and the rest of mankind.

moreover, my ancestors came from, and my emotional roots are in, that zone of dependent societies English colonialism created in the Celtic lands of western Britain, societies which early served as "an on-going laboratory" for the development of those techniques of colonial domination England so successfully applied at a later date in her overseas empire.[3]

But before we look at "the view from the South" let us briefly sketch in the shape of the world as seen from the White North; how *do* the peoples of the North see their own society and what is *their* vision of the Tricontinental South, that zone of countries south of the *limes* which runs along the southern frontier of the United States, through the Mediterranean and Black Seas, eastwards along the southern frontier of the USSR towards and south of Japan?

The nations of the White North, their peoples are aware (for do not their politicians constantly remind them?), are characterised by a technological and economic dynamism which manifests itself in a continuously expanding GNP; this expansion is in large measure a product of the "growth-mania" of which E.J. Mishan[4] and others have written. To sustain its steadily expanding output of material goods the White North has reduced much of the remainder of the world's peoples to the status of hewers of wood and drawers of water, or, more precisely, unskilled or semi-skilled workers who perforce collaborate in the pillage of their own resources to meet the industrial needs of the advanced societies. It is tacitly assumed in the North that the economic systems they have developed are the *only possible* systems, from which it is clear that economic development in the South must follow the models of the North.[5] The drive to maximise output leads to increasing economic and political integration — to the multinational corporation and the regional economic bloc, to bigger and increasingly impersonal administrative units. As Bertrand Russell observed, two men have been the principal creators of this world of the White North, Rockefeller and Bismarck:

" . . . the first in the economic world, and the second in the political, (they) destroyed the liberal dream of happiness of all inhabitants of the planets . . . substituting the monopolistic organisation and the corporate state."[6]

The White North, its peoples are aware, is not entirely homogeneous: capitalistic nations stand poised against socialist nations and the capitalist bloc itself consists of an uneasy linking, through the medium of common forms of organisation, multi-national enterprise and an imagined external threat, of a European bloc, a North American bloc and a resurgent Japan. Perhaps the unity of the White North is most apparent in its relationships with the societies of the Tricontinental South. The whole of the South is a zone whose resources are used — *and felt to be rightly used* — by the wealthy nations of the North; without these resources the affluence — or the over-development — of the North would not have been, would not now be, possible. It is a zone economically and militarily, socially and culturally, dependent on the metropolitan countries of the White North and this dependence is regarded as part of the natural order of things by these countries. It is a zone whose future development must, so it is commonly held in the North, follow one or other of the economic systems on which the development of the North has been based. It is a zone whose societies have been exposed to a wide range of manipulative techniques, extending to economic blackmail and outright aggression, by the more advanced societies seeking economic or strategic advantage. Such techniques, in their more extreme form, would rarely be employed within the White North but the peoples of the South are, it is implied, different; however, this is not always recognised by increasingly articulate elements in the South who claim to see in this differential treatment a disturbing double standard . . .

For us in the South reality has a different shape. We know that our elite groups, those whose souls you have stolen, those whom your educational systems have made more English than the English or more French than the French, see the world through the glasses you have fashioned for them — but we know these groups have no roots in the people, that they are transients heading for the trash-can of history, and we have no need to add to Fanon's devastating critique of their characteristics and role.[7]

For most of us in the South, however, the world you have created in the White North lacks the logic, the moral and intellectual cohesion, which *you* find in it. When we look at its past achievments — and we concede they were considerable — we cannot help recalling Fanon's reminder that these were made possible by the blood and sweat and toil of those whom you exploited. When we look at its present condition — its social and economic disintegration,[8] its selfishness and lack of community, its inhumanity and its lack of tenderness, we can only wonder at the blindness or the arrogance which make it possible for you to continue to proffer it as a model of development for all mankind. But if we see in your world symptoms of its terminal phase, signs of its approaching end, we nontheless recognise the immense capacity for destruction which is concealed behind the innocuous phrases of your politicians. Or partly concealed — since there are those in the White North who, sickened by the obscene combination of affluence and brutality, have ranged themselves with us in what Armand Gatti[9] terms "the guerrilla motherland" and, regardless of the cost to themselves, have exposed the realities of power and policy behind the facade of slogans. And though your White North is divided into a capitalist and socialist sector and though we see many contradictions within each of these sectors we cannot but be aware of the increasing solidarity between these two sectors when they confront our world of the

South. This solidarity is both economic (as UNCTAD II and III demonstrate) and political; it means that the policy of playing one bloc off against the other, which in the fifties and early sixties enabled us — or our elite groups — to extract certain advantages from our independence in a polarised world, has been very greatly circumscribed. As the Middle East situation shows, the two super-powers of the White North are able to pursue remarkably convergent policies when confronted with guerrilla movements which challenge the orthodoxies and dogmas of Right or Left. There are those who claim this is but a short term view and that long term perspectives are very different — but if you look at the sickening waste of human abilities, of human potential, our half-human conditions involve you will realise we cannot afford too many long-term perspectives. And, as Lord Keynes reminded you, "In the long run we will all be dead" or as the Mexicans say, in somewhat more picturesque language, "In a hundred years we'll all be bald."

I have spoken briefly of the past and present condition of your White North as it appears to us in the South. When we look to the future we find ourselves recoiling, shuddering, from the edge of the pit you are digging, not only for yourselves, not only for us and our children, but for every living thing with whom humanity shares this planet. For the price of the economic progress of which you are so proud, the economic progress which — and I use the phrase carefully and deliberately — in your madness you see continuing, even accelerating, has been the pillage for your use of the resources which constitute *the endowment of all mankind*. The price of your affluence is to be measured in terms of the depleted soils, the worked-out mines, the ravaged forests, and the broken societies throughout the length and breadth of the South. And it is to be measured also in terms of the ecological destruction your insatiable industrial machine has wrought, not only in your own lands but in the seas which wash our shores and in the remotest hinterlands of our countries.[10] You have, to achieve your frenetic pace of growth, poisoned our biosphere with the oil and the pollutants from your automobiles and your industries, with pesticides and chemicals of whose effects you are ignorant, you tamper, as if you were the Almighty's head gardener, with the genetic pool on which, in the last resort, all evolutionary progress depends. And, while we know that the socialist nations of the White North have not entirely escaped this ecological arrogance, we know that your own experts concede that:

"the vast proportion of atmospheric contaminants ... are generated within a very small fraction of the globe, those areas under direct control and manipulation of America."[11]

that, pursuing the analysis a little further:

"the present environmental destruction is increasingly the product of a structure of economic and political power that consolidates and sustains itself through the systematic destruction of the human species and the physical world."[12]

And at this point, my friends, I have two comments. First, that this world is not yours to destroy for it belongs also to *us* and *our* children and *our* children's children. Secondly, whatever some of our leaders may have once thought, may still think, the model of society you have created, the type of economic system you have perfected, those things are irrelevant to *our* future. You are headed, in spite of your power and your wealth, towards an evolutionary cul-de-sac; the next stage of human history will, we rather think, be carried forward, not by societies organised around the production of surplus and waste, but by the more austere societies most of us are familiar with, societies which achieve a maximum use of available resources, societies in which the concepts of social motivation and ecological balance converge . . .[13]

But what of our world, the world of the Tricontinental South? One of your sociologists has defined *this* world as "a universe of radical scarcity;" he continues:

"Defining and determining every dimension of man's relationship to each other . . . the inadequacy of the means of livelihood is the first and distinguishing truth of this area."[14]

And your research journals and your experts and your international agencies can provide the indices which define this universe of scarcity, this world within which we, two-thirds of humankind, live briefly, and brutally . . . And yet, however precise the indices — that in Brazil, for example, "every 42 seconds a child dies, that is 85 every hour, 2,040 every day,"[15] how much do you know of the anguished deprivation, the shattered hopes and personal suffering which lie behind the impersonal statistical measure?

Yet our understanding of our condition, of ourselves, and of you and your societies, has changed greatly in recent years. You will probably recall the description by one of your great writers, Charles Dickens, of the Parisian crowds confronting a French aristocrat: wrote Dickens:

"So cowed was their condition, and so long and hard their experience of what such a man could do to them, within the law and beyond it, that not a voice, or a head or even an eye was raised . . ."

For long, you know, we of the South were as cowed as those Parisian crowds. For long we did not question, even when we had the energy, the arrogant self-assurance with which you took for your use our farmlands and forests, our mineral wealth and the muscle of our peoples' bodies. We did not question when our laws and institutions were swept away to be replaced by those you had fashioned, when control of our destinies rested with unknown men in distant capitals, when our young men were con-

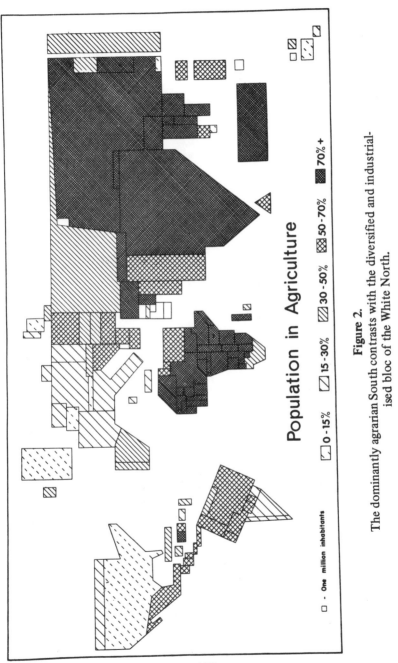

Population in Agriculture

☐ 0 - 15%   ◨ 15 - 30%   ▨ 30 - 50%   ▧ 50 - 70%   ■ 70% +

☐ - One million inhabitants

Figure 2.
The dominantly agrarian South contrasts with the diversified and industrial-ised bloc of the White North.

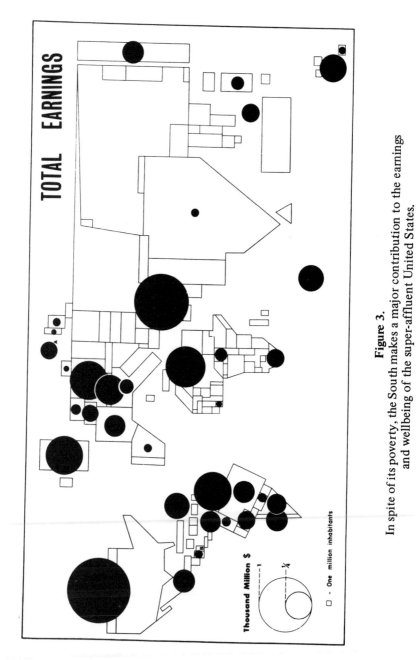

Figure 3.

In spite of its poverty, the South makes a major contribution to the earnings and wellbeing of the super-affluent United States.

scripted to fight your wars, and our lands were pock-marked with the various sorts of bases you needed, so you said, to safeguard yourselves, but which served also, we suspect, to underpin your domination of our societies. We did not, most of us, feel it to be strange that you should arrogate to yourself so many privileges in every country of the South — while we, for our part, were second-grade citizens in our own countries and scarcely tolerated, even as transient visitors, in your lands . . . And some of us who travelled and saw your wealth and power and contrasted these things with our poverty and helplessness when we returned home sometimes felt that the only explanation of our backwardness and weakness was to be found in racial factors or environmental conditions, that our condition of dependence and our poverty were perhaps predestined, that there were indeed two conditions of mankind — the damned and the beautiful — and that the divide between these two conditions was a racial divide.

And yet . . . Some of us who came to know firsthand your affluent societies of the North saw that even there one could find many groups who were exploited, whose lives were those of less-than-men, and our oversimplified explanation of the world had to be corrected, balanced . . . And we began to see that our poverty and helplessness, and the poverty and helplessness we glimpsed in parts of the North, were the product of the operation of a particular economic system — that of industrial capitalism. We saw that what had seemed a sharp divide between South and North, between the Third World and the rest of humanity, was in fact, far from clear-cut and that areas like the Southern States, the Mezzogiorno or the Celtic Fringe,[16] were different only in degree from the great belt of rural slums in which we lived. We began to understand that what you term "underdevelopment" is the product neither of climatic conditions nor racial origins but is *caused by men;* that is, as Ché taught us, the product of a deliberate warping designed to create economies complementary to the complex metropolitan economies of your imperialisms; that without underdevelopment there can, under the existing system, be no development.

And for those of you who are interested in the social and economic forces in the emerging world order I would cite this new and revolutionary awareness as possibly the most decisive single force of our time — and this is because we in the South are coming to

"perceive the reality of oppression not as a closed world from which there is no exit, but as a limiting situation which (we) can transform."[17]

And what the Chinese and the Vietnamese, the Koreans and the Lao, the Cubans and the guerrilla fighters of Africa, have demonstrated is that once the people have perceived this possibility of transforming, reshaping their world, no force on earth can stop them. You will note I use the word "reshape". I do this deliberately to remind you what these people have done is to substitute an authentic, indigenous, form of reality for the travesty of reality the White North had formerly imposed on them. And with this process a new era of world history begins . . .

The new awareness of which I have spoken has brought us a much greater clarity of vision, a new understanding of the relationship between the rich and the poor nations, and a new sense of the worth of our cultures, of our contribution to the richness of the human heritage. What we were coming to sense regarding the nature of underdevelopment has now been precisely articulated by one of our spokesmen in the United Nations. Said Carlos Rafael Rodriguez of Cuba:

> "it is by now practically indisputable that undervelopment is a historical phenomenon imposed upon the countries of of the vast underdeveloped world by those powers which, from the outside, interrupted what might have been these countries' more or less sustained growth and, by diverse methods of despoliation — always coercive and brutal during the period of colonialism, and no less coercive, but more subtle, in the neocolonialist stage — perpetrated underdevelopment as a means for taking the greatest advantage of and intensifying such despoliation. In short, the diagnosis according to which under-development is nothing but a consequence of colonialism and imperialism becomes more and more irrefutable as time goes by."[18]

Our eyes, you must understand from so forthright a statement, have been opened. And we are beginning to see not only more clearly but authentically, through the eyes of the South and not with the borrowed vision of elites trained in the White North and who until recently were our only spokesmen. Today, the shape of the world we see is different from that of the world you see, wish us to see, still strive to condition our elites into seeing.

And the problems of the world, the processes of change, these take on a different configuration, a different meaning, if you look at them from the South. What you, victims of your conditioning and of "the convenience of ignorance," see as "development" we see as a continuation of, even a deepening of, our *under*development. What you see as a "population explosion" menacing the resources on which your affluence is based, (though you never spell out your fears so bluntly), we see as an inevitable stage in our expansion, increasing our demographic potential, correcting the disequilibrium brought about by your swarming (and expansion) in the nineteenth century. What you call "aid" we see as a carefully calculated and highly profitable charity, as a weaving of fresh and a little more sophisticated webs with which to bind our people. What you describe as the export of technological know-how (a know-how to which the thousands of scientists you have imported from the South doubtless contribute) we see as a form of scientific imperialism which perpetuates our dependence. What you see as our cultural "backwardness" is such only according to the narrow criteria you have derived from your own society; according to the criteria we think are important — and we, after all, make up the majority of humanity — we find your culture and society deficient in many, many, respects.

There is no point, nor is there space, to multiply further these examples; maybe they suggest to you that it's mighty important to stress less what *you* think and to devote a little more time to trying to understand what *others* think ... And the divergent interpretations of world realities and world trends can be illustrated by taking one or two of these issues and examining them in more detail, emphasising less the conventional wisdom, (which conceals rather than enlightens) than how the issues appear to *us*. Let us look at the question of world development, the relationship of aid to such development, the impact of new technologies on the development of the South, the so-called "population problem," and the new emphasis on conservation and ecological balance.

World development: "Thems as has, gits"

Over a decade ago, you may r.. :ll, U Thant initiated the first UN "Decade of Development." A massive effort from rich and poor nations alike was to initiate the process of world development, defined as "economic progress plus social reform." Towards the end of his period as President, Lyndon B. Johnson referred, in an address to the banking fraternity, to the remarkable progress achieved. This progress and its benefits were rather less apparent to those of us who dwelled in the South; indeed even the fisherfolk of Brazil were heard to pose the question: "Development — is it for us or against us?" And the educationalist Ivan Illich, who has been one of our most dedicated articulate friends, summed up the "Decade of Development" as it appeared to us in the South; said Monsignor Illich in 1969:

> "the majority of men now have less food now than in 1945, less actual care in sickness, less meaningful work, less protection ... More people suffer from hunger, pain, and exposure in 1969 than they did at the end of World War II, not only numerically, but also as a percentage of the world population."[19]

This is a truth you do not like to acknowledge — but it is a truth which for us contains life and death.

When we turn to the statistics your agencies and your experts compile we find that what our empty bellies and empty hands tell us is indeed no product of our imagination. For example, between 1961 and 1968 the per capita GNP of the OECD countries increased by $110 yearly — and this increase is about as much as the average annual per capita GNP of most countries of the South in the 'sixties; as for the increase in the South, it was about $2.20 yearly. We have seen our share of international trade drop from 30% in 1948 to 22% in 1960 and 20% in 1968. You may point out that the exports of the South climbed from $27.8B in 1961 to $43.4B in 1968 — but much of this increase was accounted for by exports of manufactured goods and petroleum, and of these commodities 50% of the manufactured goods came from 6 territories only and petroleum exports are significant to 9 countries only. And particularly problematical is the growing trading deficit; imports exceeded exports by $3.9B in 1960 and by $6.0B in 1968, giving a cumulative deficit of $44B since 1960 ($55B if one excludes petroleum products). Confronted by these sorts of statistics do you wonder that we are mystified by all the cant about "development?" Do you find it strange that whenever the topic is raised we think immediately of St. Matthew's remarks about those who have — or of the cryptic Appalachian proverb "Thems as has, gits." For development there is, we admit, but most of this development we see taking place in the already developed, if not overdeveloped, lands of the White North.

And what we see emerging, north of the Shenyang-Guadalajara line which divides South and North, are the contours of a new geo-political unity, comprising 21 capitalist bloc nations and 8 Soviet bloc nations, linked by increasingly complex trading and financial ties, and by closely similar attitudes towards us, their impoverished Southern neighbours. Comments the economist Philippe Beaulieu:

> "The 29 rich countries are moving towards the creation of a zone of 'high development' based on the elements of modern civilisation: the mastery of an advanced technology, a high level and complex pattern of trade, and the availability of abundant financial resources. The links between this 'bloc of super-wealth' and the poor countries of the periphery are tending to become limited to, on one hand, the provision of indispensable raw materials (cotton, petrol, some metals and minerals) and, on the other hand, to some contingents of labourers since the inhabitants of the developed countries are already refusing to carry out certain types of manual work themselves."[20]

Years ago many of us talked of the growing polarisation of humanity but today it is no longer a question of "widening gaps," but rather of the majority of humanity being quite simply shunted on to one side. In Beaulieu's words:

> "Many fear that the evolution of the situation condemns the greater part of humanity to vegetate in poverty on the margin of a group of wealthy nations which will have less and less need of the poor nations."

If this analysis be correct, the choice, it seems to many of us, is between accepting irrelevance — or breaking finally all these links which have

KEITH BUCHANAN

perpetuated dependence and creating with our own resources an autonomous economic system along the lines pioneered by the Chinese.

"Calculated and Profitable Charity"

While we in the South hear rather less than we once did of Walt Rostow's "Stages of Economic Growth" — which provided the magic formula by which, one day, some day, we might attain the levels of development and affluence you have long enjoyed in the White North, we still hear an awful lot about the aid the developed nations are supposedly pouring into the countries of the South (or the pockets of our leaders). One of our economists, Mohammed Said Al-Attar, estimated the total aid granted to us in the "underdeveloped" countries at $47B over the period 1950-1961.[21] This, we recognise, is a sizeable sum; perhaps it's churlish to point out it's about as much as the USA has spent in one year on her counter-revolutionary war in Vietnam. But somehow it doesn't seem to have generated much real development. Partly this is because, as Al-Attar points out, some 45% of the aid monies went straight back to you in the White North in the form of profits, interest and repayment of principal; approximately 28% was wiped out by the deteriorating terms of trade which were to your benefit, leaving approximately 28% which could, in principle, be used for development. He adds:

"in reality, this percentage would have served to commercialise a part of the products of the industrialised countries and to make, in consequence, exorbitant and super-profits."

Partly the failure of aid to generate development rises from the fact that you take care that most of it is diverted into those sectors likely to yield you the greatest profits, not into those sectors which we hold are most important to the development of our economy or the welfare of our peoples. And by "tying" your aid to the purchase of specific items of equipment which may be over-costly or over-sophisticated for conditions in the South you introduce another element of distortion into our economies. Finally, your aid is used for political purposes,[22] buying for you allies among the "client elites" who are perhaps the sole beneficiaries of aid in many of our countries. And when we look at this balance sheet you must not be surprised if we detect behind many of your aid programmes a cold and calculating logic which has nothing at all to do with the ending of hunger and oppression but a great deal to do with pre-empting our growing determination to put an end to the subhuman conditions of life in our countries; put bluntly, what you are trying to do with your aid programmes is to channel this determination into "lines which in fact deny the liberation of the poor and their command of the development process." Yet you should understand, as Richard Hensman has emphasised, that it is only those who have suffered, those who for

179

decades have been robbed and exploited, who can create a world belonging to all; the restoration of human status for those whose humanity has been so long denied can only be through programmes "directed by the people themselves."

Al Attar's observations date from 1967. Five years later Mahbub ul Haq,[23] a senior economic advisor at the World Bank, expressed the heretical view that the South "would have been better off" had it not received the limited aid it had. By that date we in the South owed the wealthy nations of the North $60B and debt repayments were totalling $6B yearly and rising twice as rapidly as our export earnings. Aid along conventional lines was, we now see increasingly clearly, no substitute for self-help, however profitable it might be to the richer nations – and Mahbub ul Haq (speaking for himself and not the World Bank) expressed the view of many in the South when he predicted that many of the poorer countries may follow the Chinese model of "how to achieve full employment and equitable income distribution at a relatively low level of per capita income" and eschewing "aid".

The Transfer of Technology

One of the most recent and fashionable devices, contrived, so we are told, to even-up the technological gradient between the countries of the North and our countries, is the transfer of technology. This is supposed to give us the means whereby we can develop an industrial civilisation like yours (some of us are not sure we want this – but that is by the way) and is a form of aid which is pretty useful from your point of view since, far from being a burden on your balance of payments, it earns you foreign exchange. In short, we pay – and pay generously – for your technical aid.

Yet we have many hesitations about this latest ploy. We have very serious doubts about the value to our developing nations of many of the products this transferred technology enables us to produce. We note – and our suspicions are corroborated by one of your own experts, Charles Cooper, that "many of the technology agreements have aspects which have anti-developmental consequences."[24] And we don't see these technology transfers having much positive impact on our role in supplying manufactured goods.

In fact, what we would suggest to you is that most of the highly developed technologies you of the White North export – and this applies whether the "exporting" society is communist or capitalist – are of only limited value to us in the South. At times, indeed, they are demonstrably destructive; most times they are little more than a thinly-veneered attempt to perpetuate our dependence while ensuring high levels of profits for you. And that our fears and suspicions are not entirely groundless is suggested by our experience of the Green Revolution, the programme which, we are told, will solve once and for all the endemic hunger of the South but

KEITH BUCHANAN

which, the more we look at it, appears simply as yet another example of the penetration of the South by the economic institutions of Western capitalism. Concerned more — and we do not think this is too cynical an observation — with fattening the wealthy than feeding the poor and hungry.

We can see the impact of the Green Revolution most clearly in Southern Asia. There it has benefited chiefly the wealthy farmers, accelerated the growth of a landless class, and thereby aggravated tensions in the countryside.[25] And in the areas most affected by it there's evidence that *real* wages have fallen. A report by the Indian Home Ministry gives a realistic, if remarkably restrained, evaluation of its impact:

"The new technology and strategy, having been geared to goals of production, with secondary regard to social imperatives, have brought about a situation in which elements of disparity, instability and unrest are becoming conspicuous."

This Indian experience is multiplied throughout the length and breadth of the South; the imported technology can be made use of by those who can afford it and because of its dependence as imported fertilizers, imported machinery, even seeds, it increases the dependent state of our Southern economies. And maybe this is what you want — for from the times of Herbert Hoover to those of Hubert Humphrey the most powerful nation in the White North has been aware how vulnerable to political pressures food-dependent regions are and it has not hesitated to exploit this vulnerability.

Like most development under capitalism, the technologies of the Green Revolution are based on the concept of "building on the best." What you perhaps overlook are the political implications of this. As we see it in the South, what is emerging is a new instability and an instability which may pose insoluble problems to you, the policemen of the world. The richer peasant gets richer, the poorer peasant is pushed off the land and finds his way into the slum areas of our cities so that the growth rate of our urban populations is likely to continue at a high level for years to come. And have you considered just what this may mean? May it not portend a shift in some areas from the classic Chinese or Cuban pattern of peasant-based revolutionary change to a situation in which the main guerrilla focus is the city? And yet reality is still more complex for the new agricultural technology has affected only one-tenth of the grain lands in the South and these are the richer areas; the exacting demands of the new grains preclude their use in the poorer and more backward areas. Yet, as Eric Wolf has pointed out,[26] it is in such backward areas that we find some of the cradle areas for the revolutionary struggles which have re-shaped the South: the examples of China, Cuba, Algeria, Indochina and Mexico immediately come to mind. So what we see emerging as a result of your profit-hungry

181

technology is not only a social polarisation in the richer rural areas, not only an explosive urban situation — but also a growing number of potential revolutionary foci among the damned and the dispossessed of our poor countrysides (a large proportion of that nine-tenths of the South unaffected by your new technology). And in the case of the Green Revolution and so many other examples of transferred expertise the destructive impact arises largely from the fact that new technologies cannot be grafted on to an unchanged social base. We believe you are not so naive as to be unaware of this — rather do we believe that you are unable to harmonise with your policies, with your obsession with domination of the South, those transformations of traditional social and economic structures — and especially of class relations — necessary if new technologies are to bring benefit to the whole society.[27]

And we see all around us examples of your eagerness to press upon us the increasingly debatable blessings of your own very specialised brand of technology, examples of actions, which we are to preserve any sense of charity, we are forced to regard as due to your ignorance. One of the features of the South — and this you can hardly fail to notice, is the high density of population in many areas, its rapid growth, and the high rates of unemployment and underemployment. You nonetheless keep pressing on us the need for a capital-intensive system of industrialisation and you've managed to sell such systems to our elites. But this means any benefits from industrialisation accrue to a small group only, leaving the great mass of our people untouched, perhaps relatively worse off. And that this is no wild claim on our part is suggested by the comment of Dennis Meadows, director of the Club of Rome's M.I.T. project; the sort of aid the North has been giving, says Meadows:

"had the effect of moving small elites into industrialisation and freezing the vast majority of the people in poverty."[28]

And, finally, you don't really understand the ecological conditions of the South, or, rather, you believe that massed technology will enable you to dominate or tame the environment we've learned to accommodate ourselves to over the centuries. We still remember your attempt to tame the East African environment when you launched your ill-fated Groundnut Scheme. More recently, we see the ecological destruction caused in Egypt and the Eastern Mediterranean by another triumph of the White North's technology — the Aswan High Dam. Some of us in the South — whose societies were managing complex systems of water control and irrigation when your ancestors were still hunters in your misty northern forests — had doubts at the time the project was announced but we did not imagine it would so swiftly show itself as a major catastrophe, threatening the collapse of Nile-based Egyptian farming.[29]

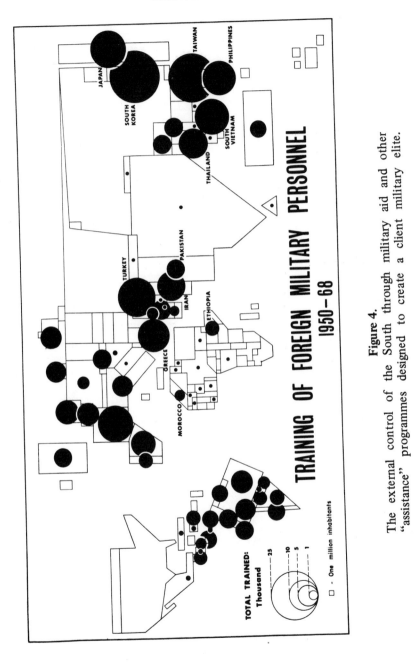

Figure 4.

The external control of the South through military aid and other "assistance" programmes designed to create a client military elite.

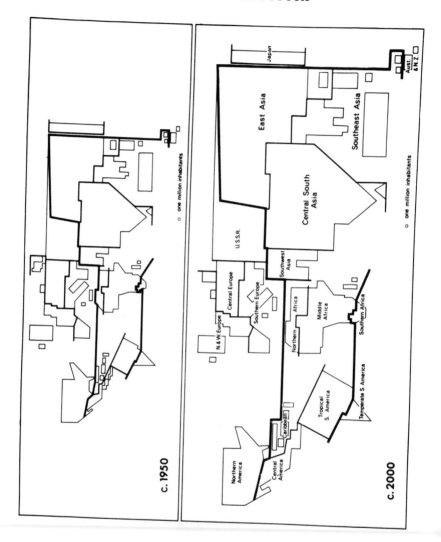

Figure 5.
The shape of the future: world population patterns in the middle and end of this century, (size of country is proportional to population).

You have a legend about the hero who sowed dragon's teeth and reaped a harvest of fighting men. Sometimes, you know, we cannot help thinking that this is what you are doing with your transfers of technology.

"People Pollution"
One of the decisive forces shaping the present world, as it shaped the world of the XIXth century, is the process of demographic growth. And we cannot help noticing that this is something which worries you greatly, indeed obsesses some groups. We are told by influential public figures, by the great foundations, and by your learned journals, that there can be no solution to the problem of poverty as long as our populations continue to grow so rapidly. This we don't quite understand since we believed that one of the important factors in the rise of industrial civilisation in the West and in the spread of this civilisation was your population growth in the XIXth century. And *you* don't understand — or are acutely insensitive — for if you did you would accept that the joys of the bed are one of the few joys we have, that when night falls we can sometimes forget the harsh realities of daytime. And can we say quite simply that we believe that the "problem of the poor" might be more effectively solved by the re-distribution of wealth or the restructuring of society than by vasectomy, the loop or the sometimes dubious techniques of contraception being disseminated by your great foundations and your governments among us, the poor of the South? Or do you perhaps fear that a redistribution of wealth would mean dismantling the super-affluent world some of you find so comfortable and substituting a civilisation predicated on the needs of the dispossessed — which means the needs of the great majority of humankind?

The views of many in the White North could not, we feel, be presented more concisely than in the phrase "people pollution" which one of your scientists has coined. But behind all the population control campaigns there lurk, we feel, political motivations — and highly dubious ones at that . . . These motivations can be pretty clearly seen in the comments of Emerson Foote, that:

"there can be no doubt that unless population growth is brought under control at an early date the resulting misery and social tensions will inevitably lead to chaos and strife — to revolutions and wars, the dimensions of which it would be hard to predict."[30]

This conveniently simplistic viewpoint has, however, been effectively challenged by many of our spokesman. For example, Felix Cruzat Alegre says bluntly the poverty of the South:

"is not caused by overpopulation, because this does not exist, but by archaic socio-economic structures."[31]

185

And we find it strange, if you really *are* concerned with poverty and misery, that you should devote so much energy, so much money, to propping up precisely these archaic and anti-human structures.

We in the South believe that the whole "demographic problem," as you term it, cannot be separated from what we think of as the "resource problem" – and the resource problem lies in the fact that some 15% of the world's population, mainly white, monopolises 85% of the world's wealth. And we, the people of the South, the great majority of humankind, have no interest at all in the stabilisation of a situation "in which our share of the earth's banquet has always been limited to the occasional crumbs from the well-stocked table of the rich." We are not the least interested in, because we see no justice in, the attempts to establish some sort of global equilibrium at our expense – for we are the ones who to date have suffered most bitterly from the consequences of this disequilibrium. Above all, since the existing gross inequalities in the distribution of wealth are the result of an economic system imposed by you of the White North, we rather think that correction is your responsibility; you just cannot lay it as a further burden on those you so long dominated.

And thinking thus, we applaud the forthrightness and the indignation of one of our great scientists, Josue de Castro, when he denounces a civilisation:

"which, after having looted the world in a manner so shameless, so inhuman and so shortsighted that it today realises that the wealth of our planet is being exhausted, now admits its bankruptcy and advises the marginal peoples to curb their birthrates so as to save the scraps that remain and leave the exclusive benefit of these to the privileged groups of the moment."[32]

Forgive us – but do you not recall the words of Pope Paul VI in *Populorum Progressio,* that "the world is given to all and not only to the rich"?

But we are in danger of becoming emotional – and one of the reasons you attack de Castro is not because of the uncomfortable facts he adduces – for these you can hardly deny – rather do you claim he should be distrusted because he introduces uncomfortable concepts like humanity, morality and compassion into scientific work. Might we suggest, mildly and diffidently, that most of your so-called "demographic experts" ignore, when they discuss the "population problem," that man is a producer as well as a consumer, that a healthy, educated and mobilised population is a *resource, the most precious of all resources.* We think your experts ignore the fact that you can't initiate successful systems of family planning without social change and education. We rather think, also, that they overlook the fact that the parents of the next generation are already born and that their numbers are such that, even if the average family size were to be cut by 50%, the absolute increment in population would, in 20 years time, still be as large as today's increment in many regions. And, at the risk of being tactless, we in the South rather think that far more important than the growth of *numbers* is the growth in *consumption* and that, if you're *really* as interested in wiping out poverty in the South as you *claim* to be, you might give some thought to the cutting-back of the extravagant consumption levels in the White North which at present appropriates some 85% of the world's resources. And you doubtless know the estimate of one of your scientists – that the United States GNP would support ten billion, yes, TEN BILLION, people living at Indian standards while the GNP of even a small country like Sweden would support 320 million people.[33]

A little austerity on your part, you know, would contribute more to the solution of the "population problem" and to the long-term development of the South than all your grandiose family planning schemes, would demonstrate your sincerity and bring us a little closer together, and, by reducing pollution levels, make your own lives rather pleasanter. In the next few years we shall be watching with interest what you do to, as we see it, put pious professions into practice ... It's really up to you to demonstrate that population control is not, as Malcolm X and many others have seen it, yet another attempt to perpetuate our dependence, it's up to you to demonstrate that it's not true, as many claim, that:

"a world order predicated upon 'population control' will invariably mean control of rich over poor, white over black and yellow"[34]

The Conservation Gambit

We in the South marvel at the skill with which your leaders and your power groups use virtually every issue – and the examples of aid and population planning are the most obvious – to perpetuate our dependence and prolong just a little longer your domination of the world. Assuredly, you have moved far from those crude old days when you sent a gun boat or a detachment of Marines to tell us just who was boss ... but the intended effect is the same.

The latest example of the weaving of new and subtler nets to enmesh us in your skilful use of the pollution/environmental issue. It's true that you have not hesitated to set up in our countries factories which could not be sited in your own countries because of your anti-pollution legislation, but generally you are playing the conservation gambit with considerable subtlety, and what we see emerging is the possibility of growing pressure on us to restrain our industrial development lest we add further to the burden of pollution which is destroying the world's eco-systems. Yet as we've pointed out earlier, most of the global pollution which threatens the viability of the human species is generated in the White North and the United States alone "is responsible for one-third to one-half of the production of hazardous waste products" (and this does not include pollution caused by U.S.-owned establishments overseas).

We must have — and we intend to have — a level of industrialisation sufficient to secure our independence. And we rather think that, since the ecological imbalance — like the imbalance in the distribution of wealth — is the result of the system you have developed and then imposed on, or sold to, much of the rest of humanity, it's up to you to start correcting this imbalance by cutting down your rate of economic growth, your emission of dangerous waste products, your destructive over-exploitation of the world's resources. And perhaps we can remind you that it is: "the political and economic inequities of capitalism (that) are ... directly responsible for the biological traumas of the earth's natural systems and its population."[35] Capitalism is not the *only* economic system and some of the nations of the South have shown that it is possible to have modern industry without large-scale pollution; that, in view of the possibilities of re-cycling, the Chinese are right in asserting that there is no such thing as "waste." But they have had to get out of the capitalist system and out of the state capitalism of the European Soviet bloc — and we rather think that one of the main trends in the future will be for an increasing number of nations to take this path. And they will do this because they are coming increasingly to recognise that the economic systems of the White North are not capable of lifting the great mass of people out of poverty, that these systems are concerned less with people than with production and more with wealth than with welfare — and because they are seeing that the so-called "economic progress" of the North promises only a Gadarene course to ecological destruction.

Perhaps, if the truth must be told, we're not convinced you'll have the wisdom — and its not really a high degree of wisdom — to recognise you cannot have infinite growth in a finite world; that the limited and basic industrial development we in the South *must* have (and we're assuming we can avoid contamination by your trash culture) can be ecologically accommodated only if you in the North *are prepared to cut back a little your own development* and move to, at the very least, a condition of Zero Economic Growth. And from your own point of view, if you are to avoid the threat of ecological disaster, further material growth in your own over-developed societies must be restricted; in the words of a U.S. scientist:

"The ecologist must convince the population that the only solution to the problem of growth is not to grow."[36]

If you *were* to accept such a drastic policy, this would relieve the pressure on our own resources (and thus obviate one of your major motives for interfering with us), would give us a chance to narrow just a little the gap that separates our two worlds and convince those of us who doubted when your spokesmen talked so eloquently of pollution at the recent U.N. Conference on the Environment at Stockholm, or when you talk with concern about the widening gap and the problem of resource depletion. Maybe it would be a small step bringing us closer to the realisation of the ideal of "one world." Maybe it will occur. Most likely it won't and all of humanity will be scacrificed to your "growth-mania," your ecological ignorance and arrogance.[37] And yet, as we see it, the ecological needs of *your* over-developed societies are convergent with the economic and social needs of *our* underdeveloped (because exploited) countries in the Tricontinental South. And with an end to the super-exploitation of the South there opens up, as the example of China demonstrates, the possibility of real and diversified development in our proletarian nations. Moreover, and here again the Chinese experience is critical, with rising levels of living and improved medical and welfare services, the "population problem" will, we believe, begin to solve itself. As for your over-developed societies, a "stationary-state economy" will demand considerable redistribution of wealth and above all reallocation of resources from the private to the public sector — in short, a drastic restructuring of society. This, you will claim, is impossible. To which we would retort, paraphrasing the words of a distinguished U.S. ecologist:

"if you don't do the impossible, you will be faced with the unthinkable . . ."[38]

FOOTNOTES

1 Introduction to *The Teachings of Don Juan* by Carlos Castaneda (Penguin 1970).

2 Richard Hensman *From Gandhi to Guevara : The Polemics of Revolt* (Allen Lane 1969).

3 See the writings of John Prebble, notably *Culloden* and *The Highland Clearances*

4 E.J. Mishan *Growth: The Price We Pay* (Penguin 1970).

5 Admirably discussed by Richard Hensman in *From Gandhi to Guevara* and *Rich Against Poor* (Allen Lane 1971).

6 Bertrand Russell *Freedom and Organisation*,

7 Franz Fanon *The Wretched of the Earth* and other writings.

8 For documentation see e.g. Philip Slater *The Pursuit of Loneliness : American Culture at the Breaking Point* (Beacon, Boston 1971) and George Steiner *Bluebeard's Castle.*

9 Armand Gatti *Journal d'un guerillero* (du Seuil, Paris 1968).

10 Concisely documented by Barry Weisberg *Beyond Repair : The Ecology of Capitalism* (Beacon, Boston, 1971).

11 Weisberg *op. cit.* pp. 70-1.

12 *Idem* p.8.

13 See, for example, Neale Hunter "The Good Earth and the Good Society" in *China and Ourselves* ed. Bruce Douglass and Ross Terrill (Boston 1970) and the essays by Stephen Andors and others in *America's Asia* ed. Mark Selden (New York, 1971).

14 *New Left Review* (London) 1963 p.4.

15 Francisco Juliao "Brazil: A Christian Country" in *Whither Latin America?* ed. P. Sweezy and L. Huberman (New York, M.R. Press, 1963).

16 See, for example, *Hunger; USA* (Boston, 1968) or the writings of Danilo Dolci.

17 Paolo Freire *Pedagogy of the Oppressed* (New York 1970).

18 Carlos Rafael Rodriguez Speech to the UNDP Administrative Council and reprinted as "The Sea is Boiling" in *NACLA Newsletter* (Berkeley & New York) Feb. 1971.

19 Ivan Illich "Outwitting the 'Developed' Countries" in *New York Review of Books* Nov. 6 1969 (reprinted in Ivan Illich *Celebration of Awareness* 1970).

20 Philippe Beaulieu "Pays riches, pays pauvres" in *Projet* (Paris) July-Aug. 1970.

21 Writing in the symposium on the Encyclical *Populorum Progressio* in *Developpement et Civilisations* (Paris) June 1967.

22 See, for example, Teresa Hayter *Aid as Imperialism* (Penguin 1971); Africa Research Group *International Dependency in the 1970's* (Cambridge, Mass., 1970) and NACLA *Yanqui Dollar : The Contribution of U.S. Private Investment to Underdevelopment in Latin America.* (Berkeley and New York 1971).

23 Cited in Richard Critchfield "The New Environment of Foreign Aid" in *Nation* (New York) May 15, 1972.

24 Charles Cooper "The Transfer of Industrial Technology to the Underdeveloped Countries" in *Bulletin of the Institute of Development Studies.* 1970.

25 See *International Dependency in the 1970's;* Harry M. Cleaver "The Contradictions of the Green Revolution" and Ali M.S. Fatemi "The Green Revolution: an appraisal" — both in *Monthly Review* (New York) June 1972; "The Green Revolution: genetic backlash" in *The Ecologist* October 1970; Steve Weissman "Why the Population Bomb is a Rockefeller Baby" in *Ramparts.*

26 Eric Wolf *Peasant Wars of the Twentieth Century* (New York 1969).

27 See, for example, Hensman's *Rich against Poor;* Susanne Bodenheimer "Dependency and Imperialism" in *NACLA Newsletter* May-June 1970 and Antonio Murga "Dependency: A Latin American View" in *NACLA Newsletter* Feb. 1971.

28 Cited by Richard Critchfield *op. sup. cit.*

29 See, for example, Claire Sterling "Written in the Water" in *International Herald Tribune* Jan.8 1971.

30 See Steve Weissman *op. sup. cit.*

31 See Pierre Pradervand "Les pays nantis et la limitation des naissances dans le Tiers Monde" in *Developpement et Civilisations* March-June 1970.

32 Josue de Castro *Le livre noir de la faim* (Paris 1961).

33 Pierre Pradervand *op. sup. cit.*

34 Barry Weisberg *op. sup. cit.*

35 *Idem*

36 For an examination of the ecological crisis and of the implications of Zero Economic Growth, see, in addition to the work of the Ehrlichs, Richard England and Barry Bluestone "Ecology and Class Conflict" and John Hardesty, Norris C. Clement and Clinton E. Jencks "Political Economy and Environmental Destruction," both in *Review of Radical Political Economics* (Ann Arbor, Michigan) Fall/Winter 1971. And for alternatives to overdevelopment see Colin Stoneman in "The Unviability of Capitalism in *Socialism and the Environment*", edited by Ken Coates (Spokesman Books, 1972).

37 See Barry Weisberg, passim and the material cited in the periodical *The Ecologist*.

38 Murray Bookchin.

dreadful behaviour one anticipates from communists. When Athens fell, and when Prague fell, the official reactions were identical. "We must strengthen NATO" said the British Foreign Secretary: "We must reinforce our Alliance's military power" no doubt said Marshal Gretchko. What neither said, however, was more interesting than what both said. It is inconceivable in the modern world that 500,000 Warsaw pact soldiers could advance to the frontiers of Austria and Federal Germany without so much as a whisper on the hot line: yet the members of the Dubcek administration were taken completely by surprise when Soviet tanks bore in upon their seat of Government. If NATO was told, (and indeed informed rumour has it that NATO received a week's notice of the impending invasion) then NATO kept the secret. Far from intervening, the Atlantic forces kept their strict distance from events. The "strengthening" of NATO, so urgent for Mr. Michael Stewart, was not a matter of increasing its capacity to fly to the assistance of its alleged supporters in Warsaw or Sofia, any more than the reinforcement of the Warsaw Pact forces was a matter of increasing their potential to assist their spiritual brothers in Greece or Portugal. The truth is simpler and more brutal: NATO keeps order in the "West", and the Warsaw Pact keeps order in the "East". If communism "threatens" Italy, that will be a problem for NATO to solve. If democratic forms of socialist organisation seem likely to erupt in Poland, then the Warsaw Pact may well decide to unleash its troop carriers. Each alliance invokes an external threat the better to prepare itself for the maintenance of internal discipline. Each requires and therefore nourishes a myth of aggressive subversion, the better to explain away the unpopular effects of its police activity. Real subversion, real threats, of course exist. They only serve to make more credible the myths. In this way both "communism" and "democracy" take on an increasingly ideological content, if we use the word "ideological" in its original pejorative sense. While each claims to uphold, indeed to be the material embodiment of, certain ideals in contrast with and opposition to the other, both in fact have rigidly encircled their original aspirations in an iron ring of state expendiences, so that "democracy" finds allies in General Franco, to say nothing of Generalissimo Chiang Kai Shek, while "communism" not only plays the diplomatic game with a will, but also goes far beyond the most illiberal of liberal democracies in its domestic restraint of dissident socialist opinion, its interference with elementary personal freedoms, and its encouragement of retrogressive practices such as censorship: to say nothing of the incarceration of its critics in mental hospitals. It has taken a long time for these real lineaments of the cold war to make themselves apparent to any significant numbers of open-minded people on either side of the divide. Radical critics have rightly spent many years in agitating for a detente, in order to minimise the danger of annihilation by nuclear war: but it has only been the attainment of a certain equilibrium between the powers, based upon their own responses to the recurrent crises in their inter-relationship, and no doubt upon their own estimation of the appalling consequences of any all-out collision, which has enabled any substantial groups of private citizens to recognise something of the real nature of the underpinning of the present world power-structure. As this dawning recognition has slowly extended itself, so at any rate among the radical minorities which have begun to form in all the advanced countries, whether capitalist or socialist, words like "imperialism" have gained a new currency, and the problem of spheres of influence has achieved recognition as an issue of crucial significance.

Bertrand Russell's was among the warning voices which helped to create this awareness: "Never before in the West" he wrote, recently,

"have so many people been prepared to look afresh at the last quarter of a century. For many years I have endeavoured to oppose the destructiveness of the cold war and the menace which it represents to all mankind. I am convinced that such opposition must be strengthened by a thorough examination of the origins and development of the cold war. To us in the West, some of the facts were at first obscured by propaganda, others by the tyranny of Stalin. Similarly, in the Third World, many were misled by the semblance of independence or the hope of economic aid. Out of this confusion has emerged the certainty of the United States of America as the wealthiest and most powerful nation in history. Its relationship to the rest of the world deserves the closest attention. There is an essential unity in the cold war, economic and foreign policies of the United States. This is created by the constant search for raw materials and markets, the imposition of poverty upon a large proportion of the world's population and the use of US military power in dozens of countries to protect the interests of American capitalism and destroy those who dare to resist. Aggression is more than a facet of imperialism: the determination to conquer, dominate and exploit is the very essence of imperialism. Such aggression is not only unjust: in the nuclear age it must be impermissible. In the face of the massive governmental propaganda to which we are all subjected, there is a need for a critical and independent analysis of these years, which is both radical and substantial, using the abundant documentation of scholarship for the purposes of clarifying issues and preparing the ground for more effective opposition to those who would exploit or destroy us all."[1]

Russell had not always held such views, and it is important to show why, at the end of his life, he so tenaciously opposed the most powerful authorities at large on earth, enduring their bitter criticism and the virtual isolation which resulted from it at a time when, had he chosen to remain silent, he could have been lionized in every corner of the world.

THE INTERNATIONALISM OF BERTRAND RUSSELL

II

Bertrand Russell was an aristocrat. Of this lapse on his part, his opponents were always rightly convinced. Neither bourgeois politicians nor proletarian theorists could readily forgive it. When he talked informally, his natural language was the language of Gibbon, which gave his writing that character of controlled mordancy which gained him the Nobel prize, not for peace or scientific activity, but for literature. His natural vision spontaneously placed men like Sir Edward Grey, or Stanley Baldwin or Bonar Law, in their historical space in the evolution of English politics, which could hardly flatter them. At the same time, although his pen always earned his living, there were those other writers who could never ignore his lineage. When, in England, he wrote of liberty, he was wont to be assumed guilty of demagogy by the Right, or patronage by the Left, on no better grounds than that his grandfather had been Queen Victoria's Prime Minister. Even his supporters have registered this fact:

> "He had an aristocrat's education, he went to what is the first or second most aristocratic college in the first or second most aristocratic university in a profoundly aristocratic society. And when he once said (and I have heard this recording over and over again) "I will not", — you know, as a form of refusal — one heard that power and background of the aristocrat. The people he used to say "I will not" to, the people he would write to, whom I wouldn't even know had a letter box, showed the confidence of the aristocrat: and he went in as one of the leading minds of his time."[2]

Yet to interpret all this as arrogance would be to mistake the man entirely. To see a human society from the top of the heap may not normally conduce to self-effacement, but in a real sense Russell's genius arose in his humility, which is again and again revealed in the pages of his autobiography. Benjamin Franklin advised his readers to "practise humility: imitate Jesus and Socrates."[3] Russell had no need to "practise". It was in his upbringing and origins to see the weakness and cupidity of men of power, and indeed he often recalled that his strange and irreverent Whig grandmother, who reared him, gave him, as a child, a bible on whose flyleaf she had inscribed the text

"Thou shalt not follow a multitude to do evil."

It was at his grandfather's house, Pembroke Lodge, that the British Cabinet had met to resolve upon the need for the Crimean War. Several of its members, Russell records in his autobiography, had been asleep at the time. In this same house the little orphan learned Euclid from his older·brother, and Shelley, Byron and Milton from his grandmother. His biographer, Alan Wood,[4] in evaluating his boyhood, speculates that although he gained from his grandmother the insight that "there are few higher virtues than moral courage in an unpopular cause", the aggravated loneliness of his childhood caused him to yearn for ordinary human affection. There can be no doubt that it made him diffident, shy to a degree.

When he entered Cambridge university, although this shyness went with him, it was mitigated by the good offices of Whitehead, who had been Russell's examiner when he gained his scholarship, and who had noticed his extraordinary talent. He formed there a number of friendships: with Roger Fry, Lowes Dickinson, and G.E. Moore, under whose influence he was to abandon the Hegelian doctrines he had learned from his tutor, MacTaggart. In 1893 and 1894 he gained first class honours in mathematics and moral sciences respectively: but when he came to evaluate the effect of Cambridge on him, he judged that its main virtue was that of intellectual honesty. Most of what he had learned in philosophy, he thought, had subsequently proved erroneous. What endured was the example of his tutors, in their willingness to admit error.

He left the university to take up an appointment as Attache at the British Embassy in Paris, because his grandmother was anxious that he should not rush into a marriage with the Philadelphia Quaker, Alys Pearsall Smith, who was a member of the circle of the founders of fabian socialism, the Webbs. After a very short stay in the Embassy, he quit the diplomatic corps, married his girl, and set off to Berlin with her in order to study the German Socialist movement. Although he became a member of the fabian society, converted his wife to religious unbelief, and returned to England to become first lecturer at the London School of Economics and publish his first book on *German Social Democracy,* this work was, as he explained in a preface to the 1965 reprint, written from the viewpoint of "an orthodox liberal".

It was after this political excursion that Russell entered upon the astonishing labour which had made his name a byword within a decade. He published his Cambridge dissertation on *The Foundations of Geometry,* and after finally purging the influence of Hegel, in 1898, he was able to complete and publish his study of Leibniz and embark upon *The Principles of Mathematics,* in which he was materially aided by Peano's notation. Meeting Peano at a Philosophical Congress in Paris was a "turning-point" in his intellectual life, he subsequently wrote, and it gave him the impetus required to start work, with Whitehead, on the *Principia Mathematica.* This labour, in turn, was to produce another turning-point, in what he regarded as his "emotional" or moral life: in Spring 1901 he went to stay with the Whiteheads for a time. Mrs. Whitehead was afflicted by heart trouble, and suffered recurrent pains which were acute and anguishing. While Russell was present she underwent a particularly dire attack, which awoke within him a sense of his own urbane complacency and aloofness from matters which should properly concern him.

"Suddenly the ground seemed to have given way beneath me, and I found myself in quite another region. Within five minutes I went through some such reflections as the following:

The loneliness of the human soul is unendurable; nothing can penetrate it except the highest intensity of that sort of love that religious teachers have preached; whatever does not spring from this motive is harmful, or at best useless: it follows that war is wrong . . . that the use of force is to be deprecated, and that in human relations one should penetrate to the core of loneliness in each person and speak to that . . . At the end of those five minutes, I had become a completely different person. For a time, a sort of mystic illumination possessed me."[5]

This revelation bit hard on Russell's reactions to the world. He become a pacifist, and found himself opposed to imperialism. While he felt his personal relationships to be deeper and richer for the advent of this experience, his social attitudes also were transformed:

"Something of what I thought I saw in that moment has remained always with me, causing my attitude in the first World War, my interest in children, my indifference to minor misfortunes, and a central emotional tone in all my human relations."

Yet during this time, and right up to 1914, he remained a liberal, and even though he took up the major anti-imperialist causes, and espoused the movement for women's suffrage, when he stood for Parliament in 1907, it was in the Liberal interest. But Russell's opposition to the war was crystallised in those still-liberal years, and followed directly upon his trauma at the Whiteheads' house. It was in 1902 that he first heard Sir Edward Grey setting out the framework of the as yet unfinalised policy of the Entente.[6] He reacted instantly, and continuously opposed it from that time onwards, saying that it was manifestly likely to lead to war.

During all the prewar years from then on, his reputation as a philosopher and a mathematician grew uninterruptedly. But at the same time that his aristocratic connections gave him an entree to the circles where war-preparations were under consideration, his independent judgment and sceptical temper ensured that he came into increasingly open conflict with the establishment of which he was so distinguished a representative.

III

So, when war broke out in 1914, he was soon to become a target for almost universal vituperation. His family position, his intellectual eminance, his privileged status, all served at the time to aggravate the offence for which today he is venerated. The war produced a crisis in

Liberalism, particularly in Great Britain. Russell felt that the Liberal administration had betrayed its fundamental commitments in unleashing a new barbarism, and he became an avowed socialist. He joined the Labour Party, the pacifist No Conscription Fellowship,[7] the Union of Democratic Control[8] and the Guild Socialist movement.[9] The moral commitment which impelled him to move in this direction may well, as he claims, have originated with his mystic experience at the Whitehead's house thirteen years earlier, although both marxists and freudians will doubtless offer their own analyses of this process in years to come. What is beyond question is that, once having decided that the authorities in Britain were bent upon a wholly insupportable course of action, Russell applied to the task of opposition all his prodigious talent for pursuing an argument through to its ultimate end, for inflexible and caustic logic, and for tenacity in support of his ideas.

"To all liberal-minded and humane men" he wrote, in an early pamphlet of the Union of Democratic Control, "this war has come as a shock and a challenge, shattering hopes, and too often uprooting life-long convictions. The horror of what is happening through Europe is so staggering that men seek to escape realisation by various means — some by such minor deeds of humanity as the time allows, nursing the wounded, providing for the relief of distress, or finding an asylum for stranded aliens; some by cherishing hopes of a regenerated Europe to emerge at the end of the struggle; and some by yielding to a fiery conviction in the righteousness of the nation to which they happen to belong. But in these preoccupations there is some danger that the larger humanity, which combats the passions out of which the war has arisen, may be obscured. If a better world is to emerge, if Europe is to be spared a repetition of slaughter and madness, it is necessary to know and recognise the causes, in the hopes and fears of ordinary men, that have made it hitherto impossible to substitute reason and law for force in the relations of nations. Perhaps at this moment an appeal to impartial reason may find little sympathy, and may seem to the majority ill-timed and unpatriotic. But peace, as well as war, requires preparation: if it is right in time of peace to make schemes for the destruction of possible enemies, can it be wrong in time of war to make schemes for the preservation of possible friends? War does not do away with all other duties, nor is it unpatriotic to suggest that there are higher goals than victory and nobler ideals than the destruction of hostile armies . . . . In each nation men are willing to die and women are willing to starve and see their homes devastated. Such sacrifices are not incurred for merely selfish ends: each nation believes that it is defending a sacred cause. Immense forces of heroism and devotion are destroying each other through a tragedy of blindness and fear. These very same forces, by clearer insight and calmer judgment, might be used for the good of mankind, instead of for mutual death. But this can only come about through mutual understanding and respect, not through partisan accusations of perfidy and greed."[10]

He then, in the midst of all the envenomed chauvinistic clamour of the time, proceeded coolly to analyse, nation by nation, the role of each belligerent, in order to demonstrate that official propaganda, everywhere, was full of half-truth, self-interest, and vulgar misrepresentation. The policy of Alliances, he claimed, was everywhere productive of disaster:

"It is the universal reign of Fear which has caused the system of alliances, believed to be a guarantee of peace, but now proved to be the cause of world-wide disaster. Fear of Russia led to the Anglo-Japanese alliance and to the alliance of Germany and Austria. The need of support in a long tariff war with France led Italy to ally itself with Austria, from fear that otherwise Austria would seize the moment for an attack on Italy. Fear of Germany led France and England into their unnatural alliance with Russia. And this universal fear has at least produced a cataclysm far greater than any of those which it was hoped to avert. Whoever is technically victorious in this war, all the nations concerned, victors and vanquished alike, must lose a large proportion of their manhood, all the economic reserves which make it possible to bring some happiness into the lives of the wage-earning classes, and all the surplus of leisure which produces the arts and the creative thought of peaceful times. None of us, whatever the outcome, can hope to return during our lifetime to the level of happiness, well-being, and civilisation which we enjoyed before the war broke out.

If civilisation is to continue, Europe must find a cure for this universal reign of fear with its consequence of mutual butchery. One way in which it might be cured is that the civilised nations, realising the horror and madness of war, should so organise themselves as to make it practically certain that no advantage can be gained by initiating an attack. For this purpose it would be necessary to avoid exclusive alliances and to form a League of Peace, which should undertake, in the event of a dispute, to offer mediation, and, if one party accepted mediation while the other refused it, to throw the whole of its armed support on the side of the party accepting mediation, while, if both parties refused mediation, the League should throw its weight against whichever party proved to be the agressor. If a sufficient number of nations entered into such a League, they could make aggressive war obviously doomed to failure, and could thereby secure the cessation of war."

With this prescription for a new League of Nations, he coupled another:

"Secret diplomacy must cease. Of all the features in our present methods which tend to defeat the will for peace, and which might be altered without waiting for the consent of other nations, the chief is secret diplomacy. Where a settled policy rather than a sudden crisis is in question, no obligation or debt of honour ought to be created without the full previous knowledge of the House of Commons and the country. So long as this principle is not observed, democratic government is a farce and a pretence. No national or human interest is served by secrecy: the only interest served is that of the official clique who are thus enabled to pursue unchecked a policy entailing terrible liabilities, and to keep the support of men who would execrate their policy if they knew what it was." [11]

These were liberal sentiments, couched in profoundly liberal language. They contrast somewhat starkly with the "socialism" of such English publicists as Robert Blatchford or H.M. Hyndman, or the "marxism" of Karl Kautsky. As Lenin expressed the matter in his assessment of Russell's English colleague, E.D. Morel:

"Marxian words have in our days become a cover for the absolute renunciation of Marxism; to be a Marxist one must expose the "Marxian" hypocrisy of the leaders of the Second International . . . This is the conclusion to be drawn from England, where we see Marxian essence without Marxian words." [12]

Yet there was implied in all this a considerable difficulty, arising from the contradictory perspectives which existed within the English pacifist movement. These contradictions, in the early days, were not revealed in distinct pacifist parties, but rather in a certain schizophrenia in pacifist advocacy. As. A.J.P. Taylor has expressed it:

"Bertrand Russell provides a striking example. The final chapter of *The Foreign Policy of the Entente* laid down Radical principles of foreign policy: no annexations: renunciation of the right of capture; universal arbitration; no alliances or understandings; "we shall not engage in war except when we are attacked." Appended to this is a footnote: "Unless a League of Great Powers could be formed to resist aggression everywhere . . . In that case, we might be willing to participate in a war to enforce its decisions." The contradiction seems startling; but Woodrow Wilson himself did much the same, when he thought to change the character of the treaty of Versailles by tying the Covenant of the League to its coat-tails. Every advocate of the League weighed with two measures. Their books described at length the misdeeds of statesmen all over the world. Then, in a short final chapter, they assumed that the same statesmen would become persistently virtuous once a League of Nations had been set up." [13]

To comprehend more fully this ambiguous viewpoint, it is necessary to follow the argument a little further. In 1917 Russell wrote *Political Ideals,* the first chapter of which he had intended to deliver at a public lecture in Glasgow, which was to be chaired by Robert Smillie, the miner's leader. Just before it was scheduled to take place, the Government forbade him to enter 'prohibited areas', among which Glasgow was numbered. "These areas included everything near the sea coast", he wrote later, "and the order was intended against spies to prevent them from signalling to German submarines. The War Office, however, was kind enough to say that it did not suspect me of being a spy for the Germans. It only charged me with inciting industrial disaffection in order to stop the war." Smillie read the forbidden lecture to a large gathering, fully expecting to be prosecuted for his pains.[14] He escaped. "The Government", said Russell afterwards, "was too dependent on coal". The fifth chapter on the little book which ensued contains a very clear summary of Russell's view of national sentiment, and his assessment of its scope and limits.

"Are the Ulstermen a nation? Unionists say yes, Home Rulers say no. In such cases it is a party question whether we are to call a group a nation or not. A German will tell you that the Russian Poles are a nation, but as for the Prussian Poles, they, of course, are part of Prussia. Professors can always be hired to prove, by arguments of race or language or history, that a group about which there is a dispute is, or is not, a nation, as may be desired by those whom the professors serve. If we are to avoid all these controversies, we must first of all endeavour to find some definition of a nation.

A nation is not to be defined by affinities of language or a common historical origin, though these things often help to produce a nation. Switzerland is a nation, despite diversities of race, religion, and language. England and Scotland now form one nation, though they did not do so at the time of the Civil War. This is shown by Cromwell's saying, in the height of the conflict, that he would rather be subject to the domain of the royalists than to that of the Scotch. Great Britain was one state before it was one nation; on the other hand, Germany was one nation before it was one state. What constitutes a nation is a sentiment and an instinct, a sentiment of similarity and an instinct of belonging to the same group or herd. The instinct is an extension of the instinct which constitutes a flock of sheep, or any other group of gregarious animals. The sentiment which goes with this is like a milder and more extended form of family feeling. When we return to England after being on the Continent, we feel something friendly in the familiar ways, and it is easy to believe that Englishmen on the whole are virtuous, while many foreigners are full of designing wickedness.

Such feelings make it easy to organize a nation into a state. It is not difficult, as a rule, to acquiesce in the orders of a national government. We feel that it is our government, and that its decrees are more or less the same as those which we should have given if we ourselves had been the governors. There is an instinctive and usually unconscious sense of a common purpose animating the members of a nation. This becomes especially vivid when there is war or a danger of war. Any one who, at such a time, stands out against the orders of his government feels an inner conflict quite different from any that he would feel in standing out against the orders of a foreign government in whose power he might happen to find himself . . .

National sentiment is a fact, and should be taken account of by institutions. When it is ignored, it is intensified and becomes a source of strife. It can only bè rendered harmless by being given free play, so long as it is not predatory. But it is not, in itself, a good or admirable feeling. There is nothing rational and nothing desirable in a limitation of sympathy which confines it to a fragment of the human race. Diversities of manners and customs and traditions are, on the whole, a good thing, since they enable different nations to produce different types of excellence. But in national feeling there is always latent, or explicit, an element of hostility to foreigners. National feeling, as we know it, could not exist in a nation which was wholly free from external pressure of a hostile kind.

And group feeling produces a limited and often harmful kind of morality. Men come to identify the good with what serves the interests of their own group, and the bad with what works against those interests, even if it should happen to be in the interests of mankind as a whole. This group morality is very much in evidence during war, and is taken for granted in men's ordinary thought. Although almost all Englishmen consider the defeat of Germany desirable for the good of the world, yet nevertheless most of them honour a German for fighting for his country, because it has not occurred to them that his actions ought to be guided by a morality higher than that of the group.

A man does right, as a rule, to have his thoughts more occupied with the interests of his own nation than with those of others, because his actions are more likely to affect his own nation. But in time of war, and in all matters which are of equal concern to other nations and to his own, a man ought to take accòunt of the universal welfare, and not allow his survey to be limited by the interest, or supposed interest, of his own group or nation. So long as national feeling exists, it is very important that each nation should be self-governing as regards its internal affairs. Government can only be carried on by force and tyranny if its subjects view it with hostile eyes, and they will so view it if they feel that it belongs to an alien nation. This principle meets with difficulties in cases where men of different nations live side by side in the same area, as happens in some parts of the Balkans. There are also difficulties in regard to places which, for some geographical reason, are of great international importance, such as the Suez Canal and the Panama Canal. In such cases the purely local desires of the inhabitants may have to give way before larger interests. But in general, at any rate as applied to civilized communities, the principle that the boundaries of nations ought to coincide with the boundaries of states has very few exceptions.

This principle, however, does not decide how the relations between states are to be regulated, or how a conflict of interests between rival states is to be decided. At present, every great state claims absolute sovereignty, not only in regard to its internal affairs but also in regard to its external actions. This claim to absolute sovereignty leads it into conflict with similar claims on the part of other great states. Such conflicts at present can only be decided by war or diplomacy, and diplomacy is in essence nothing but the threat of war. There is no more justification for the claim to absolute sovereignty on the part of a state than there would be for a similar claim on the part of an individual. The claim to absolute sovereignty is, in effect, a claim that all external affairs are to be regulated purely by force, and that when two nations or groups of nations are interested in a question, the decision shall depend solely upon which of them is, or is believed to be, the stronger. This is nothing but primitive anarchy, 'the war of all against all,' which Hobbes asserted to be the original state of mankind.

There cannot be secure peace in the world, or any decision of international questions according to international law, until states are willing to part with their absolute sovereignty as regards their external relations, and to leave the decision in such matters to some international instrument of government."[15]

The argument for international authority emerged, for Russell, from his own experience.

"Until lately I was engaged in teaching a new science which few men in the world were able to teach. My own work in this science was based chiefly upon the work of a German and an Italian. My pupils came from all over the civilized world: France, Germany, Austria, Russia, Greece, Japan, China, India and America. None of us was conscious of any sense of national divisions. We felt ourselves an outpost of civilization, building a new road into the virgin forest of the unknown. All co-operated in the common task, and in the interest of such a work the political enmities of nations seemed trivial, temporary and futile.

But it is not only in the somewhat rarefied atmosphere of abstruse science that international co-operation is vital to the progress of civilization. All our economic problems, all the questions of securing the rights of labour, all the hopes of freedom at home and humanity abroad, rest upon the creation of international good-will.

So long as hatred, suspicion, and fear dominate the feelings of men toward each other, so long we cannot hope to escape from the tyranny of violence and brute force. Men must learn to be conscious of the common interests of mankind in which all are at one, rather than of those supposed interests in which the nations are divided. It is not necessary, or even desirable, to obliterate the differences of manners and custom and tradition between different nations. These differences enable each nation to make its own distinctive contribution to the sum total of the world's civilization."[16]

That the political economy of the modern world still makes this dream an elusive one does not mean that it is simply an irrational foible. The same concern recurs. In the recent writings of the distinguished Soviet geneticist, Zhores Medvedev, one can find an almost identical utterance,[17] although there can be no doubt that he has never been able to read the relevant works of his English forebear, whose sentiments Lenin had found wholesome, but Lenin's successors could only regard with the same distaste as was made manifest by the British Government, since they are, beyond question, "disruptive" and "calculated to incite disaffection".

If science has become international in fact, so too has technology, and so too has the economic system of imperialism. The international social structure is ruptured in complex ways by patterns of concealed interest, and it is this treacherously faulted system which has both encouraged Governments to persist in pursuit of the narrow interest, as well as they can follow it, and idealist critics of governments to postulate alternatives which have often been shown all-too-evidently to be self-defeating.

In the immediate post-war period Russell came to grips with some of these problems. After the Russian Revolution, which he welcomed, and for welcoming which in an enthusiastic article he was sent to prison, he paid a disillusioning visit to the new Soviet Union, with a British Labour delegation.[18] He followed this voyage with an extended visit to China, where he lectured at the University of Peking and debated with Chen Tu-Tsu, the founder of the Chinese Communist Party. The chief, unconscious difficulty of the pacifist and socialist oppositions to the first world war had been the optic imposed upon them by their situation, in the belly of the predator itself. Things looked different from the vantage-point of the victims of depradation. If there were a plurality of imperialisms, producing strenuous advocacies each in its own behalf, there was, in every subordinate nation, a similar response to domination. This visit to China gave Russell a new perspective, which is presciently set out in his book *The Problem of China:*

"The concentration of the world's capital in a few nations, which, by means of it, are able to drain all other nations of their wealth, is obviously not a system by which permanent peace can be secured except through the complete subjection of the poorer nations. In the long run, China will see no reason to leave the profits of industry in the hands of foreigners. If, for the present, Russia is successfully starved into submission to foreign capital, Russia also will, when the time is ripe, attempt a new rebellion against the world empire of finance. I cannot see, therefore, any establishment of a stable world-system as a rresult of the syndicate formed at Washington. On the contrary, we may expect that, when Asia has thoroughly assimilated our economic system, the Marxian class-war will break out in the form of a war between Asia and the West, with America as the protagonist of capitalism, and Russia as the champion of Asia and Socialism. In such a war, Asia would be fighting for freedom, but probably too late to preserve the distinctive civilizations which now make Asia valuable to the human family. Indeed, the war would probably be so devastating that no civilization of any sort would survive it . . .

The real government of the world is in the hands of the big financiers, except on questions which rouse passionate public interest. No doubt the exclusion of Asiatics from America and the Dominions is due to popular pressure, and is against the interests of big finance. But not many questions rouse so much popular feeling, and among them only a few are sufficiently simple to be incapable of misrepresentation in the interests of the capitalists. Even in such a case as Asiatic immigration, it is the capitalist system which causes the anti-social interests of wage-earners and makes them illiberal. The existing system makes each man's individual interest opposed, in some vital point, to the interest of the whole. And what applies to individuals applies also to nations; under the existing economic system, a nation's interest is seldom the same as that of the world at large, and then only by accident. International peace might conceivably be secured under the present system, but only by a combination of the strong to exploit the weak. Such a combination is being attempted as the outcome of Washington; but it can only diminish, in the long run, the little freedom now enjoyed by the weaker nations.

The essential evil of the present system, as Socialists have pointed out over and over again, is production for profit instead of for use. A man or a company or a nation produces goods, not in order to consume them, but in order to sell them. Hence arise competition and exploitation and all the evils both in internal labour problems and in international relations. The development of Chinese commerce by capitalistic methods means an increase, for the Chinese, in the prices of the things they export which are also the things they chiefly consume and the artificial stimulation of new needs for foreign goods, which places China at the mercy of those who supply these goods, destroys the existing contentment, and generates a feverish pursuit of purely material ends. In a socialistic world, production will be regulated by the same authority which represents the needs of the consumers, and the whole business of competitive buying and selling will cease. Until then, it is possible to have peace by submission to exploitation, or some degree of freedom by continual war, but it is not possible to have both peace and freedom. The success of the present American policy may, for a time, secure peace, but will certainly not secure freedom for the weaker nations, such as Chinese. Only international Socialism can secure both; and owing to the stimulation of revolt by capitalist oppression, even peace alone can never be secure until International Socialism is established throughout the world."[19]

Meantime, the League of Nations had been formed, and had earned, with some reason, from the new Soviet Government the characterisation of "thieves' kitchen", whilst manifestly not satisfying the anti-war critics of nationalist-imperialist intrigues. A.J.P. Taylor's summing-up, in hindsight, of this process, was all-too-justified. The very pacifism of the anti-war movement was its undoing. By 1924, Russell was again in London, delivering his famous lecture "Icarus" in response to J.B.S. Haldane's optimistic science-utopia "Daedalus". This is most revealing. Supposing, he argued, kindliness could be discovered to depend on physiological causes: then a secret society of physiologists could "bring about the millenium by kidnapping, on a given day, all the rulers of the world, and injecting into their blood some substance which would fill th&m with benevolence towards their fellow creatures. Suddenly M. Poincare would wish well to Ruhr miners, Lord Curzon to Indian nationalists, Mr. Smuts to the natives of what was German South West Africa, and the American Government to its political prisoners and its victims in Ellis Island. But alas, the physiologists would first have to administer the love-philtre to themselves before they would undertake the task. Otherwise, they would prefer to win titles and fortunes by injecting military ferocity into recruits. And so we come back to the old dilemma: only kindliness can save the world, and even if we knew how to produce kindliness we should not do so unless we were already kindly . . . The only solid hope seems to lie in the possibility of world-wide domination by one group, say the United States, leading to the gradual formation of an orderly economic and political world-government. But perhaps, in view of the sterility of the Roman Empire, the collapse of our civilization would in the end be preferable to this alternative.[20]

There was another answer to this dilemma current at the same time: it was carefully formulated by Mao Tse-Tung, who had been present at the Russell debate in Peking, and who had written two letters about the event to Ts'ai Ho-sen:

"In his lecture at Changsha, Russell . . . took a position in favour of communism but against the dictatorship of the workers and peasants. He said that one should employ the method of education to change the consciousness of the propertied classes, and that in this way it would not be necessary to limit freedom or to have recourse to war and bloody revolution . . . My objections to Russell's viewpoint can be stated in a few words: 'This is all very well as a theory, but it is unfeasible in practice' . . . Education requires (1) money, (2) people, and (3) instruments. In today's world, money is entirely in the hands of the capitalists or slaves of capitalists. In today's world, the schools and the press, the two most important instruments of education, are entirely under capitalist control. In short, education in today's world is capitalist education. If we teach capitalism to children, these children, when they grow up, will in turn teach capitalism to a second generation of children. Education thus remains in the hands of the capitalists. Then the capitalists have 'parliaments' to pass laws protecting the capitalists and handicapping the proletariat; they have governments to apply these laws and to enforce the advantages and the prohibitions that they contain; they have 'armies' and 'police' to defend the well-being of the capitalists and to repress the demands of the proletariat, they have 'banks' to serve as repositories in the circulation of their wealth; they have 'factories', which are the instruments by which they monopolize the production of goods. Thus, if the communists do not seize political power, they will not be able to find any refuge in this world; how, under such circumstances, could they take charge of education? Thus, the capitalists will continue to control education and to praise their capitalism to the skies, so that the number of converts to the proletariat's communist propaganda will diminish from day to day. Consequently, I believe that the method of education is unfeasible . . . What I have just said constitutes the first argument. The second argument is that, based on the principle of mental habits and on my observations of human history, I am of the opinion that one absolutely cannot expect the capitalists to become converted to communism . . . If one wishes to use the power of education to transform them, then since one cannot obtain control of the whole or even an important part of the two instruments of education – schools and the press – even if one has a mouth and a tongue and one or two schools and newspapers as means of propaganda . . . this is really not enough to change the mentality of the adherents of capitalism even slightly; how then can one hope that the latter will repent and turn toward the good? So much from a psychological standpoint. From a historical standpoint . . . one observes that no despot, imperialist, and militarist throughout history has ever been known to leave the stage of history of his own free will without being overthrown by the people. Napoleon I proclaimed himself Emperor, and failed; then there was Napoleon III. Yuan Shih-k'ai failed; then, alas, there was Tuan Ch'-jui . . . From what I have just said, based on both a psychological and a historical standpoint, it can be seen that capitalism cannot be overthrown by the force of a few feeble efforts in the domain of education. This is the second argument. There is yet a third argument, most assuredly a very important argument, even more important in reality. If we use peaceful, means to attain the goal of communism, when will we finally achieve it? Let us assume that a century will be required, a century marked by the unceasing groans of the proletariat. What position shall we adopt in the face of this situation? The proletariat is many times more numerous than the bourgeoisie; if we assume that the proletariat constitutes two-thirds of humanity, then one billion of the earth's one billion five hundred million inhabitants are proletarians (I fear that the figure is even higher) who during this century will be cruelly exploited by the remaining third of capitalists. How can we bear this? Furthermore, since the proletariat has already become conscious of the fact that it, too, should possess wealth, and of the fact that its sufferings are unnecessary, the proletarians are discontented, and a demand for communism has arisen and has already become a fact. This fact confronts us, we cannot make it disappear; when we become conscious of it we wish to act. This is why, in my opinion, the Russian revolution, as well as the radical communists in every country; will daily grow more powerful and numerous and more tightly organised. This is the natural result. This is the third argument . . .

There is a further point pertaining to my doubts about anarchism. My argument pertains not merely to the impossibility of a society without power or organisation. I should like to mention only the difficulties in the way of the establishment of such a form of society and of its final attainment . . . For all the reasons just stated, my

present viewpoint on absolute liberalism, anarchism, and even
democracy is that these things are fine in theory, but not feasible in
practice . . ."[21]

But Mao's letters never came to Russell's attention. His own hopes, that
the movement for industrial democracy and workers' control in England
would encroach sufficient power to be able to pioneer a peaceful
transition to socialism, were painfully and brusquely dashed in the General
Strike of 1926. He continued to advocate socialism, to preach peace, to
struggle for more tolerant standards of sexual morality and for libertarian
education, and he continued his philosophical work. His central concern
with the theoretical problems of imperialism and spheres of influence
became, over the interwar years, overlaid with immediate practical tasks,
such as work for the India League, and gradually his immediate political
commitments changed.

IV

In the decade beginning in 1930, Russell remained a pacifist, although
he repeatedly insisted on the conditions and limitations within which he
held his views. In retrospect, he was to write:

"I opposed the First World War because it was unnecessary and because
the issues were those of rivalry amongst greedy men of money and
power. The devastation which followed that war gave rise to Hitler. I
was slow to approve preparation for yet another World War. I had
striven to avoid the circumstances which created Hitler. I strove to
avoid the necessity to defeat him at a cost of millions of lives. When it
became apparent that this could not be done any longer I, with great
reluctance, realised it would be necessary to go to war."[22]

Having denounced German fascism in its earliest days, he followed its
development with horror, and spent some time trying to work out
principles for passive resistance which could oppose Hitlerian conquest by
non-violent means. At the same time, he continued to argue for World
Government. In 1936 he published *Which Way to Peace?*, which outlined
arguments of this kind: subsequently he came to feel that they were
erroneous, and repudiated them, even though he remained convinced that
passive resistance could be a useful weapon against a constitutionally
ordered authority, and that world government was a necessary goal. He
was in the United States when the war broke out, and followed the news
of its progress with great distress. Returning to England in 1944, having
completed several years of intensive philosophical work, which produced
A History of Western Philosophy. An Enquiry into Meaning and Truth, and
laid the foundations for *Human Knowledge, Its Scope and Limits,* he soon
found himself in a new world. Whilst the old conflicts of imperialisms were

still very much in evidence, and the rise of the Soviet Union to become the second world power was becoming apparent, the destruction of the Japanese cities of Hiroshima and Nagasaki by nuclear devices had added a dreadful dimension to the continued possibility, indeed likelihood, of future wars: mass destruction was now entirely conceivable on a scale which could obliterate entire nations.

Russell saw the implications of the new military technology at once, and indeed predicted the development, on the basis of the experience of fission weapons, of fusion bombs. But at first, for many years, he was caught in the dilemma which A.J.P. Taylor has described. The launching of the United Nations had marked little further progress in the direction of a unified world government than had been achieved by the old League of Nations. The balance of power, uneasily poised, continued to dominate all inter-state relations in a starkly simplified form, rendered completely obvious by the ideological division of the world into two apparently clearly demarcated camps. At the same time, the dreadful experience of Stalinism seemed to indicate not only that the Soviet bloc was manifestly the most illiberal one, but also the most predatory. So when he spoke in the House of Lords on the dangers of a nuclear arms race, soon after the ending of hostilities, Russell leaned towards the United States as the most likely harbinger of any potential world authority. The Baruch Plan seemed, in 1947, to bear out this judgment, and for a few years he supported it very strenuously, and even advocated the excercise of compulsion on Stalin to bring him to accept it. But with the development of the cold war, the onset of McCarthyism quickly restored his old suspicion of the American political structure, and even before the testing of the first hydrogen bomb he found himself in increasingly strong opposition to United States' policies. He apportioned some of the blame for the failure of the Baruch Plan on the Western powers, who had quickly subverted the United Nations Organisation to serve as an instrument of their own hegemony:

> "Had it been genuinely allowed to become an impartial international body by the West, it is possible that Stalin would have acceded to the Baruch proposals. The arms race which has followed has borne out my fears and made me just as determined to prevent it from being consummate in conflict." [23]

At the end of 1954 he delivered his famous broadcast on "Man's Peril". This attracted the support of Einstein, and as other scientists signified their agreement with its warning, an appeal was launched for what become known as the first Pugwash Conference, held on Cyrus Eaton's Nova Scotia estate. This was a pioneer attempt to bring scientists from all parts of the globe into a common forum on the nuclear danger, and it benefitted from the fact that it was a non-governmental initiative. The "Pugwash movement" continued its work, and at the time of writing is scheduled to convene its latest meeting in the Fall of 1972. By 1958 Russell had helped to arouse sufficient non-scientific concern about the problem to launch the Campaign for Nuclear Disarmament, of which he was first President. Open letters which he contributed to the *New Statesman* attracted replies from N S Khruschev and Foster Dulles, and this extraordinary exchange was published as the first of a number of tracts and books on nuclear disarmament.[24] Within two years the constitutional efforts of CND had converted the British Labour Party, then in opposition, to the policy of unilateral nuclear disarmament: but the leader of that Party led a bitter struggle to reverse the decision, which finally proved possible by strenuous efforts which involved extraordinary manipulation of the trade union block votes at the subsequent policy Conference. In a context in which the constitutional political machinery was not open to change by persuasion, Russell formed the Committee of 100 for direct action against nuclear war. This body, in which he first enlisted the support of two young men, Christopher Farley and Ralph Schoenman, who were later to help him to establish the Bertrand Russell Peace Foundation, organised a series of sit down demonstrations in Trafalgar Square, outside the Ministry of Defence, at nuclear installations and airbases, and at the Holy Loch submarine base. In 1961 he was imprisoned for the second time in his life, together with his fourth wife, Edith Finch, who was actively involved in all his efforts, however demanding they might be. The message he left for his supporters as he was taken into Brixton reveals how sharply the anti-nuclear movement had differentiated itself from the political authorities by this time:

"Along with valued colleagues I am to be silenced for a time — perhaps for ever, for who can tell how soon the great massacre will take place?

The populations of East and West, misled by stubborn governments in search of prestige and by corrupt official experts bent on retaining their posts, tamely acquiesce in policies which are almost certain to end in nuclear war. There are supposed to be two sides, each professing to stand for a great cause. This is a delusion — Kennedy and Khrushchev, Adenauer and de Gaulle, Macmillan and Gaitskell, are pursuing a common aim: the ending of human life.

You, your families, your friends and your countries are to be exterminated by the common decision of a few brutal but powerful men. To please these men, all the private affections, all the public hopes, all that has been achieved in art, and knowledge and thought and all that might be achieved hereafter, is to be wiped out forever.

Our ruined lifeless planet will continue for countless ages to circle aimlessly round the sun unredeemed by the joys and loves, the occasional wisdom and the power to create beauty which have given value to human life.

It is for seeking to prevent this that we are in prison."[25]

V

Looking back on this whole period of world history, and on his own efforts for peace, Russell was to form conclusions which were acutely subversive:

"In the late 'forties and early 'fifties, I had been profoundly impressed by the horror of Stalin's dictatorship, which had led me to believe that there would be no easy resolution of the cold war. I later came to see that for all his ruthlessness, Stalin had been very conservative. I had assumed, like most people in the West, that his tyranny was expansionist, but later evidence made it clear that it was the West that had given him Eastern Europe as part of the spoils of the Second World War, and that, for the most part, he had kept his agreements with the West. After his death, I earnestly hoped that the world would come to see the folly and danger of living permanently in the shadow of nuclear weapons. If the contenders for world supremacy could be kept apart, perhaps the neutral nations could introduce the voice of reason into international affairs. It was a small hope, for I overestimated the power of the neutrals. Only rarely, as with Nehru in Korea, did they manage to add significant weight to pressures against the cold war. The neutrals continued to embody my outlook, in that I consider human survival more important than ideology. But a new danger came to the fore. It became obvious that Russia no longer entertained hope of world-empire, but that this hope had now passed over to the United States. As my researches into the origins and circumstances of the war in Vietnam showed, the United States was embarking upon military adventures which increasingly replaced war with Russia as the chief threat to the world. The fanaticism of America's anti-communism, combined with its constant search for markets and raw materials, made it impossible for any serious neutral to regard America and Russia as equally dangerous to the world. The essential unity of American military, economic and cold war policies was increasingly revealed by the sordidness and cruelty of the Vietnam war. For people in the West, this was most difficult to admit, and again I experienced the silence or opposition of those who had come to accept my views of the previous decade. In the third world, however, our support was very considerable. Cruelty has not gone wholly unchallenged.[26]

A key element in this reappraisal was played by the Cuba crisis, which broke out at the zenith of the popular strength of the anti-nuclear movement in Great Britain. When President Kennedy insisted that the Soviet missiles which were being established in Cuba must be withdrawn, all the implications of the slogan "better dead than red" came home to the world. For a few days it seemed that total destruction of the advanced nations was inevitable. Russell feverishly tried to mediate between Khruschev and Kennedy. He summarised the resultant outcome of the crisis in this way:

"From the point of view of preventing a general nuclear war, the climax of the Cuban crisis was when Khruschev ordered the Russian ships to avoid conflict with American blockading ships. From this moment, it became clear that the Soviet Government, but not the Government of the U.S., considered the survival of the human species more important than the question whether Cuba should be allowed to have the government it wanted. Until this moment, there had not been very much to choose between American and Russian policies. But when Khruschev gave this indubitable proof of his determination to avoid general nuclear war, the U.S.S.R. became the more rational of the two contestants. From an American Point of view, however, the dispute remained tense for some time after the withdrawal of the Russian ships. The Russians had been constructing nuclear bases on Cuba and importing nuclear weapons. They had, at the same time, stated that th' arms they were importing into Cuba were purely defensive. This was regarded by the U.S. as a deception and as a reason for not trus'ing Russia to carry out any agreement that might be reached. It was pointed out that all America's nuclear preparations were considered defensive. For example, Hanson W. Baldwin, in the New York Times of 7 November, said: 'The United States' contention, shared by its allies, has always been that its overseas bases were established solely in answer to Communist aggressive expansionism.' It might be retorted that the bases which Russia was establishing in Cuba were established in answer to U.S. aggressive expansionism. But the view persisted in the U.S. that all Communist arms are aggressive and all anti-Communist arms are defensive. As for 'deception', no attempt was made by the Russians to conceal what they were doing. Some of their installations were close to main roads and all were open to observation by American planes. The Russians agreed to remove all that they had done in the way of nuclear preparations and were willing to have the removal guaranteed by United Nations inspection. Fidel Castro announced, after considerable discussion with U Thant, his acceptance of United Nations inspection. But he stated that it was only just that similar inspection should take place in the invasion camps of the United States, located in Florida and Georgia.

What would American reaction be if Cuban reconnaissance planes flew over Florida and Georgia, not to mention Washington? The United States further maintain in Eastern Cuba at Guantanamo a military base in direct opposition to the wishes of the Government of Cuba. Tens of thousands of American troops are on Cuban soil in this base. Castro demanded the end of this foreign base as a further condition and sought to raise the matter in the United Nations.

How would Englishmen feel about the maintenance of a hostile Soviet military base in East Anglia, against the wishes of the people and Government, but retained through threat of immediate nuclear attack if it were interfered with economically or militarily?"[27]

Yet the greater pacific sensitivity of the Soviet Government in this crucial instance was regrettably only one of the indications of United

States' intransigence. The developing crisis in Vietnam was brought to Russell's attention very early in 1963, and in November 1964 he sent Christopher Farley to Hanoi to report on the situation. The more closely he studied the events in Vietnam, the more convinced Russell became that the Vietnamese cause was just, and that United States policy was not only indefensible, but unprecedented in its cruelty. He begun to produce a series of speeches, pamphlets and letters in defence of Vietnam, and by late 1965 had resolved to constitute the War Crimes Tribunal, which later met under the leadership of Jean-Paul Sartre, Vladimir Dedijer and Laurent Schwartz. The exhaustive work of preparing the Tribunal, which involved a large number of investigatory commissions and extensive research, was complicated by the extraordinary campaign of vilification which he encountered as his intentions became known. The tribunal was banned from meeting in England, and then in France. Journalists covered reams of paper with speculations about his senility. He was accused of acting as a mere mouthpiece for his former secretary Ralph Schoenman, although in point of fact it was precisely in connection with the handling of the complex problems of the Tribunal that he began to lose patience with his undoubtedly energetic and creative, but impulsive, disciple. If the Western press showed little charity to the Tribunal, and in the main carefully refrained from publishing its detailed documentation of the atrocities in Vietnam, the Soviet authorities were not much kinder. A curtain of silence was drawn over the Tribunal's work in much of the Russian and East European press. And yet somehow, word got through to large numbers of young people in almost every European country, and in the United States itself, and a resistance began to form. Of course, the Tribunal was only an early attempt to tell the truth. The decisive factor in this gradual change was the extraordinary example of the Vietnamese people themselves. As Russell had said at the first session of the Tribunal in London, before the government ban upon its work was imposed:

"As I reflect on this work, I cannot help thinking of the events of my life, because of the crimes I have seen and the hopes I have nurtured. I have lived through the Dreyfus Case and been party to the investigation of the crimes committed by King Leopold in the Congo. I can recall many wars. Much injustice has been recorded quietly during these decades. In my own experience I cannot discover a situation quite comparable. I cannot recall a people so tormented, yet so devoid of the failings of their tormentors. I do not know any other conflict in which the disparity in physical power was so vast. I have no memory of any people so enduring, or of any nation with a spirit of resistance so unquenchable.

I will not conceal from you the profundity of my admiration and passion for the people of Vietnam. I cannot relinquish the duty to judge what has been done to them because I have such feelings. Our mandate is to uncover and tell the truth, born of intense and unyielding enquiry."[28]

It was plain that Soviet indifference to this initiative was based on something deeper than proprietorial exclusiveness over the world Peace Movement. Russell's constant intervention for political rights for detainees in Eastern Europe, his defence of Jews facing discrimination in Poland and the Soviet Union itself, and his unremitting advocacy of democratic and humanist values, were finding their own echoes among the Russian and East European peoples. When the invasion of Czechoslovakia was launched in 1968, it seemed perfectly natural that Czech intellectuals should appeal to Russell for support, and perfectly natural also that he should give over many weeks of strenuous activity to their defence, even though he had reached the age of 96. His many statements on these events reveal the way his mind was working. Alas, he was never able to prepare the book on this question which would inevitably have followed, if he had lived a little longer.

VI

The nations are still not united. The rich not only continue to rob the poor, but threaten now to destroy themselves and the poor together unless the world can rise to meet the demand that it take control of itself again. Today we can see, as Russell often warned twenty, thirty years ago, that the hydrogen bomb is not the only way to destruction of the world. The spoliation of resources, the mad pursuit of wealth at the expense of cleanliness, human satisfactions, the existence of other species, perhaps even the very capacity of life itself to survive; all the constellation of disorders which have been labelled the "ecology problem" now bid, insistently, to overtake us before they can be solved. Russell was surely not wrong to seek the unity of the world at the same time that he upheld liberty of the individual. He was surely not wrong to seek the end of Empire, and an end to the domination of one man over another. No-one is likely to claim that all his answers to the questions implied in such issues were right: they were, as this paper argues, frequently tentative, sometimes contradictory. What seems plain is that Russell asked many of the right questions, and that only an imagination which operates freely on his scale can hope to produce tomorrow's answers. Where most men saw their local community, or their nation, as the natural boundary of their expectations and the unquestioned limit of their capacity to act, Russell saw over frontiers, and over the businessmen straddling frontiers, to dream of a world community. He saw, dimly, the possibilities of combining socialism, democracy, and the free development of the individual personality. No system which we, who follow him, may evolve, will be halfway to adequate for our fellows unless it meets these challenges, these real needs, these hopes of an aristocrat who lived after, and of a human being, who lived, we may hope not long before, his time.

FOOTNOTES

1 Preface to David Horowitz: *Containment and Revolution,* Anthony Blond, 1967, p.7.
2 Raymond Williams: *The Intellectual in Politics,* Spokesman No.3, 1970 p.5.
3 Franklin's autobiographical decalogue was mercilessly parodied by D.H. Lawrence in his *Essays on American Literature,* and never more tellingly than in the case of this particular commandment. But there is a sense in which Franklin was right to understand what Lawrence saw as arrogance incarnate as, in fact, true humility. Lawrence's contempt for intellectualism gave him a peculiarly earthbound view, sometimes reducing common feelings to insensitivity and common sense to silliness. Intellectual humility he could not understand, because it involves, unlike the abject condition normally considered "humble", real components of courage, intransigence and consistency. Sometimes, as Franklin implied, it demands even defiance.
4 Alan Wood: *Bertrand Russell the Passionate Sceptic,* Unwin Books, 1957.
5 *Autobiography,* Volume I, George Allen & Unwin, 1967, p.146.
6 This happened at a select discussion circle called 'the Coefficients', set up by Mrs. Webb. An Account of its early days is to be found in H.G. Wells: *Experiment in Autobiography,* Cape, 1934, pp 761 et seq.
7 The No Conscription Fellowship was established to organise conscientious objection, and among its moving spirits were Clifford Allen and Fenner Brockway. As early as 1915 it came under Governmental harassment, and when conscription was introduced it put up a major campaign which provoked many arrests. Its paper *The Tribunal* was edited by Russell when a previous editor was taken to prison. Russell himself was deprived of his lectureship at Cambridge in 1916, as a reprisal against this work, and imprisoned in 1918 for publishing an article supporting the Bolsheviks and attacking the strikebreaking activities of the U.S. Army.
8 The Union of Democratic Control was established by E.D. Morel to campaign against secret diplomacy and for democratic control over. foreign policy. The British Cabinet had been committed to the war without its own prior knowledge, leave alone any mandate of the people. The UDC case was put by Russell in a series of tracts, subsequently published as *Justice in Wartime.*

9 The Guild Socialist Movement was an organisation for the establishment of democracy in industry, under a system of workers' control. It gained influence in a number of trade unions, and its best-known advocate was G.D.H. Cole. Russell's *Roads to Freedom*, published in 1918, is a classic statement of its views.

10 *War: the Offspring of Fear*. Reproduced in Stansky: *The Left and the War*, NY OUP, 1969 cf pp.103-4.

11 *Ibid*, p.112-3.

12 V.I. Lenin: *Collected Works*, Vol. 21, FLPH, Moscow p.265.

13 A.J.P. Taylor: *The Trouble Makers: Dissent over Foreign Policy* Hamish Hamilton, 1958, pp.132-5.

14 Cf Robert Smillie: *My Life for Labour*, Mills and Boon, nd., pp.234-7.

15 *Political Ideals* N.Y. Simon & Schuster, pp.78-82.

16 *Ibid*, pp.89-9.

17 Cf. *The Medvedev Papers* MacMillan, 1971

18 Reported in *The Practice and Theory of Bolshevism*, Allen and Unwin, 1920. There are also interesting accounts of this delegation, and Russell's part in it, in Alexander Berkman: *The Bolshevik Myth*, Hutchinson, 1925, pp.133 cf seq., and Emma Goldman: *Living My Life*, Vol.2., Knopf, 1931, pp.794-5.

19 *The Problem of China*, Allen and Unwin, pp.182-4.

20 *Icarus*, Routledge & Kegan Paul, 1924, pp.61-4.

21 Stuart R. Schram: *The Political Thought of Mao Tse-Tung*, Penguin Books, 1969, pp.276-8.

22 Cited in *Into the 10th Decade: Tribute to Bertrand Russell*, 1962, Bertrand Russell Peace Foundation, p.16

23 *Ibid*, p.17

24 *The Vital Letters of Russell, Khruschev, Dulles* MacGibbon & Kee 1958. See also *Common Sense and Nuclear Warfare*, Allen & Unwin 1959, and *Act or Perish*, Committee of 100, 1960.

25 *Autobiography*, volume 3. Allen & Unwin 1969 p.146

26 *Ibid*, pp.171-2.

27 *Unarmed Victory*, Penguin Books, 1963. pp.53-55.

28 *Ibid*, p.216

Contributors

Gunther ANDERS was a member of the Bertrand Russell International War Crimes Tribunal and is the author of *Kafka Pro und Contra, Der Mann auf der Brücke, Off Limits für das Gewissen and Philosophische Stenogramme.*

Charles ATKINSON is a 29 year old American Trade Unionist. Since 1964 he has been an organiser with the Amalgamated Clothing Workers of America. He founded the Louisville Peace and Freedom Centre to oppose the Vietnam war. From 1970 to 1972 he studied at Ruskin College, Oxford, but has now returned to America.

Lelio BASSO is a Senator in the Italian Parliament, a leading Italian left-wing socialist scholar and jurist. He was a member of the Bertrand Russell Tribunal for the Investigation of War Crimes in Vietnam, and he founded the journal *Problemi del Socialismo,* of which an English edition, entitled *International Socialist Journal,* ran for several years.

Stephen BODINGTON is an economist and mathematician. He is a lecturer at the Middlesex Polytechnic and the author of numerous books and articles on socialism, political economy, and computer based technology. His latest book, *Computers and Socialism* is to be published early in 1973. He has written many books under the pseudonym John Eaton, which include *Marx and Keynes* and *Socialism in the Nuclear Age.*

Michael BARRATT BROWN is Senior Tutor in Economics in the Department of Extra Mural Studies at Sheffield University. Among his many books are *After Imperialism, Essays on Imperialism* and, just published by Spokesman books, *From Labourism to Socialism,* a comprehensive study of the political economy of Labour in Britain in the 1970's.

Keith BUCHANAN is Professor of Geography at the Victoria University of Wellington, New Zealand. He is the author of *The Transformation of the Chinese Earth, The South East Asian World,* and *The Geography of Empire,* published by Spokesman Books. Professor Buchanan is a member of the editorial team which produces *The Journal of Contemporary Asia.* His paper was also read at the Linz symposium in honour of the Centenary of Bertrand Russell organised under the auspices of the Vienna Institute for Development.

Noam CHOMSKY is Ferrari T. Ward Professor of Linguistics at Massachusetts Institute of Technology. He is the author of *Syntactic Structures, Aspects of the Theory of Syntax, Cartesian Linguistics,* and *Language and Mind.* His political essays were recently collected in *American Power and the New Mandarins.* His Russell lectures at Trinity College, Cambridge, have recently been published under the title *Problems of Knowledge and Freedom.* He is a member of the Spokesman Editorial Board.

Ken COATES is an ex coal-miner and is now Senior Tutor in Sociololy at the Department of Adult Education at Nottingham University, a director of the Bertrand Russell Peace Foundation, and author of a number of works on industrial democracy. He is also co-author with Richard Silburn of a series of monographs on the problem of poverty.

Vladimir DEDIJER President of the Sessions of the Bertrand Russell War Crimes Tribunal, was a partisan leader during the war, and has since gained a world-wide reputation as a historian. He is the author of the standard biography of President Tito.

John HUGHES is Vice-Principal of Ruskin College, Oxford and Director of the Trade Union Research Unit. He has contributed extensively to socialist and trade union journals and was co-author of the Penguin Special *A Special Case − Social Justice and the Miners.*

V.G..KIERNAN is Professor in the Department of History at Edinburgh University. He is a regular contributor to *The Socialist Register,* and has published numerous books and articles, including *The Lords of Human Kind.*

A.J. LIEHM teaches in the Division of Humanities at the Richmond College, the City University of New York. He was Foreign Editor of the Czechos-lovak journal *Literani Listy.* A well known political journalist and film critic, who was one of the main sponsors of the Czech Film Revival, he published an important collection of interviews with Czech writers in 1968. *(Gesprauch an der Moldau: Molden Verlag).*

Mihailo MARKOVIC teaches philosophy at the University of Belgrade. He is a member of the editorial board of the philosophical journal *Praxis.*

Lucio LOMBARDO RADICE was born in Catania (Sicily), on July 10 1916. He is a full Professor of Algebra in the Faculty of Science of the University of Rome. He has been a member of the Central Committee of the Communist Party since the 12th Congress (1969). Editor of the educational journal of PCI, *Riforma della scuola,* he has written about education *(L'educazione della mente,* 1962). He was active in the dialogue between marxists and christians (Salzburg 1965, *Dialogo alla prova* with other authors, 1965). Other non-scientific books; *L'uomo del Rinascimento* (1958), *Socialismo e Liberta* (1968); *Gli accusati* (1972), essays on Kafka, Bulgakov, Solze-nitsyn, Kundera, with a conclusion on the actual problems of socialism. This last work received the "Premio Viareggio 1972".

Jean-Paul SARTRE was Executive President of the Bertrand Russell Inter-national War Crimes Tribunal.